STO

ACPL ITEM
DISCARDED

P9-BHW-170

APR 25 '77

ENGLISH RECUSANT LITERATURE
1558–1640

Selected and Edited by
D. M. ROGERS

Volume 336

FRANCISCO ARIAS
The Judge
1621

JOHN HEIGHAM
The Gagge of the Reformed Gospell
1623

FRANCISCO ARIAS
The Judge
1621

The Scolar Press
1977

ISBN o 85967 372 3

*Published and printed in Great Britain by
The Scolar Press Limited, 59-61 East Parade,
Ilkley, Yorkshire and
39 Great Russell Street,
London WC1*

NOTE

The following works are reproduced (original size) with permission:

1) Francisco Arias, *The judge*, 1621, from a copy in the library of St. Edmund's College, Ware, by permission of the President.

References: Allison and Rogers 37; STC 741/ 14833.

2) John Heigham, *The gagge of the reformed gospell*, 1623, from a copy in the library of St. Edmund's College, Ware, by permission of the President.

References: Allison and Rogers 423 (under Kellison); STC 14907.

1950586

THE IVDGE

WHEREIN IS SHEWED,
how Chrift our Lord is to *Iudge* the
World at the laft Day ; to the extreme Terrour of the Wicked ,
and to the exceffiue Com-
fort of the Good .

*With a Preface, which it willbe neceſſary
to read before the Booke.*

Tranflated into Englifh .

*Nolite errare, Deus non irridetur : Quæ enim ſe-
minauerit homo, hæc & metet.*

Gal. 6. verf. 7.
Be not deceaued, God will not be mocked: for
the thinges which a man fhall fow, the
fame he fhall reape.

Permiſſu Superiorum, 1621,

TO
MY NOBLE,
FAITHFVLL,
WORTHY,
and moſt deare Friend,
Mʳ· G . T .

SY R,

Since I had
the Ioy to ſee
you laſt, I haue
looked a little
into the next Life , as deſpay-
ring

ring that in this, I should be
able to find any thing which
might be worthy to fill vp
that place , which is made
empty by your ABSENCE.
And now by chance , or rather by Gods good Prouiden-
ce, I haue met with a Prospe-
čtiue-Glasse, which giues me
a view of *Heauen*, and *Hell*, in
a very expresse & cleare manner, though the Countreyes
theselues be far off. I should
neuer haue beene able to fit
the Instrument towardes any
eye; but finding now, that all
was ready made (and that, so
excellently) to my hand, I
haue aduentured to frame a
case

case for it, after the English
fashion. The thing in it self,
you will not chuse but like,
for it is excellent; and I am
but too sure, that you wil loue
the part that I haue therein;
because the same Loue hath
ceeled vp the eyes of your
iudgement concerning me.
But if (abstracting from that)
you chance to like it, I shall
stand in little feare of the cen-
sure of others, who must giue
me leaue to belieue, that ther
liuesnot amõgst them all (for
ought I know) a man that can
outstrippe you in *Translating*.
Heerein I haue seene pretious
things of your doing; both in
A 3   Prose,

Profe, and Verfe, and in feuerall Languages. And I neuer
mifliked any *Tranflation* of
yours, but that one, when you
tráflated your Prefence, from
the eyes of my body, by whofe
Abféce, I am in part depriued
of being able to *tranflate* fome
of your vertues into my foule.
The leaft that I can do againft
Abfence & *Diftance*, for fo great
a wrong, is to fend them a *Defi-*
ance; and to bid them be fure,
that if they mean to make me
loue you one haires breadth
the leffe, they shal loofe their
labour. Nay they kindle me
rather, to make this expreffi-
on of my felfe; and to *acknow-*
ledge

ledge (as I may fay) *this Statute*
of my hart, before the World.
For I am fixt in giuing you all
power ouer me , and I glory
in being fubiect to fuch a
Friend .

Your, *what you*
will

G. M.

A 4

THE PREFACE.

A Learned and holy man of this age, befides the odour of his Sanctity, hath left furuiuing, diuers Monuments of his writing; and, amongſt the reſt, three bookes *Of the Imitation of Chriſt our Lord*. In the firſt of theſe, he ſheweth, vnder ſeuerall Titles, the ſeuerall Offices which his diuine Maieſty is performing to the ſoules of men; as he is our *God*; our *Redeemer*; our *King*; our *Sauiour*; our *Mediatour*;

A 5   our

our *Aduocate* ; our *Captaine* : our *Sa-crifice* ; our *Spouse* ; our *Doctour* ; our *Law-giuer* ; our *Pastour* ; our *Light* ; our *Life* ; &, to conclude , our *Iudge*. The whole booke is large ; and not only should I haue felt the paines in translating it all , but I might haue doubted of your Patience , whether or no it would haue reached, to the reading of it ouer , with due intenti-on. The last of the *Tytles* , deliuered to vs by our Authour , I haue heere translated ; and you may see, that he is a Lyon by his nayles .

In this discourse of *Iudge*, which is not founded vpon priuate contemp-plations , and much lesse, either vpon loose coniections , or streyned con-ceipts ; but euen wholy in effect , v-pon the passages of holy Scriptures (though not cyted word for word , but duely pondered, and truly para-phrased, as the best spirituall wryters are wont to do) he doth admirably

describe

defcribe the foueraigne Maiefty , the
incomparable Mercy , and the inuio-
lable Iuftice of our *Iudge.* And (as in-
cident heerunto) he deliuers vs fuch
a Mappe of the next world ; and doth
fo defcribe the *Paradife* of heauen , &
the *Zona Torrida* of hell, as may ferue,
either to rauifh vs with ioy , or ftrike
vs through with horrour , and make
vs euen wither , for woe ; according
to the feueral ftate that we may be in.
If we be members of the true Church
of Chrift our Lord ; and if , withall ,
we be in the ftate of grace, we fhall
looke with more hope vpon the ioyes
of heauen, then with feare, vpon the
torments of hell ; and fo, we fhall get
courage in the good courfe begun .
But if, on the other fide, we be cut off
from the communion of the true
Church of Chrift our Lord, by any
one errour in beliefe; or if yet , being
Catholikes , we be remaining in ftate
of mortal finne , this Treatife , I hope,
                                    will

wil help to guide vs by the hãd out of thoſe Labyrinths ; & place vs in that high way of Fayth & Charity , with-out which we can haue no tytle to heauẽ; but the iaws of hel, willbe ſure to ſucke, & ſwallow, & deuoure vs .

Let no man therfore be deceaued , or rather let no man deceaue himſelfe . God is God , and he wilbe ſerued . And it is all reaſon , that , by our beleeuing , and liuing as we ought, true Homage may be done to that infinite, inuiſible , immortall , and moſt pure Maieſty of his . And man is man ; a thing of nothing , for of nothing he was made. And as now he is, what is he , but a Pedlars-ſhop full of traſh ; or rather a very ſincke full of filth; and to what height of honour ought he eſteeme himſelfe to be aduanced , if he had but euen a ſingle leaue, to ſerue & loue ſuch an omnipotent Creator? But now, ſince beſides this , he is to be rewarded with

with an immortall Crowne of glory
for so doing (the sublime excellency
wherof , no created power can comprehend) what meruayle can it be,
that the torments be also infinite, to
which he shalbe adiudged and chayned ; if insteed of doing reuerence to
God , by imbracing an incorrupted
faith , & leading either an innocent,
or penitent-life,he enter into rebellió
and treason against him , by imbracing any errour in beleefe , or falling
into sensuality , or any one other
mortall sin, if withall, he dye therin,
without repentance.

It is not want of Charity , in
them who say, That all such as dye
with any mortall sinne vpon their
soules shall eternally be tormented in
the fyre of hell ; but it is true Charity
to declare this truth, that so, in tyme
men may know to what to trust. *S.*
Paul abounded,and ouerflowed with
Charity ; and that very *Charity* it
was

was, which obliged him to proclaim Gal. 5. v. 10. this doctrine ; That, *the workes of the flesh be manifest* , and he saith they are these, *Fornication , Vncleanes , Impudicity , Luxury , Seruing of Idolls ,Witchcrafts , Emnities , Contentions , Emulations , Angers , Brawles , Dissentions , Sects , Enuies , Murthers , Ebrieties, Commessations , and such like*. Of these (saith he) *I foretell you , as I haue foretold you , that they which do such things as these, shall not obtaine the kingdome of God*.

Now if these Sinnes doe exclude men from heauen , others also which are as grieuous , wilbe as sure to exclude them ; and the more certainly will they exclude them , the more grieuous , and enormous they fall out to be. For if simple fornication doe make a soule lyable to the paines of hell , what will not Adultry do? If for a priuate emnity with a mans neighbour, he shalbe adiudged

to

to thofe eternall and vnquenchable
flames, what fhall he not be, for deuiding the Church of Chrift our
Lord, by vnbeleeuing any doctrine,
or difobeying the gouernement therof?

    I fay the vnbeleeuing of any
doctrine, as before I faid of the committing any other mortall finne. For
this is as true, in the law of our faith,
as it is, in the law of our life, That,
Qui in vno peccat omniũ factus eſt reus;
he that offends in one, is made guilty of
all . Not that he who offends in all,
fhall not be more deepely damned,
then he that doth it but in one; but
becaufe whofoeuer fhall haue offended mortally againft any one commandment of our Lord God, which
concerneth good life, or any erroneous doctriné, in difference from the
Catholike beliefe, is moft truely declared to be a breaker of the Law of
God, and a corruptour of his truth;
                    and

and that as such a one, he shall perish,
except he repent . Woe be therefore
to them (and of woe they will be one
day sure) who bringe such false
weights into the world ; and who
prophane the law of God , and not
onely the law, but the law-giuer himselfe ; In that they allow him not to
be a perfect hater , and a seuere puni-
sher of all mortall sinne, in what soule
soeuer it be found . Whereas yet he
protesteth himselfe (throughout the
whole Current of holy Scripture)
not onely to hate , but to abhorre it .
The (1) *impious man, and his impiety are
hated by Almighty God. The* (2) *scoffer,
the* (3) *Lyer, and the* (4) *Arrogant person , is an abomination to God . The* (5)
*way of the wicked man, and euery wicked
thought of man, is abhorred of God. Thou*
(6) *wicked man, thou shalt dye the death.
Behould* (7) *the whirlewind of the indignation of God shall go forth (sayth the
Lord of Hosts) and it shall come vpon the
head*

(1) Sap.
14. 10.
(2) Prou.
3. 32.
(3) Prou.
12. 22.
(4) Prou.
16. 5.
(5) Prou.
15. 9 .
(6) Ezech.
33. 8
(7) Ierem.
23. 19.

head of sinners , like a furious tempest .

Now, if any man perhaps shall tell me, that these places, & the like , are only meant of Infidels, or such other wicked men , as shall haue spent their whole life in the offence of God ; but that christiãs & such as lead not a life so prophanly wicked as those others, are not meant heereby , howsoeuer they may commit some mortal sinne, and continue therein ; let such a one behould, how the holy Ghost taketh care to answere his obiection , by assuring vs, That, *If a man, who had been neuer so iust, should yet forsake that iustice by committing sinne , he should dye therein*. And then he can looke for nothing, but that *Day*, whereof another Prophet sayth : *That it shall come burning , like a fornace , where all proud men and all other persons working wickednes , should be like stubble, and that this day, shall set them on fire*. Nay it is a fearful thing to see, in the Prophet

Ezech. 18. 26 .

Mal. 4 .1.

B *Ieremy,*

Ieremy , how our Lord doth fweare,
That how full of priuiledge foeuer ,
& how deare foeuer a man may haue
beene to him, yet if he fall to finne, &
dye therein , he will reiect him . For
fpeaking of a finner he expreffeth it ,
in thefe wordes of Terrour : *As I liue*
(fayth our Lord) *if Iechonias the fonne
of Ioachim the king of Iuda, were a ring,*
Ierem : 22.
24.
which I did weare vpon myne owne right
hand, I would plucke it off.

So deadly doth Almighty God
hate finne, and finners ; and fo infallibly will he iudge them to be torme-
ted for the fame , in thofe eternall
ardours of hell , if they repent not
cordially thereof before their death .
And what a fit of phrenfy then, muft
that be, which can poffeffe vs fo far,
as to make vs , for any temporal and
bafe delight, to forfake , and be for-
lorne by that God of eternall Maiefty , and of infinite beauty .

But in the felfe fame manner ,
the

the Fathers and Doctours of the holy Church, haue testifyed this truth vpon all occasions. They were not Infidells, but faythfull Christians to whome *S. Chrysostome* sayd (when withall, he tooke himselfe into the number:) *Consider that without fayle, we must all departe, to stand before that Iudge, whome it will not be possible for vs to de eaue; and where, not only our actions shallbe iudged, but euen our very wordes, and thoughts; and where we shal endure extreme punishment for those things, which heer haue seemed but smal. Be alwayes remembring these thinges; & see thou neuer forget that fire which is neuer to be extinguished. Let vs therefore* (sayth S. *Ambrose*) *lament our sinnes that we may deserue pardon If our sinnes be not forgiuen in this life, we shal haue no rest in the next. The* (a) *burning of such as shal be damned, wilbe eternall, as, the fire is to be which shal burne them:* and *Truth affirmeth, that not they only*

Hom. 22 ? *ad pop. Antioch. tom.* 5.

Ambr. in psal 38.

(a) *Aug. de fide & oper. cap. 15. tom.* 4 ?

B 2 *are*

are to be sent vnto it who wanted Fayth, but they also who wanted good workes. This last is sayd by S. *Augustine*, and he also affirmeth thus in another place: *No one good deed is left vnrewarded, nor no one sinne vnpunished. At the last Day* (sayth (b) S. Gregory) *that deuouring flame shal burne such as are now polluted with carnall pleasures; then shall the infinitely wide mouth of hell, swallow downe such persons, as heere are puffed vp with pride. And they, who through their fault haue heer performed the wil of their crafty Tempter, shall fall like reprobates into those torments, togeather with that guide of theirs. And* (c) *according to the quality of their sinne, the punishment thereof shallbe ordayned, and euery damned soule shallbe tormented in the fire of hell, after the rate of her demerit.*

(b) *Greg. l.9.Moral.*

(c) *Greg. l.5.Moral.*

This is then the verdict of the Fathers and Saints of the holy Catholik Church, and of the Apostle Saint Paul; yea and so the holy Ghost himselfe

felfe, who wrote by his penne, and
which is euery where cleerly giuen,
to proue this certaine truth, That *any
one mortall finne, whether it might be a-
gainst good life, or true beliefe*, doth shut
vp the gates of heauen againft vs, &
fet open the bottomleffe Abyffe of
hell to fwallow vs, vnleffe we repent
thereof fincerely, before our death .

The hower of which death, becaufe it is fo wholy hidden from vs,
it will infinitely concerne vs, both
inftantly and exactly, to caft vp all
the accompts of our Confcience; to be
cordially forry for all our finns; to
confeffe them diftinctly; to purpofe
an amendment firmely; and to fatiffy
for them intierly. For this is a bufines
which muft not be difpatcht after a
curfory and fuperficiall manner; but
we are to confider with what care
we would confult about our eftats, if
they were in danger; or about our
liues, if they lay on bleeding . And
                B 3   heere

heer we muſt not faile to vſe ſo much
more deligéce then there, as *Eternity*
is of more importance, then a moment of *Tyme* .And in fine, we are to
do it ſo,as,at the hower of our death,
(when we ſhall go to ſtand before
our *Iudge*) we would be glad that we
had done it . For without this true
repentance which ſignifieth a flight
from ſinne with griefe ; and ſuppo-
ſeth a flight towards God with loue,
it is no Faith in Chriſt our Lord ,
which will ſerue the turne to pre-
ſerue vs out of that lake of eternall
torment.But rather,the more knowledge we ſhall haue had of him by
Faith ,the greater will our torment
be,if we do not pénance for the ſinns
which weſhal haue cómitted againſt
that Maieſty of his Which , the ſame
Fayth telleth vs to be infinite ; and
that his hatred againſt ſinne is alſo
infinite ; and that as , with ſtrange
mercy , he will aſſume to incompre-
hensi-

henſible, immortall ioy, the ſoule, which at that day he ſhall find to be free from ſinne; ſo in whomſoeuer he he ſhall perceaue, that ſin remaines, the ſame ſoule will he then inſtantly adiudg to that ſea of fire & brimſton, where it will ſaile in ſorrow, & blaſpheme, and rage, for all eternity.

To the pretious *Death*, & *Paſſion* of Chriſt our Lord, we owe & muſt acknowledg (amongſt innumerable others) this vnſpeakeable benefit (for which let all the Angells for euer bleſſe & praiſe his holy name), That through the infinite merit therof, we may be receiued to grace, by meanes of true contrition and pénance; how often, and how wickedly ſoeuer, we ſhall haue offéded that high Maieſty. But that *Death* & *Paſſion*, will neuer ſaue the ſoule of any one creature, vnleſſe both that myſtery, and all the other myſteries of Catholike faith, be well belecued, & al ſinne be cordially

B 4   dete-

deteſted; which ſinne, is a monſter, ſo fierce and cruell, as that it did coſt the very ſonne of God his life. By that life, and by that death I begge, that thou wilt giue ouer to trample with thy durty feete, in the ſacred Bloud Royall of our B. Sauiour, which he ſhed for thee vpon the Croſſe. For ſo thou doſt, preferring *Barabbas* before him, as often as thou cōmitteſt any mortall ſinne; and ſo long thou haſt continued to doe it, as thy ſoule hath beene ſpotted with that crime.

Or if thou haue ſo little of the noble in thee, as to be moued more by thine owne intereſt, then by the conſideration of that immenſe benefit, which the foūtain of Maieſty vouch-ſafed, with ſuch exceſſe of loue, to this wicked creature man; then, do I coniure thee, euen by that very intereſt of thine owne, that inſtantly thou make haſt into thy ſelfe; and that, diſcharging thy ſoule by pēnance,

ce, of whatſoeuer may be offenſiue to
the pure eyes of God, thou implore
his mercy now, which may ſaue thee
from that inflexible iuſtice of his, in
the laſt dreadful day. At which tyme,
euen this very paper will appeare to
thy extreme, and euerlaſting con-
fuſion, if thou forbeare to ſerue thy
ſelfe of this admonition. *Heauen and
earth ſhall paſſe away, but the word of* *Matth.*
God ſhall remayne for euer. And that *24. v. 30*
word hath thus aduiſed vs, and thus
aſſured vs by the mouth of the moſt
B. Apoſtle S. Paul, ſpeaking to the
Galathiãs: *Nolite errare, Deus non irri*-
detur : Quæ enim ſeminauerit homo, hæc *Gal. 6. 7.*
& metet. Quoniam qui ſeminat in carne
ſua, de carne & metet corruptionem; qui
autem ſeminat in ſpiritu, de ſpiritu metet
vitam æternam. The plaine and cleere
ſenſe whereof, is as followeth : *Take*
heed you frame not certaine fantaſticall,
and falſe opinions to your ſelues, as if you
could ouer-reach Almighty God, & eua-
B 5   *euate*

cuate his *truth*, & *make him belieue that
he gaue you a free law wherby to liue*, the
indeed he gaue. But be well assured that
the very truth is this : *Let euery man a-
liue*, consider seriously what he sowes, for
iust so, and no otherwise, shall he reape.
If you sow works of flesh (which are particulerly cited before, in this Preface,
out of a former Chapter of S. Paul
to the same *Galathians*) you shall reape
nothing but corruption, but destruction,
but euerlasting damnation. But if yow
sowe workes of the spirit, which are wholy
contrary to those others, and are there
expressed to be Charity, Ioy, Peace, Patience, Benignity, Goodnes, Longanimi-
ty, Meekenes, Faith, Modesty, Continency &, Chastity, yow shall in vertue
of that spirit (wherewith you liue, and
whereby you are to walk) passe on from
this transitory to an eternall life; & then
at the most liberal hands of God you shal
receaue a most precious crowne of immortall glory.

A

A
TABLE OF
THE CHAPTERS
OF THIS
DISCOVRSE.

HOW *the office of being our Iudge doth belong to Christ our Lord, as he is man : and of the great benefite which God imparteth to vs, in giuing him to be our Iudge.* CHAP. I.   1.

Of the great desire which Christ our Lord hath (for as much as concerneth him)   2.

him) *not to condemne any one , in his iudgmēt, but to saue them al* Chap. II.

3. *Of the benefit which Christ our Lord imparteth to vs , in giuing vs to vnder-stand, and feele the grieuousnes of sinne by the meanes and manner of his* Iudge-ment, *to the end that we may in tyme do pennance for it .* Chap III.

4. *How we are to haue great sense, of the grieuousnes of sinne, by reason of the de-monstrations which shall be made by all the creatures of God before the* Iudge-ment. Chap. IIII.

5. *How Christ our Lord, discouereth the hate which he carryeth towardes sinne , by the so particuler account which he taks thereof .* Chap. V.

6. *How Christ our Lord declares to vs the detestation which he carryeth against sinne ; whereof the wicked are conuinced by that sentence which he pronounceth a-gainst them .* Chap. VI.

7. *How Christ our Lord discouereth the grieuousnes of sinne, & the hatred which*
he

he carryeth against it, by the last sentence whereby he is to condemne the wicked,
and by the punishment which he inflicteth
vpon them. Chap. VII.

How the grieuousnes of sinne is yet
more discouered, by the causes of the
Iudgmēt, which are alleadged by Christ
our Lord. Chap VIII. 8.

How a Christian is to draw a detestation of sinne, out of the consideration of
this Iudgement of God, and great vigilancy in the leading of a good life.
Chap. IX. 9.

Of other Considerations, from which
we may draw the detestation of sinne, &
the care of leading a good life. Chap. X. 10.

How a Christian is to draw out of the
consideration of the diuine Iudgement,
a great feare of offending God, that so he
may fly far from it. Chap. XI. 11.

How it is very necessary & ful of profit, that a Christian do exercise himselfe
in this holy feare; & accompany it with
the exercise of diuine loue. Chap. XII. 12.

Of

13.   *Of how great value, and merit, this holy Feare is.*   Chap. XIII.

14.   *Of the fauours which Christ our Lord will do to the good, at the day of* Iudgement *; and of the Ioy which they shall conceaue by seeing the signes which precede that* Iudgment *; and by beholding the glory of the Crosse, which shall go before* Christ *our Lord.*   Chap. XIV.

15.   *Of the fauour which Christ our Lord will do his seruants, at the day of* Iudgment, *by separating them from the Wicked.*   Chap. XV.

16.   *Of the fauour which Christ our Lord imparteth to his seruants at the day of* Iudgment *, by giuing them his benediction, and communicating his kingdome to them.*   Chap. XVI.

17.   *Of the felicity which Christ our Lord will communicate to his seruants, in the kingdome of heauen.*   Chap. XVII

18.   *Of other benefits which Christ our Lord comunicateth to his seruants in his heauenly kingdome ; and of the fruit of gratitude*

titude, which we must gather from the Consideration of this reward. Chap. XVIII.

How all the things of this life which are good, and which giue delight, do induce vs to a defire of the kingdome of heauen.   Chap. XIX.   19.

How from this knowledge, concerning, the kingdome of Heauen, which Christ our Lord willgiue his feruants, we are to gather a refolute purpofe to fly from finne, and to fullfill the Commandments of God, and to defpife the commodityes of this life.   Chap. XX.   20.

How we are much to animate our felues, towardes the exercife of good works; confidering the great eftimation which Chrift our Lord doth make of them at the day of Iudgement; & the reward which he alfo imparteth to them. Chap. XXI.   21.

THE

THE IVDGE

CHAP. I.

How the office of being our Iudge, doth belong to Christ our Lord, as he is man; and of the great benefit which God imparteth to vs, in giuing him to vs, to be our Iudge.

A LTHOVGH the indignation, & wrath of Christ our Lord against the wicked, and the punishment which he inflicteth vpon their sins, do belong to the office which he hath of being a *Iudge*; yet so also doth it belong to him, vnder the same Title, to doe fauour to such as are *Good*, to defend them, to imparte benefites to them; and both to expresse mercy to-

C   wardes

wardes them in the *Iudgment* which
he exerciseth vpon their faults, & to
giuethē reward for their good deeds,
and for this reason it is that I wil declare the benefits and fauours which
we obtaine by Christ our Lord , in
respect that he is our *Iudge*. It (a) be·
longeth to Christ our Lord, that he
be our *Iudge*, in regard that he is a
man, and because he tooke the nature
of man vpon him; as being a most
conuenient thing , that the *Iudge* be
seene by all such as are to be iudged
by him ; and that the guilty may wel
vnderstand , and heare the sentence
that shalbe giuē against them; & that
for as much as men are composed of
a body & a soule , they may perceaue
it with their soule, and heare it with
the senses of their body . Now if
Christ our Lord , as he is only God ,
were to be the *Iudge*, he could not
then be seene by the wicked ; and the
sentence which immediatly he should
                                    pro-

(a) Why
it was
wholy fit
for the
second
Person of
the most
holy Tri
nity to be
our Iudg
at the last
day.

pronounce would not interiourly be
perceaued by them; and therefore it
was fit that he should be our *Iudge* as
man, and should passe his *Iudgment*
vpon men, that so he might be seene,
and heard by all. 1950586

This Mystery was discouered
to vs, by Christ our Lord, and Sauiour himselfe, whilest he was saying:
The Father iudgeth no man, but he hath Ioan. 5.
giuen all iudgement to the Sonne, and
he gaue him au.hority to exercise Iudge-
ment, as the sonne of man. That is to
say, Although the eternal Father haue
the supreme authority, and power of
Iudging, & that to him it doth principally belong to approue, & reward
that which is good, as also to reproue and punish that which is euill (&
the same also hath the Sonne; and the
holy Ghost the same, as being one &
the same God with the Father) yet
the office of *Iudging* exteriourly, and
after a visible manner to be seene, in
C 2   the

the Tribunall, and with the authority & Maiesty of a *Iudge* ; to giue exteriourly a *sentence* which may sensi-
bly be perceaued by such as are *iud-*
ged, this doth only belong to the person of the Sonne of God . Who by
meanes of the most sacred humanity
which he hath immediatly vnited to
himselfe , & by the power which frō
all eternity he hath as God ; and by
that which in Tyme was communicated to him as man; he is to make
this visible and exteriour *Iudgment* ,
this being an execution of the interiour inuisible *Iudgmēt*, which is made
of all the most Blessed Trinity . And
although this exteriour *Iudgment*, be
also ascribed to the Father , and to all
the Blessed Trinity , as to the prime
cause of all things, yet he who is the
immediate executour of this *Iudge-*
ment, is Iesus Christ the Sonne of the
liuing God ; because the sacred Humanity is only vnited immediatly to
the

the perſon of the Sonne, & that Humanity doth make this *Iudgment*, as the inſtrument of Diuinity.

Now (b) an immenſe benefit, and an imcomprehenſible mercy it was, for God the *Father* to giue vs Chriſt *Ieſus* for the *Iudge* of our cauſe, as he is man, as he is our brother, and our Sauiour If a delinquent were in priſon for greiuous Crymes, deſeruing death, and that he had a brother who moſt tenderly loued him, and eſteemed him, and did ſo much deſire his liberty, and his good, that to deliuer him out of priſon, and from death, he had ſpent his fortune, and had expoſed himſelfe to many troubles, and euen to the hazard of death; and if the king ſhould aſſigne that brother of the party for the *Iudge* of his cauſe, with Soueraigne power, to *Iudge* him without appeale; what kind of fauour, what clemency would it be, which heerin ſhould be vſed towards

that

(b) An vnſpeakable benefit of God who gaue vs Chriſt our Lord for our Iudge.

that man ? How full of ioy and comfort would he be, vpō the naming of
such a *Iudge* ? How confident and secure would he make himself, that the
sentence would be full of pitty , and
as fauourable to him , as possible his
cause might beare ? Well therfore ,
since all men , according to the (c)
ordinary law are faulty and guilty, &
it being necessary , according to the
diuine Iustice and wisedome , that
Iudgment be giuen vpon them ; & the
cause of all them , who haue comitted mortall sinne, being so important,
that either they must be condemned
to immense & euerlasting torments ,
or be declared not guilty , but worthy to enioy the kingdome of heauē;
what greater fauour, what clemency
could be desired, or euen thought of ,
then that God the *Father* should be
pleased to giue vs, for our *Iudg, Christ*
Iesus , who is our brother , and of the
selfe same nature with vs ; and who
loues

(c) From
which
Christ
our Lord
& his B.
Mother
are excep
ted.

loues vs with an vnfpeakeable loue;
and who doth fo much efteeme, and
defire both our liberty, & our glory,
that for the procuring therof, he hath
offered himfelf to moft bitter paines,
and fcornes, and euen to the death
of the Croffe? O how great a comfort, O how incomparable a ioy is
this, for thofe fonnes of *Adam*, who
feele the greatnes of this benefit? O
how confident, and fecure ought
they to be, that *Iudgment* fhall goe
vpon them with greate mercy; and
that the rigour of *Iuftice*, fhalbe té-
pered with much pitty; and that the
fentéce fhall paffe in fauour of them,
for as much as fhalbe poffible, without impeachment of the holy law, &
moft fweet ordination of Almighty
God.

CHAP.

CHAP. II.

Of the great desire, which Christ our Lord hath (for as much as concerneth him) not to condemne any one, in his Iudgment, *but to saue them all.*

THIS most mercifull *Iudg*, hath giuen vs some most euident testimonies, of the most ardent desire which he hath, not to condemne vs in his diuine *Iudgment*; but to deliuer vs as free & safe, & that the sentence may wholy passe in fauour of vs. One of these testimonies, and that a very admirable one, is this; That before he would come, the second tyme, to make an *vniuersall Iudgment* of sinners, & to condemne & punish (a) Marke such as he should finde to be faulty, this excellent do- (ᵃ) he came, in that first cōming of ctrine, for his, to passe a *Iudgment* vpon sinns it is ful of themselues; to destroy, and to con-truth and sume, and to depriue them of being, comfort. and

and life ; and in like manner also to
passe a *Iudgement* , against all the enimies of our soules : namely the *World,*
the *Flesh*, and the *Diuell* ; and to ouercome , and dispossesse them of all
power, and Tytle, which they might
make to men ; and to defeate those
forces which they mainteyned to the
preuidice of mens soules ; and to giue
men strength , and meanes , wherby
they might defend themselues , and
obteine perfect victory against them
all. That so , when he should come
to passe a *Iudgment* vpon men , he
might finde them free from sinne ;
and if not all of them , yet so many,
at least , as would take profit by the
grace he gaue them ; and consequently
that he might haue nothing to punish
in them . Yea and moreouer , that he
might finde them conquerours ouer
their enemies , that so he might giue
them that reward of glory , for their
victory, which he had promised to

such as should ouercome.

This is that high *Mystery* which
Christ our Lord discouered to vs in
the Ghospell, somtyme saying, *That
he came not to Iudge the world, but to
saue the world.* At other times he faith,
that he came to make iudgment vpō
the world, as he teacheth vsby the *E-
uangelist* saying, *I came into the world
to Iudge it.* And yet in another place:
Now is Iudgmēt to passe vpon the world.
Our Lord meanes to say heerby, as
himself declares, That at his first cōming when he came, in a mortal and
passible body, he came not to passe a
Iudgement vpon men, to chastise &
condemne the wicked, by doing
Iustice, and pronouncing a sentence
of condemnation against them. For
if he had come to this end, and that
he would haue passed this *Iudgement*
at his first comming; he would, in
effect, haue bin obliged to comdem-
ne all the world; for, in effect he
found

Ioan. 3.

Ioan. 12.

Ioan. 8.

found them all in sin; and euen those few Iust persõs who were free,were so,in vertue of his being come to saue them. And if that first coming of his, had beene to *Iudge* men, euen those few had also bene in state of sinne, and had beene condemned. He therfore explicates himselfe by saying, *I came not to iudg the world,but to saue it,* That is, I came not as a Iudge, but as a Sauiour, I came not to condemne sinners by doing Iustice on them, & by passing a sentence of condemnation against them; But (b) I came to saue them, by suffering and dying for them,and by communicating my Iustice and merits to them; that so I might free them from sinne, and Iustify them; and giue them the spirituall health of grace, and of eternall glory. And to this very office of sauing men, is ordeyned that *Iudgement*,which he saith he came to make in that first comming, and which he

(b) Christ our Lord deliuereth no man from the paynes of hell, by his sacred Passion, but such as first are deliuered by it from sinne,

was

was to paſſe againſt ſinnes, & againſt
the diuell alſo in fauour of men. So
doth he declare himſelfe, ſaying :
Through my Paſſion and Death ,
Iudgment is now to paſſe, and ſentence is to be giuen, in fauour of the
men of this world, againſt the diuell.
For till now, he held men ſubiect,
and captiued vnder his power and
tyranny ; but now, by the payment
which I am making for thē, they are
to remaine ſafe and free. Now, the
diuell , who is the Prince of this
world, who held men ſubiect vnder
ſinne, is to be depoſed from that dominion which he held in the world ;
for innumerable ſoules, which were
captiued in error and ſinne, are to be
conuerted and ſaued ; and remedy
ſhalbe imparted to them all, wherby
they may be deliuered from him, and
may obtaine eternall glory.

　　　So alſo, in that firſt cōming of
Chriſt our Lord to ſaue mankind,
　　　　　　　　　　　　　　　he

he made a kind of diſtinguiſhing and
deuiding *Iudgement* , betweene the
good, and the bad ; the eleƈt, and the
reprobate. For when he was preaching, and working miracles, and
procuring the ſaluatiō of the world;
ſome did profit by his comming , re-
ceauing his fayth, and obeying his
Ghoſpell, & participating of his merits. And others againe, becauſe they
would not belieue in him, nor ſerue
themſelues of his remedyes , did ſtill
remaine in their ſins; yea, & through
their ingratitude, and the hardnes of
their harts , they grew therein . And
thus by the occaſion of the comming
of Chriſt our Lord , the diſtinƈtion
grew more apparent , betweene the
faythful & the vnfaithfull ; between
Iuſt perſons, and ſinners; betweene
the eleƈt, and ſuch as were reprȯued
by God .

For they who receaued the faith
of Chriſt , & did follow him, by the
imitation

imitation of his life, & by the taking
vp of his Croſſe, according to their
(c) preſent iuſtice, were iuſt perſons;
& as long as they did perſeuere, they
had ſignes in them, of being prede-
ſtinated; and they who receaued not
the fayth, according to their then
preſent ſtate, were wicked & reprobate. This did our Lord declare, whē
he ſayd : *I came into this world, that*
they who ſee not, might ſee; & they who
ſee might be blind. Which was as much
to ſay, Vpon my comming, did this
iudgment follow, and this diſtincti-
on was made amongſt men; that many who in their ſoules were blind,
through ignorance and errour, and
vice, and who did not ſee the truth,
nor did walke in the right way to
heauen, by beleeuing in me, with a
liuely fayth, they I ſay, might ſee the
truth, and follow it . And that many
others, who ſaw, and had knowledg
of the Scriptures, and did know the
law,

(c) That is
according
to the
ſtate,
wherein
they were
at that
tyme .

law, and the Prophets ; & who both
in their own , and in the peoples opinion, & eftimation, were held wife,
and had a fpirituall light wherwith
to looke into diuine things ; they, I
fay, for their pride and ingratitude,
fhould remaine blind ; and, going a-
ftray from the right way, fhould not
find their errour and perdition .

Another diuine and moft fingular teftimony, which Chrift our
Lord hath giuen vs , of the defire
which he hath, in this iudgment of
his , not to finde any finnes which he
might punifh, nor any finners whom
he fhould be fo obliged to condemne,
is , That (d) at his firft comming he
made a law, which was to laft till the
end of the world , wherby he gaue
faculty to all finners , that during the
whole tyme whilft their life fhould
laft , they might paffe a *Iudgement*
vpon themfelues ; acknowledging
their finns , and accufing themfelues
there-

(d) Let all
Angells a-
dore him
for this
ineftima-
ble bene-
fit to men.

therof with greefe , and confessing
them to a Priest , who should hould
the place of Christ our Lord ; and sa-
tissying for them, according to the
iudgment of the same Ghostly father;
and that they performing this , he
would not , in his *Iudgment*, either
cōdemne or punish them , but would
declare them to be *not Guilty* , and
would impart the kingdome of heauen to thē. And that ,if hauing once
passed this *Iudgement* vpon themselues , they should yet return againe
to sinne, & become abnoxious therby to eternall condemnation ; yet stil
as long as their life should last , they
might returne to passe the same *Iudg-*
ment vpon themselus, as often as they
would ; and that if they should do it
according to (c) *Truth*, he would not
condemne them , but would admit
them into his company , and make
them happy . O *Iudgment* which is so
deerely sweet ! O *Iudge,* who is so ful
                                    of

(c) Con-
fessing
them all
clearely
with great
sorrow &
firme pur-
pose of a-
mendmēt

of mercy ! and how vnanfwerable is
it proued by this moſt pitteous *Iudge*,
that his intention and defire, is not to
puniſh but to pardon; nor to condemne, but to abſolue and ſaue; ſince before he comes to paſſe his *Iudgment*,
he vſeth ſo many meanes, & applyes
ſo many remedies , to the end that he
may finde no ſinnes to puniſh, nor no
ſinners to condemne.

If an earthly *Iudge*, had his prifon
ful of delinquents & theeues, & murtherers, and ſhould make a kind of a-
greement and bargaine with them,
that (f) euery one of them might
choofe what friend or kinſman of his
owne he would , and in ſecret ſhould
declare his offence to him, deliuering
to him the whole truth , and vndergoing but that penalty which he
ſhould impoſe vpon him for the ſame;
And that, vpon ſome day of the ſame
yeare , himſelfe would come to the
prifon to *Iudge* them ; and that he

D   would

(f) Confider feriouſly heerof & admire the infinit goodnes of God in that, wherein the blind world thinkes it hath hard meaſure , namely in the Inſtitution of the Sacrament of Confeſſion,

would pronounce them to be free,
who had declared their offences to
friend or kinſman of theirs; & who
had performed the penalty which he
had impoſed; and that he would only cōdemne thoſe others, who would
not haue recourſe to that remedy;
what would you ſay of this *Iudge*, &
of this agreement? You would ſay,
that there nether is, nor euer was, nor
euer will be in the world any Iudge,
who ſheweth, or is to ſhew any ſuch
mercy; nor who euer made, or will
euer make any ſuch Capitulation,
with perſons who had deſerued to
dye; nor are there any laws on earth,
which can permit any ſuch thinge.
And if there were any *Iudge*, who
would ſubmit himſelfe to the like cō-
dition, there would no delinquent
be found, who would not ioyfully
performe this agreement, and ſo be
declared for not guilty.

　　Well then, Chriſt Ieſus, the E-
ternall

ternall *Iudge*, and who is of infinite
power and Maiesty, doth shew this
mercy to all such sinners as are worthy of eternall death. And he hath
made this bargaine, and agreement
with them all; and that is yielded to
by the laws of heaue, which the laws
of earth will not endure. Let vs therfore serue our selues of this mercy,
let vs performe the articles of this a-
greement; and let vs, in tyme, passe a
Iudgment vpon our selues; let vs confesse our sinnes with true sorrow; &
let vs amend our liues, to the end that
when at the houre of our death, in
the *particuler Iudgment*; and at the end
of the world in the *Vniuersal iudgment*
we shal come before this great *Iudge*,
he may find no sinnes to punish or
condemne in vs. For it is sayd by S.
Iohn the Apostle, concerning this
Lord: *If we confesse our sins, repenting* 1. *Ioan*. 1.
our selues truly of them, before God and
his substitute, God is iust, and faithfull,

in fulfilling the promises, and rewarding the merits of Chri our Sauiour; and so he will pardon vs our nnes, through his merits, and will cleanse vs from all wickednes, as he hath promised.

O most vnhappy men who deferring to do pennance, and to make amendment of their liues, despise this mercy of God, as S. Paul sayth by making ill vse thereof; *And (g) by this meanes they treasure vp the wrath and punishment of God for themselues, against the day of his wrath, which is, that, of his Iudgement.* These lawes of mercy were not made, nor are they proclaimed vnto men, to the end that thereupon, they should take such a wicked strange presumption to sinne; but that, if they haue sinned, they should not be dismaid: but that in hope of this diuine mercy, they should instantly correct themselues, and reforme their liues and obtaine pardon. So doth the glorious Apostle

S. *iohn*

Rom. 2.

(g) Woe be to the who will needes be wicked euen because God is so infinitely good.

S *Iohn* aduertise vs ; for hauing sayd :
That if we confesse our selues well, God
will pardon vs, he instātly addeth this, 1. Ioan. 2.
These thinges haue I written, to you my
children, to the end, that you may not
sinne but that you may fly from sinne at
full speed but yet if any man do sinne,
we haue an Aduocate before the Father.
That is to say, let him not be dismaid,
nor out of hope ; but let him instantly be conuerted to God, confessing
his sinnes, and doing pennance for
the same ; because we haue an Aduocate and Mediatour before the e-
ternall Father, which is Iesus Christ
the Iust, and the very fountaine of
Iustice, who made satisfaction for al
our sinnes.

D 3 CHAP.

CHAP. III.

*Of the benefit which Christ our Lord im-
parteth to vs , in giuing vs to vnderstand , and feele the grieuousnes of
sinne , by the meanes & manner of his
Iudgement, to the end , that we may
in tyme do pennance for it .*

ANOTHER most singular be-
nefit , which Christ our Lord
imparteth to vs , vnder the quality
of his being our *Iudge* ; is to make vs
know and feele , the grieuousnes of
of sinne, that so we may be drawne
to abhorre it greatly , & to conceaue
a true feare of falling into any offence of God . This knowledg, and this
holy *Feare* do we fetch from the consideration of that diuine Iudgment ,
since notwithstanding that Christ
our Sauiour , is of his owne Nature
most pitteous, and most benigne ; &
be-

being the very fountaine of pitty and
mercy; and being moft profoundly
meeke, and fweet, and the very fountaine of fweetnes; and being fo great
a louer of men, that he dyes for them;
and fo much defiring, and efteeming
the faluation of their foules, that he
giues his life for the fame; we (ª) yet
fee, that in his *iudgment* he will come
extremely full of caufe, to make vs
horribly feare; and moft terrible wil
he be in the higheft degree, and full
of wrath and fury, & for zeale of iuftice againft finners He will come
fitting downe, vpon thofe horfes of
the heauen which are the cloudes; he
will come in a warlike manner, accompanyed by all the fquadrons and
armies of heauen; he will draw with
him the whole world of creatures,
being all ranged & placed in forme
of battaile againft finners. Yea, and
euen the very Saintes, and Bleffed
foules themfelues, who are fo full of

(a) The
terrour
wherwith
Chrift
our Lord
will ap-
peare, at
the later
day.

Matt. 25.

Sap. 5.

Sopho.c.1.

pitty

pitty, and haue beene the Aduocates
of sinners, will come armed, & shall
be made both Iudges, and the Ministers of diuine Iustice against them.
He shall haue, for the Messenger
Psal. 96. which speakes of his comming, a
most furious fire, which shall burne
and purge all corporeall creatures; &
a most hideous frightfull sound of
mysterious trumpets, whichshal sped
themselues ouer the whole world; &
shall make all creatures tremble; and
shal passe and pierce euen to the low-
est bottome of hell, and shall make
those soules spring out of those infernall habitations of theirs, full of horrible confusion, to resume their bodyes and appeare in *Iudgment*. In this
manner doth the Scripture describe
the comming of Christ our Lord to
Iudgement.

Let vs now consider, who it is
that canseth this mutation of Christ
our Lord. Who changeth him in so
                                    strange

ſtrang a faſhion? Who maketh him,
of moſt pittifull, ſo extremly fierce?
Who, of moſt profoundly meeke, ſo
full of wrath? Of muſt delightfully
ſweet, ſo full of fury and terrour? Of
peaceable, ſo giuen to warre? Of a
refuge and ſhelter for ſinners, to be
growne ſuch a ſeuere puniſher of the
faulty? Sinnes (b) they are which
cauſe this great mutation, and which
do ſo farre eſtrange him from that
moſt benigne, and ſweet condition
of his. The hatred and profound
deteſtation which he hath of ſinne;
the liuely feeling he hath, to ſee himſelfe ſo foulely offended; the greiuous
weight which our faultes do carry
in his diuine preſence, wherby his
will is tranſgreſt, and his law deſpi-
ſed, do make him grow ſo frightfull,
and ſo very fierce, towards the doing of iuſtice, and taking vengance
vpon ſinners. So ſaith the Apoſtle of
Chriſt; *Iudas Thadæus*, ſpeaking of

(b) See
heere, if
ſinne be
not a dan-
gerous
compani-
on to liue
withall.

Iud. 1.

D 5   this

this *Iudgment* : *Marke well*, *for our Lord doth come accompanied with the innumerable troupes of holy Angells to passe a iudgment vpon all wicked men; to conuince them of all the euill workes which they haue comitted, and of all the euill words which they haue spoken, contrary to the law of God ; and to pronounce a sentence of condēnation against them*

Since then the hatred which God doth carry against sinne , is so very great ; since the punishment which he will execute vpon sinners in that *Iudgment* of his is so immense; O it is full of reason , that from the faith and infallible notice which we haue of this truth , all we , who are beleeuers, should fetch a knowledge of the grieuousnes of sinne ; and a perfect detestation of the same, and a profound griefe and sorrow for such sinne as we haue already cōmitted; & much feare in respect of them which

we

we may commit heerafter. That so
we may fly them, and be freed from
the fury of that diuine *Iudgment*, and
from that sentence of eternal damna
tion, which is to be thundered out
against sinners. For (c) this is the true
reason, why this *Iudgment* is discouered, and notified to vs, as *S. Paul*
affirmed whilst he was preaching to
the *Athenians* to this effect: *God doth
now anounce the truth of his Ghospell, to men; to the end that all men, and
in all places, may do penance of their sins;
since he hath, with firme deliberation,
ordeyned a day, at which tyme he will
iudg the whol world with great vprightnes of iustice; giuing to euery one, that
reward and punishment which his workes
deserue. And this Iudgment he will
passe vpon the world, by the meanes of
Christ our Lord; who, as man, hath authority from the eternall Father, to giue
visible Iudgment vpon all men.*

(c) The
true vse
which we
are to
make of
conside-
ring the
terrour of
the day
of Iudge-
ment.

Act. 17.

CHAP.

CHAP. IIII.

How we are to haue great feeling. of the grieuousnes of sinne, by reason of the demonstrations which shall be made by all the creatures of God before the Iudgement.

TO the end that from the declaration of the office which Christ our Lord hath of being the *Iudge*; & of the *Iud ement* which is to passe vpon the whole world, we may draw the great fruite of knowing and feeling the greiuousnes of sinne, and of abhorring it , and doing penance for it; and , that we may also draw from thence , a feare of sinne, and of the punishment therof, we will go declaring those points, and misteries of this diuine *Iudgment*; which may best discouer to vs the immensnes of the hate, which God doth carry towardes

wards sinne; and of the punishment
which he inflicteth vpon sinners. The
first point which doth discouer to vs
the hate which God doth carry toward sinne, is, that in this his terrible *Iudgment*, he will not onely punish the sinners who did offend him
by their sins, but (a) he will, after a
sort, punish all the Creatures of the
whole world, wherby sinners were
assisted and serued. The *Sunne* shall
grow darke; not as now it doth som-
tymes, by naturall causes; or in respect
that any cloude may ouershadow it;
or becaufe the Moone may cast it self
betweene it, and the earth, (as it
hapneth in the cafe of an Eclipse)
but it is to be obscured, by a supernaturall and miraculous caufe; and fo it
is to be vnderstood, that for a while it
shall loose the whole light it had. The
Moone shall also loose her light. The
Stars shall fall from heauen either becaufe when they are without light,

Matt. 24.

(a) How
insensible
creatures,
shall after
a fort be
punished,
for ha-
uing been
made the
instrumēt
of mans
finne.

Ioel. 2.

it

it ſhall ſeeme to be , as if they were
fallen , or els for that , in very deed,
they ſhall diſlodge themſelues from
that high firmament , where they are
fixt,and for ſome tyme ſhall fall from
thence, and deteine themſelues in the
ayre , till they returne againe into
their place.

The *powers* of the heauen ſhalbe
moued ,that is,thoſe celeſtiall bodies,
with their naturall vertue ſhall trem.
ble, and ſo ſhift their places, as in an
earthquake the earth is wont to do ;
or if it be vnderſtood of *Angells* ,the
meaning is , how in that day , they
ſhall make ſome kind of ſpiritual de-
mõſtration, & motion of great admi.
ratiõ.The *Sea* ſhalbe troubled, & ſhal.
be moued in a moſt wõderful mãner,
and with the waues thereof, ſhall
make ſuch a hideous noyſe, as will a-
ſtoniſh the whole world ; & oppreſſe
and afflict with exceſſiue feare and
horrour, the harts of mortall men , &
will

will make them euen whither againe
with woe . The *Earth*, shall tremble, 2. *Pet.* 3.
and shalbe open in many partes, and
shall disclose euen the pits of hel. The
Ayre, with the same *Earth* , and *Sea*,
shall burne by that most ardent ouerflowing of fire, which shall consume
al the liuing bodyes, of fishes, beasts,
and men . God in his law, comman- *Deut. c.* 13.
ded the children of *Israel* , that when *v.* 20.
they should be to fight against the I-
dolatours, and Pagans (who dwelt
in the Land of Promise , and whome
he was pleased to punish for their
sinnes) not only that they should kill
the men , but euen the very beasts ,
which did them seruice ; and so in
particuler he (b) exacted this of
Saul, when he went to fight against (b) A signe
the *Amalecites* ; and because he did of this
not punctually comply with this co- truth in
the old
mandment, but suffered some of the Testamēt
Cattle to liue, God was offended, & 1. *Reg.* 3.
Saul was punished .

Let

Let vs now fee why God did not content himfelfe, with caufing the men who had finned to be put to death, but the beafts alfo, which had no fault. It was to make men vnderftand and feele, that finne is fo great a mifcheife, and is fo worthy to be abhorred and punifht, and that God doth indeed, fo much abhor it, that it is a moft côuenient thing, not onely to punifh finners with eternall tormêts & death, but to deftroy alfo, and confume, and as it were to cha-ftice, the creatures wherof they did ferue & help thêfelues towards their finnes. Therfore is it, that refoluing in the *Vniuerfall Iudgment* to chaftice the wickednes of all men, in a moft complete manner, he will not content himfelfe to deliuer ouer finners them felues to thofe eternall ardours of fire, & thofe other immenfe paines of hell; but to the creaturs alfo wher-of they made fome vfe in finning, he

giues

giues as it were a kind of payne, and
punifhment, in deteftation of the fins
themfelues ; as alfo, to the end that
they may be purged, and cleered frō
that indecency, and deformity which
grewto them, by the feruice, which
they did to finners. For thus it is, that
the *Sunne*, the *Moone*, & *Stars*, which
did illuminate finners whileft they
were committing their finnes, fhalbe
depriued by him for a whyle, of all
the light, & beauty which they haue,
& he fhall conuert it into thick darknes. And as for the *Sea*, & the *Earth*,
& *Ayre*, which gaue food to finners,
& did maintaine them, whileft they
were offending God, he will make
them as it were feare, and tremble, &
will depriue them, for a tyme, of the
naturall quality and difpofition they
haue; and will confume, and kill all
thofe liuing creatures, and plantes,
which were the food of finners ; and
wil deftroy al thofe buildings, which

E   were

were the habitation of wicked men.
And thus, through the mutation, &
demonstration, & desolation which
in the *Iudgment*, God will shew in al
the creatures which serued sinners, he
doth teach and testify the infinite hatred which he hath against sin . And
he doth induce, & perswade vs , that
now, through the knowledge of this
truth, we may be drawn to abhor &
detest them; and that with a peniten-
tiall & holy life, we may cleanse our
soules, as well as possibly we can, frō
al fault & offence of his diuine Maiesty . *S . Peter* (c) doth admonish vs of
the good effect which we are to draw
from the change which is to be made
vpon the creatures, by saying to this
effect : *Since there is a day of the vniuersall Iudgement to come wherin all the
creatures, for hauing serued sinners are
to be purged with fire and burnt ; inferre
my brethren from hence, how diligent ,
and constant it is fit for you to be , in the
leading*

2. *Pet.*3.

(c) This
truth is
insinua-
ted by S.
Peter.

leading of a good life; and how holily and
purely you are to converse in this world,
and how vigilant, and carefull, it will
becom you to be, in performing the works
of piety towards God; and of mercy towards your Neighbour; expecting with a
liuely fayth, that day of our Lord; and
approaching and drawing neere to him
with speed, not with paces of the body, but
with the desires & affections of the soule,
desiring and louing this day, and preparing to see your selues at that tyme, accompanyed with purity of life, and with
the exercise of vertue.

CHAP. V.

How Christ our Lord, discouereth the
hate, which he carryeth towardes sin,
by the so particuler account which he
taketh of them all.

ANOTHER mystery of this diuine Iudgement, discouering the
mighty

mighty demonftration, and deteſta-
tiō which God doth expreſſe againſt
the faults whereby he is offended; is
the ſo particuler accompt which he
will take of vs, & which we all muſt
giue, of all the facultyes or powers,
& al the ſenſes, both of our body and
ſoule; & of all the creaturs which we
haue vſed; and (a) of all the workes
which we haue performed, all the
wordes which we haue ſpoken, and
all the thoughts which we haue conceaued, how little ſoeuer they fall
out to haue beene; without leauing
out, ſo much as any one idle word, or
any one idle thought. We ſhall giue
accompt of how we imployed our
Vnderſtanding; if we did ſet it on
worke, vpon the inquiry and ſearch
of God, and his truth, and in contemplating on him, & his holy Cõ-
mandments, and the workes of his
handes, and the diuine words of his
mouth. As for the memory, we ſhalbe

(a) If you beleeue this point of fayth to be true I ſhall not need to wiſh you to looke wel about you.

be queſtioned, if we haue vſed it, in calling our Lord God to mind, to-geather with his preſence, his good-nes, his power, and all his benefits, and mercies. We ſhalbe arraigned vpon the point of our Will, if perhaps it haue beene buſyed, in the loue, and eſtimation, and deſire of God, and the accompliſhment of his Law, and of his will; and in the ſearch of all thoſe thinges, which concerne the glory of our Lord God.

We ſhall (ᵇ) giue account, of how we put the ſenſes of our body on worke; if we imployed our eyes vpon behoulding this fabrike of the world, and theſe Heauens, and Ele-ments, and the other works of God, that ſo, behoulding in theſe creaturs, the trace, and ſent which they carry in them, of all his diuine perfections, we may raiſe our ſelues vp by them: So to conſider with our ſoules, the power, and the wiſedome, and the

(b) We ſhall not only giue account of our ſinnes, & the facul-ties of our mind, but alſo of the ſenſes of our body and of the vſe of all Gods cre-atures.

E 3 good-

goodnes, and the beauty of God, and
by this meanes, to loue and praise him
with our whole harts. So also, if we
imployed our ears, to hear the words
of the true God; and those instructi-
ons, and doctrines, & admonitions,
and examples, which were profitable to the soule; and in hearing the
sweet musicke of mans voice; and of
the instruments which he can vse, &
of the birds also of the ayre, so to stir
our selues vp, towardes deuotion, &
to contemplate the much sweetnes
of that Celestiall musicke; and so to
loue and esteeme the blessinges of
heauen. And concerning the Smell,
if we imployed it onely, vpon those
things which are necessary for mans
life; & through the sent of creaturs if
we aspir'd towardes the sweet sauour
of vertues, and of good example; &
of the glory of the next life. So also
for the Tongue, if it was mouing in
the prayse of our Lord God, & in offering

ring him deuout prayers, & in lear-
ning and teaching thofe thinges,
which are neceffary both for our felues and our Neighbours; and in dif-
couering, and confeffing our finnes
for the obtayning of pardon, and re-
dreffe thereof, and in taking but that
food, which was neceffary for the
fuftenance of our life; and in drawing out of the guft & fauour of corporal meate, a confideration and feeling of the vnfpeakeable fweetnes,
and fauour of thofe fpirituall foods of
grace, and glory. So alfo, if we haue
imployed the fenfe of Feeling with
our handes, and all the reft of our body, vpon the onely taking of thofe
thinges, which were neceffary for
the fame body; and profitable for our
foule, and for our Neighbours, and
for the vfe of our life, and for the exercife of the workes of Charity and
Mercy.

  This good vfe of all the powers

    E 4   of

of our ſoules & ſenſes of our body doth
our Lord God demaund of vs , when
he ſaith , *Keepe thy ſelfe , and keepe thy*
ſoule , with great care ; and of this are
we to make a very exact accompt ,
in his diuine *Iudgement* . Wee ſhall
alſo giue accompt in the ſame *Iudg-*
ment of all our ſinnes of ſpeach ; ſuch
as are vaine Oathes , Reproaches ,
murmurations , curſings, ſcoffing of
our neighbours , and words of anger
and impatience , of lying, of ſowing
diſcord : Of theſe and others which
are either laſciuious , or curious, or
vaine, *of euery idle word* , ſaith Chriſt
our Redeemer , *ſhall men giue a compt*
in the day of Iudgment ; and that word
goeth for *idle* which is neither neceſſary, nor profitable . Accompt muſt
alſo be giuen of all ſinnes of deed ;
ſuch as are diſobedience to parents ,
and other Superiours , reuenge , ill
intreaty of our neighbours, diſhone-
ſty, iniuſtice, vſurping & detayning
the

Deut. 4.

Mat. 12.

the goods of others againſt right,
vnlawfull bargaines, pride in gouernement, exceſſe in the furniture
of houſes, of clothes, of expences
otherwiſe, and in the intertaine-
mēt of ſeruants; exceſſe alſo in dyet,
in play, and in other ſuperfluous and
vaine things: Of all theſe, and of all
other euill deeds, accompt muſt be
giuen, as *Eccleſiaſtes* ſaith; *All things* Eccleſ. 12:
which are done by man, both good & bad,
ſhall be preſented in that diuine Iudge-
mēt, to be there examined; & for euery
work which ſhalbe found erroneous
and ill, he ſhalbe puniſhed. We ſhall
giue accompt of al our thoughts, ſuch
as are raſh Iudgmēt; conſents which
are giuen to reuenge, or els vncleanes
or voluntary delights, in any thing
which is ill; or to inward hatred; or
in fine, to thoughts which are vnprofitable For as the Wiſe man ſaith,
God will examine, & iudge the thoughts Sap. 1
of the wicked.

E 5   Beſides

Besides this, we shall giue (c) accompt of our sinnes of Omission, which are the most in number, and ly most hidden from our sight. For hauing forborne to pray, to read good bookes, to fast, to performe other penances, and mortifications, and to confesse, and communicate. For hauing omitted to do the workes of Iustice, and mercy, in certaine cases, and at certaine tymes, when either some particuler precept, or the great necessity of doing those workes, did oblige vs to them. For hauing fayled to comply with many dutyes of our calling, and offices, to which we were bound by the obligations either of God or man. We shall giue accompt, how we haue profited by those spirituall and supernaturall graces, which God hath giuen vs; such as are his *Sacraments*; the guifte of *Fayth*; the Doctrine of the *Ghospell*; good *Sermons*, holy exampls, vertuous

(c) A point of great moment and little thought on.

vertuous conuersations, the admonitions, and reprehensions of our
Superiours, and Ghostly Fathers;
and the interiour inspirations which
God hath giuen vs. We shall giue account, how we haue vsed our naturall and temporall benefits, as namely
our *Health*; if we haue imployed it
vpon the seruice of that Lord who
gaue it; Our *Tyme*, if we haue spent
it profitably ; our *Reputation*, if we
vsed it to the glory of God, and the
good of our Neighbour. Our *Estate* &
temporal goods, if we haue imployed
them, onely to the succour of the true
necessities of our selues, our family,
and our neighbours, and of those
things which are profitable to the
life of a Christian man, and to the
honest Condition of euery one.

The accompt which is to be giuen for these sinnes of *Omission*, and
the punishment which is allotted to
them, Christ our Lord declared in
that

that *Parable* of the *Talents*, when he told that vnprofitable seruant, that the *Talent* which God gaue him, (which are his naturall and spirituall guifts, as also his temporall goods) was not well imployed by him, nor vsed in those workes which were agreable to God; and he said thus to

Matt. 25. him; *Thou negligent and wicked seruant, since thou sayst that I am rigorous, and that I expect more then I laid out, why didst thou not put out that* Talent, *to profit which I gaue thee?* That is, *why didst thou not make the right vse of what I gaue thee, imploying it well in the exercise of vertue, in the increase of merit, and in the multiplication of good works?* And so, when he had rebuked this sloathfull seruant, he commaunds the ministers of his Iustice, to execute the sentence, which he giues against him, when he sayth, *Take that vnprofitable seruant, and cast him into exteriour darknes, which is that of Hell;*

where

where there is lamentation, and euerlafting torment, through the paines of
intollerable both heat and could, & other
torments alfo, which are to be endured
there.

CHAP. VI.

How Chrift our Lord declares the dete-
ftation which he carryeth againft the
finnes of wicked men ; whereof they
are conuinced, by the fentence which he
pronounceth againft them.

THESE are the things, wherof
a man is to giue accompt in that
diuine *Iudgment* of God. And this is
that, which now is to be confidered,
that fo he may know how deeply
God doth feele the weight of finne,
and confequently how to moue himfelfe to deteft it. And withall let him
ponder, how after, that Chrift our
Lord hath demāded this accompt, of
the

thē whom he findeth to be culpable; for not hauing complyed with these obligations; but proceeded contrary to his commaundements: How, I say, that most iust *Iudge* will conuince them in that terrible *Tribunall*, before all the Inhabitants both of heauen and earth, saying to them in his man. ner.

(a) If this do not mooue thee, pray to God that it may, for els thou art in ill case.

You (a) men, why haue you thus *offended mee? why haue your done me so many Iniuries, I being your God, of infinity Maiesty, Goodnes, and Wisedome? I being your Creatour, your Father, and your Sauiour, who for you did giue my life, and shed my bloud? Why haue you spoken so many wordes in affront of me? Why haue you wrought so many wicked deeds, in dishonour and disobedience to my Law? Why did you consent to those bad desires, and thoughts, whereby you came to cast me vnder the feet of those creatures, esteeming & louing them more then me? Me, whom you ought to haue*

pray-

prayſed, & glorifyed with your tongues; whome you ſhould haue ſerued, and obey. ed with your workes ; whome you ſhould alwayes haue deſired and loued with your whole harts; for whom you ought to haue giuē your liues & a thouſand liues, if you had been Maiſters of ſo many. Why haue you ſo diſhonoured me, tranſgreſſing & trāpling vpō my Precepts? Why haue you exchāged me, with ſo extreme contempt, for thoſe moſt baſe aduantages and gayns of earth, and for thoſe moſt vaine de-lights, & guifts of creatures? Since you confeſſed me by your wordes, to be your Lord and God, why would you deny me by your workes? Tell me you men ſince I haue imparted to you ſo many ſupernatu-rall guifts, which I gayned for you, by my Paſſion, & Death; A guift of Fayth, and Baptiſme, whereby I made you Chriſtians; a guift of Grace, whereby I adopted you for my Children : ſo ma-ny Vertues, whereby you might adorne your ſoules, & be enabled to worke well;

The

The guift of Sacraments *, which might conferre and conuey my* Grace *into your soules ; and innumerable inspirations, which might quicken you vp towardes vertue: and so many most high, and most pretious guifts, which I purchased at my so great cost ; why haue you set them at so low a rate ? VVhy haue you despised thē, and permitted them to passe away, without being of any profit to you at all? More account did you make of the vanity of your descent, according to your linage of flesh & bloud, then of the fayth of Christians, and the adoption of the sonnes of God.*

More account did you make of money, which is made of dead mettall; & of the goods of this life, and of the vaine punctillios of honour, then of the blessing of my grace, and of those immense, eternall treasures of my glory : I hauing giuen you such a holy Law *, a Doctrine so pure, so profitable, and so celestiall, that you might obserue and keepe it ; hauing*
                                    giuen

giuen you so many Prophets, Apostles, holy Doctours, & so many Preachers, and
teachers of my Ghospell, to the end that
they all might coun aile & perswade you
to the observation of my Commandmēts,
and to the accomplishment of my will; yea
and my selfe, being come visibly downe to
earth in flesh & bloud, to teach & preach
this Law to you, by the very wordes of
myne owne mouth, why haue you made
no more account of this law, nor complyed with my will, nor obeyed my wordes?
Why would you rather do that which Sa-
thā that did tempt you to, thē that which
was commanded you by me? VVhy would
you rather follow, and obey that peruerse
enemy, who abhorred you, and endeauou-
red nothing but your damnatioī, then
me, who am your God, & who was your
Father, & who loued you, and did procure your saluation & euerlasting glory?
Tel me yet further, O you vngrateful mē,
since it is I who gaue you life, & health,
and temporal goods, & space of tyme,

F

that

that you might sacrifice it all to my ser-
uice; how commeth it to passe, that you
would needs imploy it in offence of me? I
gaue you life *, I say, and* health, *and*
strength, *whereby you might haue ac-*
quired vertues, and haue exercised good
*workes, and so you might haue (*b*) merk-*
ted eternall happines. And you on the o-
ther side, haue imploied it in the pursuite
of vaine honour, & of pleasing men, for
certaine interests which passe and perish;
and in the search of those deadly delights
which now are carrying you on, towards
eternall torments. I gaue you temporall
meanes, for the necessary supply of this
life, and that you might relieue the mi-
series of your Neighbours; and you haue
wasted them, vpon the foolish complemēts
of the world, and vpon banquets, which
serued not for necessitie but for gluttony;
and vpon certaine a'tires, & ornaments,
which did but serue for vanity; and vpon
sports, and other vicious imployments. I
gaue you Tyme *, to the end that you*
might

(b)throgh
the passiō
&promise
of Christ
our Lord
good
workes
arriue to
be meri-
torious,
andnot of
themsel-
ues.

might imploy it vpon praying, and rumi-
nating, and meditating vpon my benefitts
and mercyes, and vpon the Mysteryes of
my law, and in performing workes which
might haue relation to euerlasting life;
but you haue wasted it vpon vnprofitable
conuersations, and vpon wicked deedes,
which deserue to be rewarded with eter-
nall fire.

    These complaintes doth God
make againſt ſinners, by his Prophet;
and there will he make them at that
day, with greater demonſtration of
miſlike, then euer, till that tyme, he
will haue ſhewed. And thereby he
will conuince them all, & they ſhalbe able to make no excuſe or deféce,
nor haue ſo much as one word to anſwere; and ſo ſhall that be fulfilled
which the *Pſalmiſt* ſayth, *All wicked-*   Pſal. 106.
nes, that is, all wicked men, ſhal haue
the mouth ſtopped vp.

    Let vs now conſider, what e-
uery one of theſe ſinners will thinke

within himfelfe, in that point of the
diuine *Iudgement*, when (c) he fhall
see a Theater made round about him,
of all the creatures, both of heauen
and earth; and that himfelfe is placed
in the middeft of them; & that both
all the Angells, and men, and Diuels
are looking on him. And when he
fhall obferue, that his finnes are pu-
blifhed, and proclaymed before them
all; and not only his wicked words,
and workes, but euen all his bad defires, and thoughts; & when he fhall
perceaue that all that lewdnes which
he committed in the moft retyred
corners; yea and thofe impurityes,
which did not fo much as iffue out of
his hart, fhall then be cleare and pa-
tent to all the world. To fee that all
thofe Diuels fhal ftand accufing him,
& that his own very confcience is ftil
vpbraiding & cōdemning him. And
to fee the *Iudge* himfelfe offended, &
enraged againft him; and that he behoulds

(c) Make
this cafe
thyne
owne be-
tymes; for
one day it
wilbe thy
cafe, whe-
ther thou
wilt or no

houlds him with a countenance full
of terrour, and of reuenge, for iniu-
ryes receaued; and to fee that hideous
pitt of hell, all open, in expectation
to fwallow him vp; and to fee himfelfe fo euidently conuinced, & that
he hath no word to plead for himfelf.
And (d) that finding himfelfe hem- *(d) A fad*
med in, by fuch an exceffe of afflicti- *confide-*
ons, & fuch incomparable miferyes, *ration but*
muft cer-
he cannot fly away, nor hath he any *tainely*
one hole wherein to hide his head; *true.*
nor any one thing to alleadge, nor a-
ny one perfon to whome he may appeale, or by whom he may be fuccoured. For to defend himfelfe againft
the *Iudge*, is impoffible, fince he is of
infinite power. To deceaue him with
falfe informations, cannot be, fince
he is of infinite Wifedome. To work
vpon him by way of prefents or pe-
titions, is not to be thought of, fince
he is infinitely iuft. To goe in fearch
after Patrons, and Aduocats, is loffe

of labour. For in that day, neither
the Angels, nor the Apostles can intercede for any one, no nor euen the
Queene (e) *of heauen, and the mother*
of mercy, can plead the caufe of finners in that day. The gate of pardon
and fauing mercy, is then clofed vp,
againft all the wicked; & all the iuft
and bleffed foules, fhall approue of
the diuine *Iuftice*, in that day; and
fhall reioyce, in that it is to be executed ; becaufe fo it is fit for the glory
of God our Redeemer. And then fhal
that be perfectly fullfilled, which the
Pfalmift fayth: *The Iuft man, feeing the*
punifhment, and vengeance which is to be
taken vpon the wicked fhall reioyce, not
for the payne which thofe finners
fhallbe fu biect to; nor out of any defire of reuenge ; but only for the zeale
they haue to the glory of God, & for
the loue they beare to his diuine *Iu-*
ftice.

(e) A hea-
uy and
moft def-
perate
cafe.

Pfalm, 57.

CHAP.

CHAP. VII.

How Christ our Lord, discouereth the grieuousnes of sinne, and the hatred which he carryeth against it, by the last sentence wherby he is to condemne the wicked, and the punishment which he inflicteth vpon them.

ANOTHER Article of the diuine *Iudgement*, which doth admirably discouer the excessiue hatred which Christ our Lord doth carry against sin, is the last sentence which he will thunder out against the wicked. As soone as he shall haue published their sinnes, & conuinced them thereof, he wil deuide them from the company of the Iust; and then turning his terrible and fierce countenance towardes them, he will pronounce this most hideous sentence against them. *Depart* (a) *from me, you* (a) Our Lord deliuer vs from so great a misery.

F 4 *accur-*

accursed into that eternall fire which is
prepared for the Diuell and the wicked
Angells. Depart from me, who am
an infinite good, and the fountaine
of all benediction, of grace, of comfort, of ioy, of life, of saluation, & of
glory. If then, they be deuided from
that only fountaine of al Good, what
kind of miserable thinges will they
find themselues to be? It is plaine
that they must find themselues without comfort, without grace, without
ioy, without repose, or ease; and ful,
on the contrary side, of all misery, of
all mischiefe, & of all paine. Depart
all you accursed; because *cursed are*
they, who breake the Commandments of
the true God; for the greatest ill of all
ill, is sin, and to this ill do they submit themselues who do any thing against that which our Lord comāds.
So sayth *Dauid*, & so doth the church
sing euery day, when she speakes to
God, *Cursed are they, O Lord, who de-*
                                      part

part from keeping of thy Comaundmentes. *Pfal.* 118.
In particuler manner are they *accurfed*
in the Law, who doe not offer the
firft fruits, and tithes of thofe things,
which God had giuen to them; and *Matt.* 3, 1.
curfed alfo are thofe others, who hauing promifed fome beaft, in facrifice, to Almighty God, do offer him
fuch a one, as is leane and lame, and
worth nothing Into all thefe curfes
haue you fallen, becaufe you haue
broken the Commandmets of God,
and gaue him not the honour, and
glory, of all the good deeds which
once you wrought, nor of all the benefits which you receaued. And hauing confecrated and dedicated your
foules to our true God, by *Fajth*, and
Baptifme; and being obliged to giue
him the beft and chiefe part thereof,
which is your loue, and obedience, &
fidelity, and a watchfull care to doe
him feruice; you did not giue this to
God, but to the world, and to your

owne will; and for thefe reafons you are indeed accurfed, and your felues are the authors of your malediction.

Let (b) vs now confider, whither it is, that he fends them, when once he driues them from himfelfe. *Go*, faith he, *you accurfed, into euerlaſting fier*; & becaufe in this life you fought for contentments, for delights, and gufts according to your owne will, againſt the will of God, you ſhal now be burnt, body, and foule, with a moſt furious and impetuous fier, againſt your will. And becaufe by ſinning you haue offended and defpifed God, who is infinite Good, and an infinite Maiefty, that fier ſhall be infinite in the continuance therof. And who now ſhalbe the miniſters of Iuſtice, to torment thefe accurfed creatures? And with what companions ſhall they be forted, in that torment of eternall fire? *Go*, faith our Lord, *into eternal fire, which is prepared*

(b) Be attentiue, to fee whither the wicked are to be fent, whē they are once driuen from God.

red for the diuell and his wicked Angells.
For the principall authors of any wickednes, the punishement is principally to be prouided; and becaufe the
deuill, was the firft author of finne,
therfore was the torment of eternall
fier, prouided firft for him. And becaufe wicked men did follow the
deuill in the fault, they fhall follow
him alfo in the paine. And becaufe
they chofe to obey the perfwafion &
will of the deuill, rather then the
commaundement and will of God;
they fhall therfore haue him for their
tormentor, and companion, in that
euerlafting fier.

O what kind of paine, what
kind of torment is this which is prepared for the wicked! O what an (c)
huge Sea of paines and torments is
this; fo very incomprehenfible, thorough the intenfenes and fiercenes,
and fo infinite in the continuance
therof! The thing, which in this life
doth

(c) It is
fad fwim-
ming in
this fea.

doth moſt of all torment , and doth
cauſe moſt exceſſiue paine , is fire .
But the fire of this life , doth worke
after a limitted manner; according to
the naturail power which it hath ; &
it cannot paſſe beyonde thoſe con-
fines . Wheras the fire of hell , how-
ſoeuer it be of the ſame nature with
this of ours , yet worketh it as a ſu-
pernaturall inſtrument of God ; and
ſo it receiues no other tax or limit, but

(d) An
excellent
conſide-
ration .

the onely will of God . And (^{d}) as the
thinges which God doth take for
Inſtruments , whereby he ſheweth
mercy to ſuch as ſerue him , are ſub-
lymed by himſelfe , aboue the power which they had in nature ; and
are enabled to produce admirable
effeᶜts ; As namely he exalteth the
water of *baptiſme* , ſo farre as to be the
inſtrument of iuſtifying a ſoule ; and
the *Balſamum* of *Confirmation,* and the
Oyle of *Extreme Vnĉtion* , to giue
ſtrength and increaſe of grace ; ſo the
fire

fire of hell, which is fo deadly fierce
of his owne nature, is fupernaturally
ftrecht vp, to inflict a kind of paine
and torment which is incomparably
more great, and fierce, then that to
which the whole power of nature
can arriue. And fo it fhall not onely
torment the body, but the foule with
all. And it fhall not leaue anie one
part, or power either of body or foule vntormented; and the torment &
greife which it will caufe, fhalbe
greater then all, which either we can
fay, or thinke.

     The Prophet (e) *Iſay* doth fig-
nify thus much when he faith, That
Topheth, which is hell, *is prepared for
the wicked by God the eternall king, from
the begining of the world*. It is mightily
deepe, for it is in the very Center of
the earth. It is mightily wide and
capable, for the receiuing of all fuch
as fhalbe damned. The nourifhment
and food which fhall maintaine it, is
               fier

(e) Reade
and trem-
ble.

Iſa. 30.

fier, which shall neuer be quencht (as euen heere, the fier doth neuer go out, if alwaies it haue matter to intertaine it,) for the breath of God, as if it were some torrent of brimstone, doth inflame it. His meaning is, that as a mighty quantity of brimstone will inflame this fier which we haue, & as longe as the brimstone lasteth, so longe, doth the fyre also last; iust so, the will of God will kindle that fier of Hell; and as his will is eternall, so the fier can neuer haue an end. Now this fire, being supernaturally so fierce, and furious, to torment and burne; the wicked will not also faile to be very (f) well disposed, and prepared, to be tormented and burnt. Therefore doth the Prophet *Malachy* say, That they shalbe like straw. *The day of our Lord,* sayth he, *shall come burning like a fornace of fire: & such as are proud withall the workers of wickednes, shallbe like straw to be infla. med*

(f) How conbustible the wicked shallbe in the last day.

Malac. 4.

med; and the fire of that place shall burne
them. And S. Iohn Baptist saith, that
they shall be as straw; when he telleth
vs, that Christ our Lord shal come to
iudge. He shall carry, saith he, in his
hand his Fanne; and like a labourer he
shall cleanse his barn, which is his Church;
and he shall lay vp, in his granaryes, his
cleane and choice corne, which are the
iust: & the straw (which is the wicked)
he shall cast into vnquenchable fire. This
chaffe and straw, are thinges which
be easily kindled by the fire, & they
make a mighty flame; and so the wicked are made apt, and well disposed,
by the diuine iustice to be burnt, in
that eternall fire, both in body and
soule.

But yet, although they shall be
burnt like chaffe and straw, and to
be penetrated by the fire, from side
to side; yet are they neuer to be consumed, but they shall liue for euer,
and for euer shall their paine endure.
The

Iob.20. *The wicked man shall pay for his sinnes* (sayth *Sophar*, the friend of *Iob*) *but he shall not be consumed*, *nor shall he*
D. Thom. *loose either his being*, *or his life*. This
in additio- fire, to which Christ our Lord will
nibus q. deliuer the wicked, is to be increased
74. by that other fire, which shall come
before him ; and wherewith, as hath
been said, he will purge all the inferiour creatures. And he will also
purge those iust persons, whome he
shall finde aliue when he comes to
iudge; which persons shal dye by that
forerunning fire ; and in a very short
tyme they shal be purged, & they are
(g) Marke to rise, with all the rest. And this very
now, or (s) fire, when once the sentēce shalbe
neuer. giuen, will wrap vp all the wicked,
both in body and soule; and the earth
opening it selfe, in many places, that
fier, shall discend with them all,
through those ouertures of the earth,
into the bottomles pitt of hell ; and
the earth, shall then shut vp it selfe,
some

& some do hould, that the waters shal then returne to couer the earth, as they did when God first created thē. For the cause of his discouering the earth from vnder the waters, was to giue conuenient habitation to men, and beasts; and that cause growing once to cease, the waters shall returne into their due place, and the wicked shall remaine locked vp in the center of the earth, enuironed vpon all sids, with that fire of hell. And (ʰ) being couered first with the whole globe of the earth, and next with the profoundnes of the Sea, they are neuer to get out, from that lamētable place, and that euerlasting fire. For as S. Iohn affirmeth, *They shalbe tormented in it day and night, for all eternity.*

Titelm. l. 7. de Cælo c. 4. Latiel. l. 4. Meteor.

(h) The braue spirits of our tyme, will be mightily to seek whenthey come hither.

Apoc. 20. 14.

Nor shall this torment of fire, whereby the wicked are to be tormented go alone; but togeather with that they shall suffer other most bitter paines; whereof euery one wilbe

G   a kind

a kind of hell to the damned. They
shall haue such a cruell and fierce
rage of hunger, (¹) that if it were
possible, they would teare in peeces
and eate themselues; and this so raging hunger they shall euer feele, in
all the moments of their tyme, nor
shall they euer be at peace. Withall,
they shall haue a most (k) scalding
thirst, which will afflict them in all
extremity. If a man who were sicke
of a burning feuer, should be, for
some dayes, denyed a draught of water, towardes the appeasing of his
thirst; he would feele so much torment by it, that he would rather
chose death, then it. And what then
shall they feele, who burning in that
hideous fire, are possessed with such
a most raging thirst: wheras yet they
shall not get the least drop of water,
for all eternity. For, as *S. Iohn* affirmeth, *The smoke of their torments shall*
ascend, for euer and for euer; and neuer
shall

(i) The
deadly
hunger of
hell.

(k) The
scalding
thirst of
hell.

Apoc. 14.

shall they rest, either by day or night.
They (1) shall also continue in that euerlasting prison, bound hand and foot; and so are they to be cast into that fire, as Christ our Lord signifyeth, when giuing sentence againft him that came into the *Feaft* (which is the bosome of his Church) *without his wedding garment* (which is charity and grace) he sayd thus to the Ministers of his Iustice : *Bind him hand & foot, and so caſt him bound into exteriour darknes, where shalbe weeping, & gnashing of teeth.* That is, the wicked shall remaine obſtinate, & hardned for euer, without meanes of remedy, or deliuery. And this is, to haue the hands and feet tyed vp; To be incapable of doing any one work or conceauing any one good deſire; in such sort, as that whatsoeuer they shall do, or thinke for all eternity, is to be wickednes and sinne. And as a man, who being bound hand & foot

(l) The indiſſoluble chains of hell.

Matt. 22.

G 2   and

and caft into the bottome of the fea, cannot fwimme nor fcape from being drowned ; fo thofe wretches can neuer wraftle out of thofe paynes . For if there could be any remedy, it muft be by pennance , and amendement of their liues ; but that can neuer be , becaufe they are to remaine obftinate in euill, and difabled to do any thing which is good .

These miferable damned creatures, fhal alfo be fubiect to moft (m) offenfiue fmells, which fhall extremly afflict and torment them . This is fignifyed by S. *Iohn* who fayth, *That into that lake of fire (which is Hell) the Diuell fhalbe caft* (who is the occafion of the paynes of Hell, and of death , (for which caufe he is called fometymes, by the name of death, and hel it fe fe) *& that into the fame lake, all the wicked who are not written in the booke of life fhalbe alfo caft; and that this lake of fire, shall burne with brimstone;* which

(m) The filthy fmells of hel .

Apoc. 14. 19 .20.

Aug . de ciuit. Dei l. 20.c.14.

which signifyeth the detestable smell
of that horrible prison, which is caused supernaturally, either by brimstone, or some such thing.

These and innumerable other
paynes there are, in that most hideous prison; and although they be all
so immense, as that they exceed all
expression; yet the (n) greatest of them
all, is hauing lost the glory of God;
and then being to want it for al eternity. For as the greatest good, and
suprem felicity of man, is to see God,
and to enioy him: so the greatest misery, and mischiefe, and torment, is
for euer to want the sight of God, &
the possession of his celestiall Kingdome. This is that, which aboue all
things, doth torment those most vnhappy soules of the damned; to see
that they might haue gained an infinite good, and that they had tyme &
commodity for it; and that through
their owne fault, & negligence they

G 3   gained

*Riber . in
Apoc.c.19
num.37.*
(n) If
thou be-
lieue not
this truth
it is a sign
that thou
art extra-
ordinarily
in ill case.

gained it not , nor did ferue themfelues well of their tyme , and of thofe
other meanes which were giuen thē
by our Lord for that purpofe . And
to fee , that innumerable other men
of their owne naturall condition, &
fraile like themfelues , doe , for the
good imployemēt which they made
of the guifts of God, obtaine to enioy fo great a good, and to poffeffe it
with a perpetuall fecurity ; whereas
they, by their negligence, or malice,
loft it : The remēbrāce heerof, which
for euer fhallbe imprinted in their
minds, will be fo liuely and frefh, as
that they will neuer be able to caft
it off ; and this will breed in them an
intollerable griefe beyond all griefs;
and a moft vehement indignation ,
& a hoat boyling rage againft themfelues, for hauing fo loft God . But
yet this torment doe they not feele ,
for the refpect of God ; for they doe
not loue, but do abhorre him, but on-
　　　　　　　　　　　ly

only for the interest & profit which
they might haue had by his glory.
And this torment of indignation is
that, which Christ our Lord, did
signify by the gnashing of teeth,
which springeth from the inraged
wrath of the hart. That (o) excel-
lent writer *Rusbrochius*, doth ponder (o) Note
the grieuousnes of these torments ve- this cer-
ry excellently well; and particulerly so piously
he sayth, That the hauing lost the deliuered.
glory of God, is the greatest of them
all; and he expresseth it, by these
wordes: *Belieue me, that whatsoeuer*
can be sayd of the paynes of hell; if it be Rusbroch.
compared with that which there is felt, Epist. 1.
in very deed is lesse then a drop of water
is, in respect of the whole Sea; and yet
neuerthelesse, all those paynes of hell put
togeather, are nothing, in respect of that
one only payne, which is felt by hauing
for euer, lost the sight of God. And of
this paine, S. Iohn Chrysostom said: Chrys. in
If thou put before me a thousand hells, Matt. c.7.
hom. 14.

G 4　　　　　　　　*they*

they are not all so great a mischiefe, *as is
to loose the glory of Christ our Lord, &
to be abhorred and driuen away by him,*
with those (P) *wordes* : I know you
not.

(P) O infi-
nite affli-
ction.

CHAP. VIII.

*How the grieuousnes of sin is yet more
discouered , by the causes , which
Christ our Lord alleadgeth as the
reasons of his* Iudgment.

A NOTHER point very worthy
of Consideration in this diuine
Iudgment which discouereth also the
mighty hatred which Christ our *Iudg*
doth carry against sinne , which sheweth also the greiuousnes of those
paines wherewith he is to punish the
same , are the faults which he relates,
and which he alledgeth at the tyme
of his *Iudgment* , in the sentence of
damnation, which he pronounceth
against

against the wicked, saying; (a) *I was hungry and you did not giue me to eate*; *I was thirsty and you did not giue me to drinke*; *I was a stranger and you did not harbour me*; *I was naked and you aid not cloth me*; *I was sicke and in prison & you did not visit me*. For it is euident, that amongst all mortall sins, the very least, and they whereof men make least accompt and scruple, are the forbearing to succour their neighbours; euen in those cases of necessity wherin yet they are bound to do it, by the precept of Charity. And for this reason, Christ our Lord, who had no meaning in this relatiõ, which he makes at the tyme of his *Iudgment*, to reckon vp all those sins for which he is to cõdemne the wicked (for that would be a long (b) busines) did only speak of such as go for the lightest, & vpon which men vse to make the least reflection; wherby all men may gather and inferre concerning those

Matt. 25
(a) So that men shall not be iustifyed by faith alone, sinçe they are to be cãned for want of Charity.

(b) That is, it wold haue bee-ne longe for Christ our Lord, to haue spoken of alla mans sinnes, in that speach of his.

G 5   other

other great sins, for which he is to passe the sentence of condemnation vpon the wicked. And this following circumstance a man is to consider and ponder, euen in the very bottome of his hart: If (c) these sins of Omission, and negligence, in the performing of the workes of mercy (which in reason, and in the estimation and iudgment of all men are the lightest of all mortall sins) be yet neuertheles so abhorred by Almighty God, as that, in the vniuersall *Iudgment*, he doth publish them in a particuler manner, as being very grieuous, and worthy of eternall condemnation; and will complaine against them, as against faults which are full of iniury, and affront, against his diuine and eternal Maiesty; and will proceed against such as fell into them, as against his enemies; and will excommunicate them as *cursed* people, dryuing them away for euer out

(c) A most necessary consequéce which deserues to be deeply pondered.

out of his company, and the communion of the Church triumphant; and
will deliuer them ouer into euerlasting fiers; and will execute the same
paines vpon them which are suffred
by the very Diuells themselues, in
whose infernall company they are to
be tormented, & that for euer; what
will he not be sure to do to wicked
men for the sins of comission, wherby
they offend their neighbours; which
are more expresse sinnes; and wherin, there is more malice shewed;
and which are committed by men v-
pon more deliberation. If the ouer-
sights and voluntary negligences in
not giuing bread to him who is hungry, or drinke to him who is thirsty,
or clothes to him who is naked, or
visits to him who is sicke & impriso-
ned, in cases when piety doth oblige
men to it, are yet so abhorred by
Christ our Lord, and so seuerely punished, what will he do to men for
those

those impieties, when a sinfull man
will take from another the goods
which he had honestly gayned; and
if he robb him, or vsurpe it otherwise
by vnlawfull and vnconscionable
waies; and for those other sins, when
one man takes the health and life
from another, by wounding, and
killing him, or doing it at least in
his desire; and when he depriues him
of his honour, and good name, by
murmurations, detractions, and reproaches; or when he takes from him
his wife, or his daughter, or his kins-
woman by fornications or adultries,
or the like? And (d) if negligence in
releeuing the corporall necessities of
ones neighbor when there is comodi-
ty for the same, be so abhorred and
punished by Allmighty God; how
much more will he abhorre and punish any slacknes in releiuing the necessities of soules, by teaching the ig-
norant, those things which are necessary

(d) The
spirituall
workes
of charity
are of far-
re more
impor-
tance,
then the
corporall

ceſſary to ſaluation; by reprehending their vices; and by admoniſhing and exhorting them to a good life, in caſes of neceſſity and obligatiõ. Thus doth the bleſſed *Laurētius Iuſtiniaꝛus* ponder this truth in theſe words: *If* *Chriſt our Lord in his Iudgment do ſo* *exactly and preciſely examine & chaſtice* » *the faults which are comitted*, in failing » to ſhew thoſe works of mercy which » are expreſſed towards the bodies of » men which dye; what kind of exa- » men, and what kind of puniſhment » wil he impoſe vpon their faults, who » forbeare to ſhew the ſpirituall works » of mercy which they ought to haue » imparted, for the ſaluation of ſoules, » which are immortall ? Let him that » readeth this conceaue rightly, and be well aſſured that there is no doubt, but that, as this latter fault is greater, ſo ſhal the examen be more rigorous, & the puniſhment more ſeuere. And if the denying of any ſpirituall beni-

Laurens à *Iuſtin l.* *de humilit.*

ſit

fit which is due to his neighbour for the good of his soule, be a fault of so high quality, how much more will it be so, to rob the soule of life, by giuing it wicked Counsell, and by teaching it false doctrine; and by inducing it to vice by all perswasions, and lewd examples. Let the good Christian passe on, and consider & ponder yet more deepely, that the sins

(e) Sinnes comitted immediatly against God, are the greatest of all others.

which are (e) committed imediately against God, such as are the crimes of infidelity of seuerall kinds, of superstitions, and blasphemies, and Sacriledges in breaking vowes and promises made to God; and of periuries which draw God as a witnes of lyes, and falshood, be greater sins then they which are committed against our neighbours; and consequently the hatred which God doth carry against them, and the punishment which he wil execute for them, is incomparably greater.

From

From *(f)* hence the Christian man will gather the great necessity that he is in, to abhor in a most profound internall manner, all kinde of sins; and to flye them with a most watchfull care; & to feare them with his whole hart. For if the lighter sort of sinnes, and they wherof men are wont to make least accompt, are so publikely to be recorded & reproued in that diuine iudgment, & tobe sentenced as worthy of condemnation, and punished with eternall torments; the case is plaine, that the sins which are more greiuous, and in greater hurt & preiudice of our neighbours; and they againe which are of more imediate iniury, and affront to God himselfe, shalbe proclaimed in that diuine iudgment, to the greater confusion of sinners; & they shalbe more sharply rebuked by Christ our Lord, and more grieuously punished. And although the other torments were also

(f) The true vse which is to be made of this consideration.

so eternall , yet these shalbe greater and more intense then they. For this truth was reuealed to S . *Iohn* by the Holy Ghost , who sayth: *So much as* *the wicked man hath glorified himselfe* *and hath deliuered himselfe ouer to vici-* *ous pleasure: and so much more, as he pre-* *sumed of himselfe , and lifted vp his face* *of pride against God, affronting his diuine* *Maiesty with greater sins ; and so much* *more as he yeilded obedience to vice, in* *contradiction to the law of God: so much* *greater torment shalbe imposed vpon his* *body ; and so much more greife and sor-* *row shalbe inflicted vpon his soule .*

Apoc. 18.

CHAP.

CHAP. IX.

How a Christian is to draw a detestation of sinne, out of the consideration of this Iudgement *of God; and great vigilancy in the leading of a good life.*

THESE (a) are the points and articles of that diuine *Iudgment*, which discouer to vs the hatred, that God doth carry against sinne . And these we are to consider , with great attention; that so we also may gather this fruit out of the diuine *Iudgement* to abhorre sinne extremely, to grieue vnfaygnedly for those which we haue committed, to feare it with our whole harts, and to fly from it with cõtinual care. For it is all reason that we should abhorre that which God doth so highly abhorre ; and that we should be mightily grieued , for ha-

(a) For Iesus sake read ouer thisChap- ter with sober and sound at- tention ,

H   uing

uing committed such things against
God, as he mislikes so much, & wherby he is so much offended. And it is
most iust, & fit, to feare a *Iudgment*,
which is so seuere, and ful of terrour;
and such torments as are so excessiue
and so without all end. And now,
that we may with the more efficacy,
rowse our selues vp towards a perfect
hatred of sinne, and a feare of the
diuine *Iudgement*, let euery one of vs
go casting vp his accompt, after this
manner.

(b) Resol-
ue thy
selfe to
suffereter-
nally in
helif thou
refuse the
grace,
which
God is de-
firous to
giue thee
euen very
now, if
thou wilt
concurre.

God (b) *who is my Creatour, hath*
resolued, that the day shall come, when he
will Iudge *me, and from this* Iudgment
it is impossible for me to flye. So also hath
he resolued, that he will reward me in
this Iudgment, *according to my works.*
If he find me in the state of Grace, *and*
with the stocke of a good life in my hand,
he will giue me the reward of eternall fe-
licity. If he find me in mortall sinne, and
that I haue ill imployed my life, he will
                                    driue

driue me out of the sight of his glory, &
wil condemne me to euerlasting torments.
Now, that I consider my selfe, I see that
I haue lead a carelesse kind of life, & that
I haue committed many offences against
his holy Commaundmentes. If now, he
should call me to his Iudgment, I am
sure that I should be condemned; for I
haue not done pennance for the sinnes,
which I haue committed, nor haue I yet
reformed my life. At least I am in much
doubt of my saluation; for the pennance
which I haue done, was luke-warme; &
I haue sought to mend m life, but slack-
ly. It is necessary therefore, now, & euen
very now, that I change my course, that
I betake my selfe to my pennance, & that
I do it in good earnest. I will obey the
voyce of God, who commands me by Ecclesiasticus, saying: Before thou come
to the diuine Iudgement, prouide thy
selfe of workes, which may be holy
and iust, to the end that it may succeed well with thee. Before thou come

into the hāds of God, to be iudged by him, aske thy selfe the question, examine thy conscience well: passe an vpright Iudgement vpon thy selfe; reprouing thy selfe with griefe, & punishing thy faults with pennance; and so thou shalt find mercy in the sight of God; thou shalt find him a fauourable Iudge, and he will cast the sentence on thy side.

(c) Attention.

Let (c) the Christian man consider further, in the bottome of his hart, & let him reason thus within himselfe. If I (d) knew now that the end of the world and the Vniuersall Iudgment were to be held within ten or twenty yeares; it would more seriously worke vpon me, and would make me more carefull to do penance, and to endeauour a totall renouation of my life; and I should more cordially feare the Iudgement, and eternall punishment of God, & the sinnes which make me subiect to euerlasting damnation. Yet certainly, for as much as concerns me, the day when I shall dye, is after a

(d) Of the litle difference, which there is to be for vs in substāce betweene the day of our death & the day of the last Iudgement.

sort

fort the *very day of the* Vniuerʃal Iudgement, *and of the end of the world.*
For the chiefe of that which paʃʃeth in the Vniuerʃall Iudgement, *and which maketh it to be feared ʃo much, is the irreuocable ʃentence of eternall damnation which is then to paʃʃe vpon the wicked; &* (e) *that where a man ʃhall then be lodged he ʃhall lye for all eternity. And he ʃhall then, no more, haue any vʃe of any creature of this world; or of tyme wherin he may do pennance, or procure ʃaluation. Now this is, in effect, the ʃame thing, which is to be done with me in the houre of my death. For then I ʃhall be iudged; and if then I be found guilty, an irreuocable ʃentence of damnation ʃhall paʃʃe vpon me; and where I ʃhall then be caʃt, I ʃhall remayne for euer; and in the* Vniuerʃall Iudgment, *there is no more to be done, but to confirme and proclaime the ʃentence, which was giuen in the particuler* Iudgment. *And in the houre of my death, for as much as concerneth me,*

(e) This maketh not againſt purgatory but ʃheweth only that if a man dye in ſtate of ſinne, he ſhall continue ſo for euer: and if in ſtate of grace, he ſhall alʃo for euer continue ſo; thogh till all be ſatisfyed, he ſhal ſtay in purgatory and then he flyes vp to heauen.

the

the whole world is at an end ; & so is the
vse of all the creaturs therof: since I shall
returne to it or them, no more ; and so is
the Tyme also at an end , wherein pennance might haue beene performed , and
merit might haue been procured. If therfore it be so, that the houre of my death ,
is to be the same thing for me, which the
Vniuersall Iudgment; and the end of
the world, and the same it is to be for all
men ; and f since it is most certain that
the day of my death , will arriue eare
long ; and that according to my age , and
to the tyme which men are wont to last
it cannot exceed twenty, or thirty years;
and since it is so casuall, as that perhaps it
may be eare night; it followeth, as a most
iust and necessary consequence , that I
should, euen from this very instant, dispose my selfe to do pennance for my sins ,
with greater care; and to make a totall a-
mendment of my life; & to do that which
Christ our Lord commandes me, saying:
Watch , for you know not the houre
                                                    when

(f) The
certainty
of death
and the
yncertian
ty of the
houre of
our
death.

Matt ô 24.

when your Lord will come; *and that also which the Apostle* S . Peter , *in the* name *of the same Lord , doth aduise me saying*: Brethren the day of our Lord will come like a theefe *Now the theef who steales by night, comes without giuing any news of himselfe ; and then he doth it, when he is lookt for least . Iust so will christ our lord come to iudg vs in the end of the world, and in the houre of our death , and no man shall know when he is to come; & the tyme willbe at hand when many willbe least ready for it . Doe you therefore earnestly labour to lead a vertuous life, that so you may be free from sinne, and that .there be nothing in you which may deserue reproofe ; but that , with a quiet and safe conscience you may expect our Lord , when he shall come to iudge .*

2. Pet. 3.

CHAP. X.

Of other Considerations, from which we
may draw the detestation of sinne, &
the care of leading a good life.

LET a man also consider with
himself, the sentence, & punishment which followeth this *Iudg-*
ment ; and let him be perswaded to
feare God, vpon this ensuing reason.
What (a) are those things, which a
man in this life will not do, for the
auoyding of paine and griefe ? A
man who is in prison, and expects or
feares a sentence of violent death,
what doth he not, for the deliuering
of himselfe ? He thinks of nothing,
but how he may escape ; he neuer giues ouer to make friends, who may
intercede for him ; he humbles himselfe to all such as are able to do him
fauour, and to giue him helpe; he
spends his meanes vpon Atturneyes
& Lawyers, and in sending presents
to

(a) Is it
possible
that thou
shouldest
be so mad
as not to
be able to
frame this
argument
in thyne
owne per-
son.

to such as may do him any good. A
mã who lyes sicke vnder great pains
which torment him day and night
without ceasing, being caused by
some surcharge of humours, which
he hath in his body, or by some sto-
ny grauell, which perhaps he hath
in his bladder, or by some Me-
lancholy, which is lodged at his
hart; what will he not do for his re-
couery? How willingly doth he imploy what he hath, in giuing fees to
Phisitians, and in paying of Apo-
thecaries bills, for druggs, which
way giue him ease? With what faci-
lity and diligence, doth he take pur-
ges; and permit that issues be made,
and buttons of fire be applyed; yea
and he endureth to be cut & opened,
offring himself to one extreme paine
& daunger, to excuse another which
is a greater, if he can tell how.

If this be so, what then will it
be fit for me to do, that I may free my
self

selfe from those miseries & torments,
to which the wicked must be sentenced, in that diuine *Iudgement*. Which
(b) besides that they are, in theselues,
extrem, beyond al that can be said or
thought; they are neuer to haue any
end, but in their contynuance, they
are to equall the eternity of God himselfe. For as God, in his owne nature
is eternall, so are those torments to
be eternall, by the determination of
God, which can neuer faile. Although these torments were no greater then for a man to be cast into fire,
such as heere we haue, (but so as
that he shold not dye of it for the space of thirty yeares) the very thinking
of it, would strike into him extreme
horrour; and there is nothing ima-
ginable which a man would not do
to keepe himselfe from vndergoing
such a torment. Nay although it were
no more, but that a man were to remaine thirty yeares, laid in a bed;
with-

(b) Tor-
ments
both into-
lerable, &
eternall.

without being able once to rise or stirre from thence, it would be of intollerable paine to him; and he would performe things of very great difficulty and labour, to deliuer him-selfe from the same.

But what then will it be, to re-maine in the fire of Hell, together with all those other torments, which there are felt; and that, for the space of all eternity; and what then will it not be fit for a man to do, that so he may not be to endure those tormēts? And (c) to the end that a man may haue some little tast of this eternity, let him thinke of so many thousands of yeares which are to passe ouer the head of the damned, as there are grains of dust in the whole world, or drops of water in the sea, or moates in the ayre; and that at the end of all those thousands of yeares, they shall not get out of those torments, but still shalbe, as if they did but then

begin

(c) If thou desire to vnderstād eternity thou must procure to take it thus in sunder.

beginne to suffer, and that then as many more thousands of years are so to passe; and then againe as many more; and that still, that wheele shalbe running round without any end. And let him also knowe, that by this so large contynuance, his torments are not yet to cease, nor to be in the diminution of a haires breadth; but that they shall be as (d) liuely felt at the end of so many thousandes of yeares, as at the first instant. Because those torments, do not worke after a naturall manner, that so they might be the lesse felt by custome, but they worke as instruments of the diuine Iustice, which is inuariable; and doth conserue them at the end of innumerable yeares, in the same force and fury which they had at the first. O with how great reason did the Prophet *Hieremy* exclaime to God & say: *Who is he that will not feare thee, O thou King of the Nations? Thyne is* ſu-

(d) The tormentes of hell are not made more tollerable by a custome of enduring them a while.

Hier. 10.

supreme Dominion, and there is none like thee in wisedome and power.

By these Considerations, a Christian being assisted by God, will get, out of the diuine *Iudgement*, a great remorse and griefe for sinne, which doth so much offend God, and which is so greatly abhorred, and so greiuously punished by him. And(e) with this griefe, he is to accuse, and reprehend, and condemne, and with penances and mortifications, to inflict punishment, and take reuenge vpon himselfe. So did holy *Iob*, when he confessed saying : *Place me before God, and I will come to Iudgement, and consider what he is to do with me ; and I will loade my selfe with reprehensions.* For as S. *Gregory* (f) sayth vpon these wordes : *A man contemplating the so strict, and perfect examen, which God doth make of his sinnes in that terrible Iudgment of his, he turneth in, vpon, & against himself, & he reprehends himself*

with

(e) The cure of sin is pennance.

Iob. 23.

Greg. ibid. (f) Thus S. Gregory sayd & thus he did,

with griefe and forrow , for the offences which he hath committed againft God. The (g) faithfull feruant of God, is also to drawe from this diuine *Iudge-ment*, a great watchfulnes and deligence , to confider well , and with attention, al the workes that he doth; and to fee that they be good , and be wrought with a pure intention of pleafing God. Not being negligent in the performing of exteriour workes , & much leffe, giuing place in his hart to the defire or loue of any thing that is ill , or confenting to any thing which is contrary to the will of God; nor principally to feeke his owne intereft in any thing, but onely the glory and good pleafure of God . To the end, that when our Lord fhall come to iudge vs, he may find vs prepared , and may meete with nothing in vs which he will punifh.

This Counfell was giuen vs by *S. Paul,* who faid , *You know well my bre-*

(g) A man is to carry a quick & watchfull eye ouer all his workes.

Theff . 5 .

*brethren, that the day of our Lord is to
come vpon vs like a theefe in the night.*
For although it be true, that when he
will come to make the *vniuersal Iudgment*, he will do it with great Maiesty
and very manifestly to all the world;
yet, for as much as concernes the tyme, the day, and houre, wherein he
is to come, aswell in the *vniuersall
Iudgment*, as in the *particular*, he will
do it suddenly and conceald; and so
as that men shall not know either of
the houre or day. He will come like
a theefe, who hath a mind to robbe,
when men are sleeping and incon-
siderat; so I say will he come, suddenly, & at vnawares to passe his *Iudgment*, vpon many when they liue ca-
relesly in their sinnes. Therefore (ʰ)
we who are faithfull Christians, and
who by liuely faith are made the sonnes of light; we, I say, must not
slumber, nor giue place to the sleepe
of negligence and sinne; as others are

(h) Take
heed of
sloath in
Gods ser-
uice.

con-

content to do , who want this faith. But let vs watch in prayers and good workes , following the light of faith, and the word of God;and let vs carry our selues in al things,with sobriety: That is , we muſt be very temperate & moderate, as the Euāgelicall law, & as the example of Chriſt our Lord, and of his Saints doth exact at our hands ,both in our eating, drinking, clothing , ſleeping , ſpeaking , and whatſoeuer els . This fruit doth holy *Iob* draw out of the conſideration of of the diuine *Iudgement* , as himſelfe expreſſed ſaying, *I did obſerue & examine my workes, with much reflection & care, to the end that none of them might be wicked ; and to the (¹)end alſo , that all they which were good , might be well done ; for I know that in thy Iudgement, thou art not to let any ſinne paſſe without puniſhment* .Which yet is to be vnderſtood of (ᵏ) ſinns, which formely ſhall not haue beene purged and diſcharged by pennance.   CHAP.

Iob . 19 .

(i)It is not ſnough to doe good thinges, but they muſt alſo be well done.

(k)When due pennance is done for ſinne, it is no longer lyable to any puniſhment.

CHAP. XI.

How a Christian is to draw out of the Consideration of the diuine Iudge-ment, *a great feare of offending God, that so he may fly far from it.*

THE faythfull Christian, from the consideration of this diuine *Iudgement*, is to draw a very reall, & true feare of God. And this feare of God, and of his *Iudgment*, is the most particuler and proper fruite, which from that *Iudgment*, is to be drawn. So doth the Psalmist signify, when he speakes to God, and sayth: *O Lord* Psalm. 18. *I haue feared thy Iudgments ; and vpon the consideration how thou dost exercise them vpon the wicked, I haue conceaued an excessiue feare .* And *Salomon* his 2. Paral. 6. Sonne, speaking to God in the prayer which he made in the Temple, declared the same truth by saying : *Giue*

I   *O Lord,*

O Lord, to euery one, in thy Iudgment, *the reward which is fit for their workes ; & according to the desire of their harts, to the end that they may feare thee, and may walke in the way of thy Command-ments, all the dayes of their liues.* And the Angell, whome *S. Iohn* saw, did say: *Feare our Lord, for the houre of his Iudgement is come.* When a (¹) man delights in wickednes, & yet calleth to mind the diuine *Iudgment*, & the punishment which God doth exer-cise vpon sinners, he doth conceaue a *feare* of the payne; and being prin-cipally moued by that *feare* he abstai-nes from sinning, which *feare* is a *feare* of slaues, and therfore it is cal-led *seruile* . And although this *feare* be good, and doth grow from a root which is supernaturall, it is yet im-perfect, and insufficient for the ob-tayning of euerlasting life, or for the iustification of a soule · Nor is it me-ritorious, but it is a ground from whence

Apoc. 14.

(a) A ser-uile feare.

whence iuſtification may riſe, and it
is a diſpoſition towards grace, wherby we may merit; and this it is wherof the Wiſeman ſayth: *That the* Feare
of God, is the beginning of Wiſedome. Prouer. 1.
Which is as much as to ſay, That it
is a beginning for the obteyning of
an experimental knowledge of God,
which growes from Charity. And
ſo doth *Eccleſiaſticus* declare it ſaying,
The feare of God, is the beginning of Cap. 25.
the loue of God. But (b) when a man (b) Of fi-
who loueth vertue, and is reſolued lial feare.
to ſerue God, doth by cõſidering the
diuine *Iudgment*, ponder the grie-
uouſnes of ſinne, by meanes of the
ſeuerity of the ſame *Iudgment*, & the
exceſſiue greatnes of thoſe paynes,
wherewith God doth puniſh it, and
theruoon he doth incline himſelfe to
a great feare of ſin; and doth tremble to thinke of doing any thing,
which may offend the pure eyes of
God, this *feare* is a *feare* of ſonnes; &
ther-

therfore it is called a *filiall feare*; because he feareth God his heauenly
Father, more then he doth the punishment, which otherwise is due to
him for the same.

So also, when a faithfull seruant
of God, through the desire which he
hath to flye from al offence of his diuine Maiesty, and in all thinges to
comply with his holy wil, doth settle
himselfe after a sincere, and serious
manner, to consider the *Iudgements*
of God, and those eternall punish-
ments and tormentes, whereby he is
to take vengance vpon the wicked,
thereby to moue himselfe so much
the more, to a feare of those *Iugdmēts*
and paynes; and the more to animate
himselfe to flye from all offence of
God, and to keep his diuine Commandments; this feare, howsoeuer it
carry a kind of respect to paine, is
not yet to be accōpted a *seruile feare*.
Nor doth it spring from selfe loue,

but

but it is a *filiall loue*, and it growes
from Charity. Becaufe (c) in thefe
thinges which are morall, and voluntary, the nature and denominati-
on of the work, is principally taken
from the end at which it aymes. And
as a man who fhould fteale money
wherby he would enable himfelfe to
commit an adultery, were more to
be efteemed an adulterer then a theef;
fo the iuft man, who difpofeth himfelfe to feare the punifhment, due
to finne, that fo he may feare and
abhorre the finne, is rather to be ac-
compted to feare the finne, then the
punifhment. So therefore the feare
of this man, is a holy feare, and belongeth to a fonne, & friend of God;
& this very *feare* maketh a man iuft
and holy, yea it is euen iuftice and
fanctity it felfe This *feare* doth make
a man acceptable to God, and is meritorious of eternall life, and it maketh alfo the workes which proceed

(c) A clear
proofe of
the truth
which he
deliuered
before of
the two
Feares.

I 3   from

from thence, to be acceptable to God
and meritorious both of grace and
glory. Holy (P) *Iob* sayth of this *feare*,
The feare of God is wisedome it selfe.
And *Ecclesiasticus* sayth, *To feare God
is entire and perfect wisedome*. *A seruile
feare* is sayd to be *the beginning of wisedome*; because it disposeth a soule
towards *wisedome*: and so is this *filial
feare* sayd, *to be very wisedome it selfe*,
because it imbraceth wisedom, it loc-
keth it vp, and it doth perfect, and
increase it. For he that hath this feare
hath the guift of holy wisedome togeather with it, which is that principall guift of the holy Ghost, wherby God is knowne and loued. And
through the exercise of this holy
feare, this guift is increased; and for
this reason the Wiseman sayth of this
feare: *That it is the fountaine of life*,
because it giueth spirituall life to the
soule, and from thence do spring the
workes of life; since they be such
as

(d) The
places of
holy
scripture
reconci-
led which
seemed to
differ.
Iob. 18.
Ecclef. 1.

Prou. 14.

as are (e) meritorious of eternall life. For they, who after this manner do *feare* God, as *Ecclefiasticus* fayth, do procure with diligéce, to pleafe God in all things.

Let vs therfore , much , and many tymes côfider this diuine *Iudg-mēt*, that fo we may draw a holy *Feare* from thence , and grow therin , and conferue our felues therby, in a vertuous life, fo long as we fhall contynue in this pilgrimage; fo doth Saint *Peter* aduife vs faying , *If you call him Father, as indeed he is (who is alfo our God, and our Lord , and who as a moſt righteous* Iudge, *fhall iudge, & reward euery one according to his workes) moſt iuſt and reafonable it is, that during all the tyme of our being in pilgrimage in this world (as perfons who are banifhed from the houfe of our Father) we should liue in fuch feare, as becommeth his children.*

(e) throgh the grace of God in Chriſt ourLord, & throgh his promife. Ecclef. 18.

1. Pet. 1.

I 4   CHAP.

CHAP. XII.

How it is very necessary, & ful of profit that a Christian doe exercise himselfe in this holy Feare; and accompany it with the exercise of diuine loue.

(a) A doubt cõcerning the exercise of the actes of Feare and Loue, cleerely solued.

BVT to this, one (a) may say, by way of question; Since the act, & exercise of the *Loue* of God, is more excellent, and acceptable then that of *Feare*, why is it not better to exercise our selues alwaies in the *loue* of God, and in the consideration of his benefits and mercies, and of his goodnes, and *Loue*, and the rest of his deuine perfections, which may induce vs to *loue*, then to be considering his diuine *Iudgment* and the paines of Hell, which oblige vs to *feare*?

(b) The first answere.

To (b) this I say, first, That the act & exercise of *loue*, is more excellent and acceptable to God, then any other act

of

of vertue, when that *loue* of God, is
cleane and pure from faults, & from
felfe loue. But (c) if a perfon fhal only giue himfelfe to the exercife of
diuine *loue* (for as much as *one* doth
caufe a kind of fecurity and comfort
to the foule) a man may grow from
thence, many tymes, to be flacke in
vertue, & forward to commit faults,
and come to be remiffe in doing of
pennance, and mortifications, and
admit of certaine delicacies, and fo
increafe in felfe loue. And he may
alfo come to prefume vpon himfelfe;
conceauing that he doth greatly loue
God; and by that very meanes, he
goes difpofing himfelfe, to loofe the
fame loue of God, by cōmitting veniall finnes, & by increafing in them;
he arriueth alfo to fall at laft, into
mortall finne, wherby he doth wholy
loofe *loue* and grace. But in the meane
tyme, this negligence which grew
to end in mortall finne, doth not

I 3   grow

(c) Take
heed thou
walke not
in the way
of fpirit
without
aduice.

grow from that very *loue* of God,
which of it selfe is all good, and per-
swadeth vs also to all good; but(d)
it groweth from the infirmity of mā,
and from his bad inclination, and so
it is wholly the fault of man; who, as
he vseth many other things ill, so also
he vseth ill, the *loue* of God.

It is therfore both very profitable, and very fit, & euen necessary,
that the good Christian, do ioyne
the holy Feare of God, to the *loue* of
him; and that as he is to exercise himselfe, in some considerations which
may moue him to *loue* God, so also
he may exercise himself in some other,
which may moue him to *feare* him.

And although it be true, that at
the first when a man is but begining
to serue God, it is more necessary that
he bestowe himselfe more vpon the
consideration of *feare*, then that of
loue; yet is it also very conuenient,
euen for them, who haue beene long
in

(d) So
weake is
man that
he may
well be
suspected
euen whē
he mea
neth best.

in his feruice , and are very well ad-
uaunced therin ; that although their
cheife practice , may be in the exercifes of the *loue* of God , yet , that many
tymes, alfo, they do intertaine themfelues in the thoughtes of his diuine
Feare ; and vpon thofe confiderations
which may help them to it . And (e)
thus , accompaning this holy *Feare* ,
with the *loue* of God , the inconue-
nience , and daunger , & loffe wherof we haue fpoken , wil ceafe ; which
yet will be fure to grow through the
frailty of man , if he fhall onely imploy himfelfe in the exercifes , and
confiderations of *loue* . For this *Feare,*
when it is ioyned with *loue* , keepeth
a man from being negligent in Gods
feruice ; and it leaues no place for any
faults to be cōmitted againft God ,
how veniall and light foeuer they be ;
and it keepes him from giuing ouer
his penances and mortifications , or
from vfing tepidity therein . Nay it

(e) The
remedy of
this dan-
ger.

cau-

causeth him to contynue them with care, leaft els he fhould indeed grow tepide; & it teacheth him to humble and defpife himfelfe, giuing no place to pride, but fearing ftill his owne frailty, and the *Iudgement* of God. Al this is wrought by this holy *feare*; & the fame is witneffed by *Ecclefiafticus* who faith, *The feare of God, driues fin away from the foule*. It driues it away by penance, after it is committed, & it driues it away, by caution and refiftence of temptation, before it is comitted. And in another place, he faith, *He that feareth God, is negligent in nothing; but feare makes him carefull, and watchfull, towards euery thing that is good*. For this, did the Apoftle *S. Paul*, when he was perfwading Chriftians to procure the purity and fanctity of their foules by efficacious, fecure, & certaine means, aduife the to help themfelues heerein, with the holy *feare* of God; faying, *Let vs*
cleanfe

Ecclef. 1.

cleanse our selues from all vncleanes both 2. Cor. 7, of flesh and spirit . That is to say , *from all sinne; as well that which may be committed by these exteriour powers of our body , togeather with the consent of the mind , as that other which is committed by the onely consent of the mind without the body. And let vs perfect our sanctification, which is that purity & sanctity which we receiued , either in baptisme , or by penance .* Let vs go conseruing & increasing it with good workes, and by the exercise of vertue , and by continual reuewing our watchfulnes and care, in flying al that is offensiue to God . And let vs do all this, with *a feare* of his diuine Maiesty . And *S.* D. Thom. *Thomas* giuing a reason, why the A- in 2. Cor. c. postle saith not , *that we should doe it* [7] *with the loue , but with the feare,* deliuereth these words : The Apostle saith not , *with charity, but with feare of God ; To teach vs that the affection of loue, which we are to carry towards God,*

is

is to be accompanyed by a solicitude, and reuerentiall feare. For this loue, cau-seth security, wherby many tymes a man groweth carelesse and negligent in the seruice of God; but he who accompaineth that affe*ct* of loue with feare, is watch-full in the seruice of God, and runs dili-gently towards it, and flyes speedily frō any offence of him. This is deliuered by S. *Thomas*. And for this reason it wilbe fit, many tymes, to vse the cō-siderations of the diuine *Iudgement*, from whence this holy & chast *feare* may be fetcht. And so we may com-ply with that, which the holy Apo-stle aduiseth vs saying: *Worke your saluation with feare, and trembling.* Which is as much as to say, *With an interiour feare to offend God, which may be so great, as that it may appeare by your exteriour vigilancy and care to performe your workes, whereby you may obtayne that true and euerlasting saluation.* S. *Bernard* (f) left this truth, confirmed

both

(f) A sweet & secure guide for vs to fol-low.

both by his doctrine, and example, *Bernar. in Cant. ser. 7* in these words: *Happy is that soule wher in Christ our Lord hath set the print of his two feet ; and wherin he hath left the markes and footesteps of them both, which are the feare of his diuine Iudgment, and the hope of his diuine Mercy. For the consideration of the diuine Iudgment alone, breeds disconfidence and despayre ; and the memory and consideration of his mercy alone, doth occasion a sly deceipt of a mans selfe. & ingendreth a very dangerous kind of security. And so haue I experimented in my selfe. For the benignity of God sometymes hath graunted to me (miserable creature) that I might sit downe at the feet of Iesus Christ my Sauiour, and that I might with entier deuotion, imbrace the one foot of feare ; & at other tymes, the other foot of confidence, and of loue. And if at any tyme it hapned to me, that, being forgetfull for his mercy, I detayned my self long in the consideration and apprehension of the di-*

uine

uine Iudgment, I grew all difmayd, &
diftempered with an incredible kind of
feare, and a miferable confufion; and all

Pfal. 8. trembling, I would be crying out with
the Pfalmift, O Lord, who fhalbe able to
conceaue or comprehend the power of thy
wrath! And who, through the feare he
hath, fhalbe able to meafure out the greatnes, and mightines of that indignation, which thou wilt execute againft finners in the other life! And (s) if, on the

(g) See & other fide giuing ouer the confideration,
imitate and exercife of this feare, I detayned
the great my felfe long in the confideration and
humility meditation of the mercy of God, I fhould
of this be grown to fall into fuch a deale of care-
excellent leffe negligence, that euen then already,
Saint, and my prayer would become more remiffe &
learne my felfe more floathfull towards a good
heereby workes, and I fhould be more difpofed to-
to know wards laughter, and fuch idle intertay-
thy felfe. nements; more free and liberall in my
fpeach, and more vnfetled both in my
inward & outward man. Being therefore

*fore taught by experience, which hath bin
a faythfull Maister to me, I wil sing to
thee, O Lord, not only* Iudgement, *nor
only* Mercy , *but* Mercy *&* Iudgment
*both togeather ; and both thefe meanes
of iuftification will I exercife, and ufe as
long as the tyme of* Pilgrimage *, in this
banifhment of myne fhall laft , and till I
arriue to be poffeffed of that moft happy
ftate, wherein all mifery, and all caufe of
compunction and feare , fhall ceafe , and
all my glory fhall b. to prayfe thee for all
eternity .*

This faying is of S . *Bernard,*
wherin by the teſtimony of what he
experienced in himſelfe , he confir-
meth that, which the holy Scripture
and the doctrine of the Saints doe
teach , concerning the neceſſity ,
wherein all the ſeruants of God are ,
(towards the keping of themſelues
ſtill his ſeruants) to ioyne holy *feare*
with *loue,* and the conſiderations of
the diuine *Iudgement* , & the puniſh-
K   ments

ments inflicted by his Iustice, with
the considerations of the mercy of
God; and of the fauours & benefits,
which he cōmunicateth with a most
liberall hand, to such as keepe his
Law.

CHAP. XIII.

*Of how great value, and merit,
this holy Feare is.*

THIS is the first way of answ-
ring that which was demaunded.
The (a) second is, that when we
speake of *seruile feare*, & of accompaning the same with the *loue* of God,
it is true, that the exercise of *loue* is
much more excellēt thē that of *feare*.
For as we haue said, seruile feare,
which hath the eye vpon punishment
is imperfect, and but of beginners, &
it is found euen in them who are not
yet in state of grace; nor can it be
merito.

(a) The
second an-
swere of
the for-
mer obie-
ction.

meritorious, nor wholly acceptable
to our Lord God. But speaking of *fi-
liallfeare*, wherby a man *feareth* and
flyeth from sinne, because it is the of-
fense of God; and of that *reuerenciall*
feare, wherby the soule reueareth his
diuine Maiesty; and doth humble her
selfe to him, by doing his diuine wil;
and comparing this kind of feare
with the *loue* of our Lord God, and
considering that which indeed doth
passe in iust persons; it is not an exercise lesse excellent, nor lesse pleasing to God, nor lesse meritorious
then is that of *loue*. For (b) this holy
feare springeth out of the true *loue* of
God; and imbraceth the same *Loue* as
the fountaine, & roote from whence
it springs. For from louing of God,
doth grow the feare of offeding him;
and from the loue of vertue, groweth
the feare of loosing it; & frō the high
estimation which the soule makes
of God, and the fulfilling of his will,

(b) Filiall
fear riseth
out of
loue.

K 2   doth

doth growe a profound reuerence of
God, and the keeping of his law, and
the feare of doeing any thing which
is contrary to the fame. And fo the
good Chriftian, whilft he is exercifing the chaft feare of a fone of God,
he doth alfo exercife the *loue* of God.

So faith S. *Augustine*, The *feare*
through which a man loues not vertue, but flyes from the punifhment of
vice, is a *feruile feare*; and this feare
is that, *which shutteth Charity out of
doores*, and the fame *Charity* which
alfo fhutteth out this kind of fear, doth
produce and breed that other *chaft*
feare, through which the foule feares
to finne, though it were neuer to be
punifhed. And this is that holy feare,
which iuft mé do exercife in the confideration of the diuine *Iudgement*;
becaufe, as we haue declared, through
the great defire which they haue to
pleafe God, and to do according to
his wil in al things, they difpofe them-
                                    felues

*Aug. in
pfal* 113.
ferm. 25.

felues to confider the diuine *Iudgmēt*, fo to know the better, and as it were to feele, the greiuoufnes of finne, and the punifhment, that falls vpon it; and the much that God abhors it; & fo to procure a forrow and hatred of finne, as being an offence of God; and to feare it much, and to fly from it with great care, as being contrary to his diuine will; and fo exercyfing this *chaft* feare, which is an effect & fruit of diuine *loue*, he exercifeth loue with all, which is the caufe of that *feare*: for this it is, that we haue faid, that the iuft man exercifing this *filiall feare*, doth not loofe the leaft graine of the excellency and merit of his *loue*; and that the exercife of *filiall feare*, is not leffe pious and acceptable to God, then that of *loue*. For in fine this is the *feare* of Saints, to all whome the *Pfalmift* fpeakes by faying *O all yow Saints feare our Lord*. *Pfal.* 33. And this is that *feare*, which hath for

K 3   a rea reward, That it obteyneth of God what it will, as the *Psalmist* doth also witnes, saying, *God will fullfill the will of them that feare him; and will heare their praiers, granting all which they aske.* To (b) conclude, this is that *feare* which maketh men happy in this life, through the liuely hope, and pledge it giues of glory; in the other life it will giue the possession therof. For a truth it is, deliuered by the holy Ghost, *Blessed is the man who alwaies liues in the holy feare of God.*

Psal. 140.

(b) True hope ri-seth out of filiall Feare.

Prou. 28.

CHAP.

CHAP. XIIII.

*Of the fauours which Christ our Lord
will do to the good at the day of Iudgement ; and of the ioy which they
shall conceaue , by seeing the signes ,
which precede that Iudgment ; and
by beholding the glory of the Crosse ,
which shall go before Christ our Lord.*

GREAT are the benefits which
we find in that diuine *Iudgment* ,
& the fruits which we gather thence
by our considering that which Christ
our Lord will shew vpon the wicked.
For , as we haue declared , it doth
cleerly discouer the greiuousnes of
sinne , and how mightily it is abhorred by our Lord God , and it moueth
vs to a hatred, and a feare therof. But
yet greater are the blessings which
we find in the *Iudgement* of God ; and
the profit which we reap from thece,

K 4   by

by confidering that which Chrift our
Lord will then do for his feruants ; &
the fauours which he will impart, and
the felicity which he will communicate. For in this , doth he difcouer his
goodnes , and the much that he loueth fuch as are good ; and the eftimation which he makes of vertue ; &
he awaketh and prouoketh vs much
to loue him, and he doth animate and
incourage vs much , to labour hard
in his feruice, and that for the pleafing
of him , and complying with his holy will , we muft imploy our felues
in all kind of vertue. Let vs therfore
go declaring the fauors which Chrift
our Lord will impart to the good , in
this his *Iudgment* ; to the end that we
may gather this fruite from thence.

(a) How
differetly
the fame
things do
worke v-
pon the
good and
the bad.

A great (a) benefit and fauour
shall it be for the good, that thofe
very fignes which are to precede the
diuine *Iugdment* , as namely the dar-
kening of the Sunne, the Moone , &

Starres

Starres, the swelling vp of the Sea,
the opening of the earth, withal the
rest, which are to strike such excessiue horrour into the wicked; and
will cause in them such an extreme
affliction and dismay, so far, as that
they shall goe like persons euen distracted and mad with griefe, & shal
euen be dryed vp and withered, thorough the deadly paine and sorrow,
which they shal receaue, as our Lord
himselfe declareth, saying: *Men shall
whither with the feare they wilbe in of* Luc. 21.
*those miseryes which they expect, and of
which, those signes are the forerunners:*
That these very signes, I say, shal giue to those iust men, the seruants of
God whome they shall find aliue,
great strength & courage great confidence and security in God; & shall
cause them great alacrity and comfort, and they shall go all refresh't,
and fully at ease, as being animated
with a new spirit of hope and ioy.

K 5   For

(b) The great reasons, which good men haue to be glad of death, and the day of Iudgment

For (b) iuſt men, who cordiallydoe loue Almighty God, do much deſire to leaue the miſerable eſtate of this life, where God is ſo many wayes offended; and when themſelues cannot forbeare to fal into ſome defects; which although they be light & veniall, yet for as much as they goe againſt the will of God, they feele thē much, and much paine by them; & where they alſo find, that they haue many impedimentes to keepe them from communicating with God, & from louing him, and taſting him as they deſire: Theſe perſons do extremely couet the ſtate of immortality & glory, where they ſhall moſt perfectly, both in body and ſoule, enioy the fauours and benedictions of God as the Apoſtle declareth (c) ſaying: *We know that all creatures*, that is to ſay, *all the whole machine of the world* (*which conteyns all the ſenſible creaturs*) *is groaning vnder the weight, and muta-*

(c) The ſenſe is of the B. Apoſtle, and it is opened and explained by our Authour. Rom. 8.

tability, and corruption, which it is fubiect to.

And as a woman who being in labour of her child, doth expect to bring
him forth; fo doth it remaine with a kind
of wearines, and griefe, from the very
first beginning of the world, till this in-
ftant; defiring & hoping to fee it felf free
from this corruption and mutabil ty; &
to be all renewed, according to the imitation, and refemblance of that glorious liberty of the fonnes of God. And we the
difciples & feruants of Chrift our Lord,
who haue receaued the chiefe, and first
fruits & gifts of the holy Ghoft, doe figh,
& groan withal the affectiõ of our harts,
towards the perfect & complete adoptiõ
of the fonnes of God; which is the glory,
not only of our foules, but euen of our
bodyes alfo, whereby the whole man fhall
be deliuered from all mortality, and corruption, and from all euill inclination &
concupifcence; and fhall perfectly enioy,
both in body and foule the redemption,
                                    which

which was wrought by Christ our Lord.
This is of the Apostle . And for as
much as this desire is of iust persons,
and that, in it selfe,it is so very internall, and so vehement ; when they
shall see the signes of the diuine *Iud-*
gement,they shal know that the tyme
is then close at hand ; wherein that
desire of theirs is to be satisfyed , and
when they are to be possessed of that
happy state , and wherein they are
to be free both in body and soule frō
all corruption and misery both of sin
and pennance. And they shallbe ful
of glory in their soules ; and their bodyes, being adorned with the glorious stole of immortality,are to enioy
God eternally in his kingdome .

(d) The
ioy which
the elect
will haue
to see thē-
selues so
neere the
end of
their
hope.

Now (d) by this so certaine, &
secure hope, that God wilbe so gracious to them, as to graunt that they
may possesse, & enioy that immense
good,which they so mightily desire,
and to which , then , they shall be
brought

brought fo neere, they will reioyce,
and be reuiued in a wonderfull manner ; and giue ſtrange thankes to
God, for hauing brought them to fee
that day, and for hauing continued
them in his feruice ; and vouchfafed
to giue them fuch tokens & pledges
of his glory . All this did Chriſt our
Lord vnfold , in the Ghofpell . For
hauing reckonedvp the figns which
are to appeare before his comming
to *Iudgement*, and the feare and forrow wherewith they ſhallbe receaued by the wicked ; turning then his
difcourfe to his difciples (and in their
perfons to all fuch as would be their
imitatours, and were to be aliue at
that tyme) he fayth , after this manner: *When theſe thinges ſhall arriue ,*
which are to precede my comming , do
you lift vp your heads. Be not difquieted,
be not difmayd , giue no place to ſorrow ,
none to feare, or to diſtruſt, as the louers
of the world will do, who will go with
                                        the

the head all hanging downe like men af-
flicted and dismayd But haue you great
confidence, conceaue great courage , be
cheerefull and reioyce, and with this con-
fidence and ioy lift vp your harts & your
face, to God, for now your redemption
draweth neere. The tyme approacheth,
and so doth that most happy state and
complete redemption, which now with
my Passion and Death I am about to gain
for you, and that is, both security from
all knd of misery, and immortall glory
both to body and soule.

      Another great fauour to the
iust, willbe, to see, appearing in the
ayre (and that high vp neer heauen,
and before the person of Christ our
Lord) the signe, and standard of the
(e)Happy most holy (e) Crosse, not made of
soules, wood, or mettall, but of other most
which glorious matter, and more brightly
heere shining, & incomparably with more
are deuo-
ted to the beauty, then the sunne; and in pro-
Crosse of portion so very large , that being
Christ
our Lord plac'd

plac't on high, it may be seene ouer
the whole earth, by all the inhabitāts
thereof. For a matter and motiue it
is of incomparable comfort & ioy,
for them to see in such high honour
and glory, that Crosse, which they
adored, as the Image of Christ, and
which they loued, by enduring and
suffering affronts and paynes for his
sake. When (f) a worldly man doth
hate any thing, or any person, and
seeth it or him aduanced to honour,
it puts him to payne. Wicked men, in
this life, did abhorre the Crosse of
Christ, becaule they did extremely
loue the pleasures and delicacyes, &
transitory honours of this world, &
they detested to suffer paine & sham
in the vertue, and for the loue of
Christ our Lord. So doth S. *Paul* expresse it saying : *There are many who*
line and conuerse among you (of whome I
haue aduertised you many tymes, & now
againe I repeate it with griefe & sorrow
of

(f) A pro-
found, &
yet a plain
conside-
ration.

Phl. 3.

of my hart.) who are the enemies of the Crosse of Christ, since they giue themselues to delights and delicacyes, and to ambition and pride, which the Crosse of Christ doth condemne; and they flye from penance, and mortification, and abstinence, and from the exercises of humility, to which the Crosse of Christ doth perswade and teach. When therefore these men shall see, in that diuine Iudgment that the Crosse of Christ is so highly honoured, and made so glorious, which they with their workes did so abhorre, it shall replenish them with paine and griefe. For thereby they shall more cleerely see their errour, and the eternall condemnation, which is prepared for them. For that, is to be the end of such men, as the same Apostle declareth saying: *Whose end, is death, and the destruction of their soules.*

(g) The same consideration continued.

On (g) the contrary side, whosoeuer he be that doth greatly loue any
ny

any thing or person, he reioyceth &
taketh comfort to see that it is honored & esteemed by others. And now
for as much as the seruantes of God
do cordialy loue the Crosse of Christ
which is, To mortify theselues with
thinges of difficulty to flesh and
bloud; and to suffer paines, and tribulations, and affronts for his loue,
and in the imitation of his Passion.
For as S. *Paul* sayth: *They who are of* Galat. 5.
Christ, and who re liuely m mbers of
him, and who haue hi spirit and who
are gouerned by him, doe crucify their
flesh, and chastise it with penances, and
by willingly imbracing those affronts &
paynes, which God presents. And by af- (h) And
flicting their flesh, in this manner, they haue we
doe withall, destroy and kill the vices, not reason
and ill desires which sprout from thence. to loue it,
Now when the seruants of God, shal since it
see that Crosse, (h) which they lo- was the
ued so much, and wherein they did instrumēt
so greatly reioyce, become exalted, on.

L   and

and so glorious, and so highly honoured by Almighty God; and so reueared by the whole world, they shal receaue thereby, excessiue ioy, and consolation; to see how well they chanced in following the Crosse of Christ our Lord; and they shall hold it as an expresse signe of the glory, which God will giue to them. For, a truth of God it is, which is pronounced by his Apostle: *That whatsoeuer tribulation or paine or trouble is suffered int his life for the loue of God (which how long soeuer it lasts is but momentary, since it liues no longer then we liue) & which how grieuous soeuer it may seeme, yet to the soules that loue God, and are assisted by his holy grace, is light and easy) doth worke in vs, and that as a meritorious cause a weight of most soueraigne glory, ouerflowing beyond all measure, and exceeding all that which we can so much as euen imagine: & this is not to be of temporall glory, but a glory which shall neuer end.*　CHAP.

CHAP. XV.

*Of the fauour which Chrift our Lord wil
do his feruants, at the day of* Iudgement, *by feparating them from the
wicked.*

ANOTHER benefit & fauour,
and that a great one, will Chrift
our Lord, do to his feruants in the
day of *Iudgment*, and that will be to
feparate them from the company of
the wicked. This was fignified by
Chrift our Lord, who faid : *When the
fonne of man fhal come to iudge,* he fhall
fit vpon the throne of his Maiefty, &
all the nations of the earth fhalbe af-
fembled before him ; and, as the fhep-
heard deuides the fheepe from the
Goates, fo fhall he deuide the good
and bad from one another. The good
he calleth *fheep*, for the innocency,
fimplicity, meeknes, & fruitefulnes
in good works wherwith they aboūd

Matt. 25.

L 2   and

and the wicked he calleth *Goates* , for
their barrennes in doing any thing
that is good ; and for the ill odour of
their vices , and the impetuousnes of
their passions , to which they are su-
bieĉt . Three things there are , which
do principally afflict and torment the
good , when they are in company of
the bad . First , they see before their
eyes , many and great offences committed against God , and they are
not able to preuent them . This
(a) is a greiuous torment ; and the
more they loue God, & the fulfilling
of his lawe, so much greater is the
griefe which they conceaue , by seeing him offended , and it despised .
This did *S . Peter* explicate, when he
said of *Lot* , *That he was a iust man &*
as such he could not indure to see sins có-
mitted , and yet he dwelt among such
men ,as tormented his very soule ,by their
sins .

(a)He that
finds not
this griefe
in his hart
is not so
much in
loue with
God,as he
perhaps
conceaues
2.Pet. 2.

   Another thing which afflicteth
        good

good men, when they liue and conuerſe with ſuch as are wicked, is the
danger (b) wherin they are, of loo-
ſing the vertue which they haue. For
as the example of the good, doth induce men to the loue of vertue, ſo
doth the example of the wicked to
the loue of vice. For this cauſe, did
the Apoſtle ſay to the *Corinthiãs* who
were men of vertue: *Do not ſuffer your*
ſelues to be deceiued ; depart from the cõ
pany and communication of the wicked ;
for euill wordes do preiudice and corrupt
good workes, and ſo make men bad of
good. For as much therfore as (d)
good men do vnderſtand their owne
frailty ; they do greately apprehend
their ſpirituall hurt; therfore do they
feele great paine, by running hazard
of falling into ſuch a thing as ſinne,
which they do ſo much abhorre.

(b) Thou
little
knoweſt,
the ex-
trem dan-
ger into
which ill
company
doth caſt
thee.
1. Cor. 15.

(d) The
more ver-
tuous mẽ
are, the
leſſe they
preſume
vpon thẽ-
ſelues.

    The third thing which afflicteth
good men, who finde themſelues in
the company of wilfull ſinners, is

feare to be punished ioyntly with
them. For although , in this life, God
doth not punish the soule of one , for
the sins of another ; yet (e) it happe-
neth, that for as much as concerneth
temporall things, God sendeth punishment sometymes to some who are
good, for the sins of other with whõe
they liue. As he did , to the Children
of *Israell* , who for the sins of *Acham*
(who tooke some parte of the enemies spoyles against the commaund-
ment of God) retyred his hand of
succour from them all, and disconti-
nued the strength , which he had giuen them ; and so they were subdued
and slaine by their enemies . And
God declared , that he sent that puni-
shmẽt for the sinne of *Acham*, saying;
*The children of israel, shall not be able to
resist their enemyes , but they shall flye
from before their face ; because they are
polluted, by his sinnes, who tooke that ,
which was solemnely forbidden .* I will
no

(e) The
iudgmẽts
of God,
are some
tymes se-
cret, but
they are
euer iust.

Iosu. 7.

no more declare my selfe in fauour of you , till you punish him. And so *A-cham* being punished , God returned againe to shew them fauour. Now this course of Gods punishing , in temporall things some one, for the sins of another, may be taken by Almighty God (without the least iniustice to any one , because he is the absolute Lord of all things , and he doth whatsoeuer he doth vpon perfect reason) *to declare,* as S. Austine sheweth , *what a wicked thing sinne is , and how profoundly it is hated by him.* And this is to be vnderstood , when the good, who liue amongst the wicked, do not yet participate with them in their sins ; for when they do partake or consent therin, and doe (f) not reprehend or correct them , as they ought , then God doth not onely chastise them in temporall things, as of the body , or goods , but also in those other which concerne the soule;

Augu. in Iosue q. 4. D. Thom. 2. 2. q. 108. art. 4.

(f) It is no smal sinne for a man not to reprehend sinne in due tyme & place .

L 4 and

and that not onely in this life , but in
that of the other alfo , according to
the quality of the fault.

Thefe are the things which put
good men in paine, when they are in
cōpany of the wicked . And fo it wil
be a moft fingular benefit, and of fupreme confolation and ioy , for the
good to fee themfelues feparated , &
that for euer, from the fociety of the
wicked . And to knowe foe cleerly ,
that then no longer they fhall be able
to fee with their eyes , nor to heare
wi h their eares, in thofe eternall habitations of theyrs , any thing at all
which may be of the leaft offence to
G d. But that whatfoeuer they fhall
either heare , or fee , is to be nothing
els, but the praifing and glorifying of
his diuine Maiefty with fupreme per-
fextion. And to knowe , that then
they fhall not be able to haue fo much
as any occafion , or daunger of it, nor
that there fhall be any one, in heauen,
who

who may giue them example of finne
by deed, or perfwade them to it by
word. For all they whom there they
are to haue for companions, & that
for euer, are to be Saints; and fo truly Saints, that they fhall neuer ceafe,
not fo much as for one little, fingle
moment from louing God, with the
very higheft top of all perfection, &
from doing the holy will of God in
all thinges, with vnfpeakable comfort and ioy. And yet further to
know that then they are free for e-
uer, from all kind of punifhment; &
from all danger to fuffer any. For as
for any finnes of their owne, they
cannot be punifhed for any fuch, becaufe they can commit none; and as
for the finnes of others, they cannot (g) How
be punifhed for them, becaufe they euery one
haue not, nor cannot haue the com of the E-
pany of any fuch as can finne. But ioy in the
on (g) the other fide they are to haue glory of
an augmentation of glory, for the each o-
ther.

L 5   moft

moſt holy ſociety which they ſhall
enioy of the Bleſſed, through whoſe
glory their glory alſo ſhall increaſe.
For the immenſe ardour of loue,
wherewith they will be carryed to
God, will be the cauſe why they ſhal
take particuler guſt, in that loue,
wherwith euery one of thoſe bleſſed
ſoules, ſhall glorify,& loue Almighty God. And ſo alſo the ſupreme loue
which euery one of the ſame bleſſed
ſoules ſhall beare ech other, wil mak
thē receaue particuler ioy, by euery
one in particuler. O moſt bleſſed
creatures, who are to liue in ſuch a
ſociety; and who are to enioy ſuch a
communication of felicity for all e-
ternity. If it be a great benediction
to enioy the ſociety of good men,
heere on earth; what kind of bleſſed-
nes will it be to enioy the company
of bleſſed ſoules? If it be a matter of
much profit and comfort to participate in the communication of the
guifts

guifts of grace ; what kind of profit,
what kind of comfort will it be, to
haue communication with so many
Saints both men and Angells, in the
guifts of glory ? O with how much
reason is it savd: *Bleſſed are they, O
Lord, who dwell in thy houſe; they shall* Pſal. 83.
*prayſe thee there, through the eternity
of all eternityes , Amen.*

CHAP. XVI.

*Of the fauour, which Chriſt our Lord
    imparteth to his ſeruants at the day
    of Iudgment, by giuing them his
    benediction, and communicating his
    kingdome to them.*

THIS benefit and fauour, is followed by another , which yet is
greater . For the good, being once
ſeparated from the wicked, & being
plac't vpon the right hand of Chriſt
our Lord ; this celeſtiall King ſhall
caſt

caſt towards them his moſt gracious countenance, being all full or ſuauity, and delight. And paſſing his ſentence of fauour on them, he will ſay, *Come yee bleſſed of my Father*. The benediction of God is the good guift of God; and ſo, to be bleſſed by him, is to be filled withal thoſe good gifts and graces; which God communicates to his ſeruants. That is, withal thoſe principall benefits, which the Saints haue heere on earth (when once they are made pure and cleane from all imperfections) and withall thoſe others alſo, which the Angells doe poſſeſſe in heauen; &, which is more, with all thoſe goods & graces which the King of heauen himſelfe, doth poſſeſſe and enioy. For, as S. *Iohn* affirmeth, *When he ſhall appeare, we ſhallbe made like to Ieſus Chriſt our Lord, participating of his power, of his beauty, of his wiſedome, of his goodnes, of his ioy, of his glory.*

1. Ioan. 3.

He

He (a) calleth them *Bl ssed of his Father*, to declare the fountayne, & first offspring, from whence all the benefits of grace and glory spring, and this is the eternall Father; and besides, because all that which the Father operateth, is also the worke of God the Sonne as he is God; as also it is the worke of God the holy Ghost. For the Diuinity, the Goodnes, and the Power, is the very same in all the three Persons; and to attribute them all to the Father (as to the first Authour of all that is good) is to offer them also to the Sonne, as he is God; and it is also to offer them to the holy Ghost, who is one God, with the Father, and the Sonne. O happy men, who are to receaue such a bene-diction! A benediction, giuen by Christ our Lord, in the face of heauen and earth, & of all the creaturs! A benediction authorized by all the most Blessed Trinity, as the Authour and

(a) How grace and glory proceed from God the Father and how also from the other persons of the most B. Trini-ty.

and fountaine of the same! A benediction which comprehendes all the
chiefe guifts of grace, & al the guifts
of glory! A benediction full of benefits, vnspeakable, most high, and truly heauenly, which containe all the
most chiefe and choice part of heauen! A Benediction of eternall benefit! A Benediction irreuocable,
which can neuer be changed, as long
as God shallbe God! O how highly
is this benediction to be esteemed! O
how much is it to be desired, & procured, which maketh men so truely
happy, as our Lord himselfe declareth saying: *Come and possesse the king-*
dome, which is prepared for you from the
beginning of the world.

(b) The
great dif-
ferences
which are
betweene
an earthly
& a hea-
uenly
kingdom.

Kingdoms (b) *& dominions you had*
on earth, but temporall kingdoms & do-
minions they were & of little valew &
cōfort; or rather ful of miseries; & what-
soeuer they were, they are now growne
to an end. Laying aside those miserable
king-

kingdomes which already are ended, come
and possesse another kingdome, which is
celestiall & full of incomparable happines;
a kingdome of infinite value; a kingdome
which eternally shall contynue. And
although euery one of you is to be a king of
this kingdome, and is to raigne and possesse the same; yet the kingdom is still but
one. For all of you are to be subiect and
obedient (but it is to be with supreme
loue) to this Soueraigne King, in whose
company you are to raigne. And because all of you are to be of one hart and
of one will, vnited by most perfect loue,
in such sort that the blessings belonging to
any one in particuler to be of you all (so
farre forth as to reioyce therin) and they
of you all to be of euery one (to reioyce
with them, to whome in particuler they
belonge) this kingdome is also to be but
one. Yet still, though this kingdome be
but one, you shall all be kings, and you all
shall raigne. For the kingdome is infinite
in the greatnes of the felicity, which is
possest

possest therin ; and it is infinite also , in the contynuance , since it is eternall. And to the end that you may discerne the altitude of this kingdome , and the great affection wher with it is giuen you , Behould , it hath bene prepared for you since the beginning of the world .

(c)Of our election to the kingdom of heauen and the preparation , which is made for vs toward the same.

The election (c) of the inhabitants of this kingdome was made before the world was created ; for they were chosen and predestinated from all eternity to raigne therin . But the preparing of those things which concerne this kingdome , and the putting of those meanes in practice , which had relation to the obteyning therof , did begin at the beginning of the world . From that tyme, were framed those most sumptuous pallaces , those most beautifull habitations , and those most glorious feats and thrones , where the inhabitants of this kingdom were to liue & raigne . Then were created and were made

made happy thofe firft Cittizeus of
this kingdom, which are the Angels,
who were to keepe men company
therin , and to augument the glory
which men were to poffeffe in this
kingdome. And fo alfo from the firft
begiuingof the world,ther were gifts
of graces which came to be communicated to men,wherby they were to
obteyne this kingdome.And for God
to create man,and withal to communicate iuftice & grace to him,wherby
he might procure this kingdome, all
that was done at once ; & from that
tyme, to this, nothing hath beene
done, but to difpofe and help men ,
& giue them meanes that they might
come to poffeffe and perfectly intoy
this kingdome,in glory both of body
and foule. This is that moft bleffed
fentence , which Chrift our Lord
will giue in fauour of his feruants; &
that being done , he will inftantly
rayfe them vp togeather with him-

M

felfe

selfe, and will inuest them with the most glorious possession of his celestiall kingdome.

CHAP. XVII.

Of the felicity which Christ our Lord will communicate to his seruants, in the kingdome of heauen.

(a) A most excellent most sweet, most profound, & yet most plaine description of the ioyes of heauen, throughout this whole Chapter. (b) The place of the kingdome of glory.

LET (a) vs yet more particulerly cōtemplate the Maiesty of this kingdome, which Christ our Lord imparteth to his seruants; and of that felicity which is possest therein; to the end that we may gather that fruit, which it is fit for vs to feed vpon; which is nothing els, but the disposing of our selues to the obtayning of this kingdome, by an imitation of the vertues of Christ our Lord. And (b) first, the scituation and place of this kingdome, is that supreme heauen, which for the glorious

rious brightnes and splendor which
is found therein, is called Empyreal.
The altitude and capacity, and beauty & admirable designe, the grace
and suauity of this place though it be
such, as no tongue of flesh and bloud
can declare; yet to giue vs to vnderstand, some part of that which there
is found, by a comparison of those
thinges which heere we know, S.
Iohn describes it in the *Reuelations*
after this manner. He was carryed *Apoc.21*
in spirit, to a mountaine which was *& 22.*
great and very high; and he saw that
holy *Hierusalem* the celestiall Citty,
full of the clarity of God; all built of
perfect, pure and most resplendent
gould, like cleane, pure glasse. It had
a wall about it of Iaspar, both very
thicke, and very high, the foundati-
ons wherof, were adorned with pretious stone. In this wal, were twelue
gates, and euery one of them, was
made of a most pretious pearle and

that

that pearle alone, did make the gate.
This Citty had within a very spacious open place, all paued with gold,
most pure & most resplendent, & in
the midst of that place, there was a
riuer of infinite sweetnes. A Temple
also there was, to adorne this Citty;
and a light to illuminate it; and this
Temple and Light was God himself,
and therfore it must needs be farre
from hauing any necessity of any other Temple or Light.

(c) We
who are
sensible
creatures,
as well as
spirituall,
must be
raised towards spirituall
things by
such as
are sensible; and
therefore
the vse of
ceremonyes, and
Images, is
very necessary.

By these wordes S. Iohn describeth the scituation of the Kingdome of heauen, and the habitation
of the Saints. And although it be
true, that there are not there, any
of those mettalls of gold or siluer, or
any of these pretious stones of earth
(for all these thinges are poore and
base, and of no valew) yet (c) he deliuereth himselfe thus, that by those
thinges which are the most pretious
and beautifull of the earth, the soule
may

may rife to confider the greatnes &
beauty of heauenly thinges, vnder-
ftanding euer, that thofe, are incomparably better then thefe. And as the
whole globe of the heauens, is fo far
exceeding the earth in greatnes, that
the whole earth is but as a point, or
in effect as nothing, in comparifon
of the heauens ; fo is it in all the reft
as well as in greatnes . And all the
brightnes, and beauty , and fweetnes of thinges of this world , being
compared with thofe of heauen , are
as if they had not, fo much as the leaft
being at all . So that the aduantage
which the habitation of heauen doth
carry beyond this of the earth is fuch
that it exceedeth all comparifon. For
in fine fuch it is, as is fit to be carryed
by the houfe of the Creatour in refpect of a creatures houfe ; and by the
Citty of God, in refpect of the Citty
of men; and by that fphere of felicity and eternall ioy, in refpect of this

Center of miferyes, and this valley
of teares.

(d) Mans
supreme
happynes
confisteth
in the vi
fion of
God.
Apoc. 22

The (d) chiefe felicity which
is enioyed in this foueraigne Citty
by cleare vifion, is God himfelfe.
His feruantes, fayth *S. Iohn*, in this
Citty of God fhal feç his face. What
vnfpeakable happines, what Abifle,
what immenfe kind of fea of all felicity, will it be to looke the Diuinity
of God in the face, without the in-
terpofition or interpretation of any
creature? To (e) fee that diuine ef-

(e) A moft
fweet ex-
plication
of the
moft blef-
fed Trini-
ty.

fence, in three perfons; and three diuine perfons in one, and the felfe
fame effence; to feç the power of the
Father, the wifedome of the Sonne,
& the goodnes of the holy Ghoft? To
feç how the Father, from all eternity, engenders the Sonne, communicating to him his diuinity; and how
the Father and the Sonne, as one &
the fame eternall fpring or roote, do
by fpiration, giue proceeding to the
holy

holy Ghoſt, and communicate their diuine eſſence to him? To ſee how all the perfection of God, is in euery one of the three diuine perſons; and how al the perfectiõ, that any one of the diuin perſons hath, the very ſame is poſſeſſed by either of the other diuine perſons. What kind of incomparable ioy wil that be, ſo cleerely to behould an infinite Good, which is all amiable, all ful of infinite beauty, of ſuauity, and of delight. And not only to ſee it, in ſome manner, which might be leſſe excellent, but to behould it with the eyes of an incorruptible ſoule, and they moſt brightly clarifyed by the light of glory; & euerlaſtingly to loue it, without ceaſing, & that with a moſt perfect loue, and to poſſeſſe it with a perpetuity of ſecurity.

After (f) the rate of the *knowledge* of any thinge, growes the *loue* to be; and after the rate of the loue,

(f) Of knowledge, Loue and Ioy, and how they grow out of one another.

M 4   is

is the *ioy* for that which is so much beloued; and that *knowledge* which the
Saints haue of God, being the greatest which can possibly be had (since
it is the cleare sight of God, the *loue*
must also be so great, as that greater
cannot be conceaued.

     The (g) soule is moued to loue
a thing, which it knowes, because it
is good, because it is beautifull, because it is profitable, because it is
delightfull, because it concernes the
soule, and is, after a sort, belonging
to it. And so much more as that thing
is good, more beautifull, more profitable, more delightfull, more concerning it, and more belonging to it,
so much more doth the soule (if it
know that thing well, and be hinde-
red by no impediment at all) delight
in it, and *loue* it, with a more intense,
and perfect loue. Well then, since all
these reasons, and tytles, & motiues
of loue, are found to be in God, with
                infinite

(g) The
motiues
of loue.

infinite perfection (and the foule
cleerlyfeeing God ,and meeting with
no impediment which may hinder
loue) with what *loue* fo intenfe,andfo
immenfe, will it be fure to loue him?

By (ᵸ)feeing that he is *infinite*
goodnes,there is ingédred in the foule,
a moft copious riuer of*loue*; By feeing
that he is *infinite beauty* , there is produced in it , another moft abundant
riuer of *loue* ; By feeing how full of
aduantage it hath bene , and is , and
euer will be to the foule ; and that in
fome forte it is euen infinite , there
flowes from the foule another riuer
of *loue* , fo wide , and deepe , as that
it hath neither bottom nor brim . By
feeing that it is an *infinite delight* ,and
fweetenes , and that it concernes the
foule fo much , and that fhe doth fo
dearly truly belong vnto it ; and that
it is her creator , her father, her God;
and that all her being depends vpon
it;there is alfo created in the foule an-

(h) The
riuers of
ioy which
ouerflow
a foule
which is
in glory,

other moſt copious and moſt abundant riuer of *loue* ; and all theſe riuers
of *loue*, meeting then in one, the ſoule
of euery Saint in heauen growes to
haue in it an vnbridled boundles Sea
of loue.

He that (i) *loues* a thing, doth
wiſh it well; & if he may *ſee* the good
he wiſhes , it giues him *ioy* ; and the
more he *loues*, and the more he *deſires*,
and the greater that the good is , ſo
much the greater is the *ioy* .Now thē,
ſince the Saints in heauen do loue
God , with a whole boundleſſe Sea of
loue; and ſeeing that he poſſeſſeth all
the good which they can wiſh (as
namely that he is God himſelfe) and
that , together with God , he is infinitely happy ; who can ſay what delight, who can ſay what ioy they ſhall
receiue ; ſince it is bound to be great
according to the rate of their loue.
Infallibly they ſhall poſſeſſe a whole
immenſe Sea of diuine *ioy* ; an immenſe

menfe Sea fhall they poffeffe, of celeftiall and fupreme delights. This is
that delight and ioy, which the foule
receiues from God himfelfe, being an
infinit good; when once she is poffeft
of a cleare vifion of him, and that by
loue. O (k) *ioy*, which ouercomeft all (k) Infinit
ioy! *O ioy*, which imbraceft all our ioy.
good! *O ioy*, without lymit! O eternall *ioy*! *O ioy* which art the euer running fountaine of al *ioyes*! *O ioy* which
knoweft how to fatiffy all the defirs,
and canft fill vp all the hollowes and *Matt. 25.*
empty places of the foule ; and doft
poffeffe whatfoeuer we fhall euer be (l) The
able to think! To this *ioy* doth Chrift vnfpeak-
niuite al his faithfull feruants, & this able ioy,
doth he giue them, in reward of their which
vertue, faying, *Reioyce O thou good &* haue by
faithfull feruant, enter into the ioy of thy feeing the
Lord. the moft
glorious
Another (l) felicity which the humanity
bleffed foules fhall haue, is to behold of Chrift
the moft glorious humáity of Chrift our Lord.
our

our Lord; and to enioye it , and to see him (euen as he is man)in so excessiue Greatnes , and Maiesty, and glory. And to see him withal so amiable, and so affable, & so deerly sweet, towards all those happy soules;and to see that that Lord, who is man as they are , and who with his passion and death did for the loue he bare them , redeeme them from eternall damnation; the same man , I say , is the infinite and eternall God . O how will they *loue* that most sacred humanity, which loued them so much,& which did and suffered so great things for them? O how will they reioyce to see that humāity so mightily sublymed , and vnited by an incomprehensible manner, to the person of the Word? O how wil they glory in his felicity? O what delight & sweetnes wil they receiue, from such a sight and from such a loue ? For as the prophet saith

Isa . 33 . *They shall see the king in his beauty.*

Another

Another (m) supreme felicity
for those happy soules, shalbe to see
the loue which God carries towards
them; and wherwith the eternall fa
ther, did, from all *Eternity* loue, and
choose them, & did, in *Tyme* bestow
his Sonne vpon them ; and deliuer
him ouer to death for them; and to see
that this loue, in it selfe, is infinite,
and the very same wherewith God
loues himselfe. The (n) seruant of a
King, will much esteeme, that the
king do him fauour, bestowing some
important place vpon him in his
house, with good prouision belonging to it. But much more will he e-
steeme it, and much more contentment & cōfort will he receiue, to see
himselfe beloued, by that king ; and
that he is a fauorite of his. And thogh
he haue but some coniectures of this
loue, and that it may easely be cooled
and changed into a disaffection ; yet
doth he neuertheles esteem it more,
$\qquad$ then

(m) It wil
be an ine,
stimable
ioy to see
how infi-
nitly God
loueth
them,

(n) This
truth is
prouedby
a fit com-
parison.

then all the other fauours which the
king doth him . For by louing him ,
he giueth him his hart , which is incomparably more , then if he gaue
him a part of his fortune . What then
will a Saint in glory feele in himselfe
when he shal see, that he is so beloued
by God ; and although the benefits
which God hath done him are very
great , yet the loue he beares him is
much greater ; and although they are
most precious benefits which there
he is enioying, by the guyft of God,
yet much more pretious is the loue .
For this *loue* is the root & fountaine
of all the benefites , and guiftes , and
graces which he hath comunicated ;
nay this *loue* , is euen very God himselfe . Now then to knowe this loue
of God , not by coniecture, but by
seeing it expresly in God , with as
great clarity as that wherewith he
seeth God himselfe ; and still to see
with the same clarity that this *loue*

cannot

cannot be loſt, no nor changed, but that for euer it ſhall remaine inuariable, with the ſelfe ſame permanency wher with the truth of God himſelfe ſhal remain, of which truth it is ſayd *that it ſhall remaine for euer*; O how highly wil the *Bleſſed* eſteeme & value this *loue* of God! O how imcomparable ioy will they receiue to ſee théſelues ſo beloued by God *!*

Pſal, 118,

When *loue* is great, it hath this property & power, that by the band of the ſame *loue*, it makes (o) him that loues, become the ſame thing with him that is beloued, and that he lodgeth his whole hart in him; & that with the chaynes of loue he becomes impriſoned, and euen captiued by him, who is beloued, & that he depend wholy vpon him; willing that which he wills, and communicating to him all his goods. Now then, ſince the Bleſſed ſoules, knowing that this is the property of intenſe

(o) Of the vnion, of ſeuerall things which is made by loue.

tenfe loue, and feeing themfelues fo
beloued by God with this loue which
hath no meafure, nor had no beginning, nor will hauè end; what kind
of immenfe, incomparable ioy, wil
this be to them? Without all queftion
except the ioy which they fhall haue
in the felicity of God, whome they
loue more then themfelues, this o-
ther is their greateft ioy, to fee themfelues fo beloued by him, who is omnipotent, and who is infinite beauty
and glory, and the infinite fountaine
of all Good. Of this *Loue* God himfelfe giueth teftimony, faying by the
Prophet *Hieremy* : *With eternall loue*
I haue loued thee ; and therefore did I
in tyme shew mercy to thee, and I cal-
led, and drew thee to my friendship and
glory.

Hier. 31.

CHAP.

CHAP. XVIII.

Of other benefits which Christ our Lord cōmunicateth to his seruantes, in his heauenly kingdome ; and of the fruit of gratitude, which we must gather from the Consideration of this reward.

BESIDES these benefits which are the chiefe, there are others yet, which are enioyed by happy soules in the kingdome of heauen, which are also of inualuable value, and of incomparable ioy. One of them is, to be in cōpany of the Blessed; where there is such a multitude of (a) Angelicall spirits, distinguished into nine Quires, as that they are in greater number, then all the men, which haue beene, which are, and which shall euer be; yea more, then all the corporeall creatures of

(a) The incomprehensible number of the Angels.

N   the

the whole world put togeather. And
where there are so many Patriarkes,
and Prophets, and Apostles, and A-
postolicall men, and Martyrs, and
Confessours, and Virgins; and so
many others, who by pennance haue
made their way to heauen, & whom

Apoc. 7. S. *Iohn* (who saw them in a *Reuelation*) sayth, to be so many, as that they
cannot be numbred. And (ᴾ) all of

(b) The
dignity & them, are the sonnes of God, and
excellen- *Grandes* in the Court of God; and
cy of
thofe ce- Kings in the kingdome of heauen;
leftiall in- and all of them, most perfect in ver-
habitants. tue, and most sanctifyedly wise, and
most beautifull, and full of immense
glory; and all of them, so well content, and at ease, that they desire nothing but what they haue, because

(c) What they haue as much, as possibly they
a noble
conuersa- can desire. And (ᶜ) notwithstanding
tion will that they are so very high in dignity,
this be? and glory, yet withall, euery one of
them is most profoundly humble;
all

all affable, and milde, and of moſt
ſweet condition. And being ſo innumerable as they are, they yet doe
all, know one another much better,
and in a more intrinſecall manner,
then a man on earth can euer arriue
to know himſelfe. And they all do
treate, and communicate with one
another ; and they loue one another
with ſuch a loue, as doth incomparably exceede, the loue which any
Mother can beare to a child . For
in them all, there is but one affection
and will, which is that of God , by
the vnion, and conformity of wi'l,
which euery one hath with his ; and
the felicity of all, euery one eſtee-
meth as his owne ; and the glory of
euery onein particuler, is held as proper to euery one . And (d) ſo, euery
one of the Bleſſed hath as many particuler ioyes, as there are Angels, &
Saints in heauen. For euery one of
them reioyceth at the others good, as

(d) Euery
one of
them hath
exceſſiue
ioy in the
glory of
any other.

at his owne; and he enioyeth the ioy
of another, as his owne ioy; and so
much more will one happy soule be
glad of the glory of any other, as he
shall see God to be more glorifyed in
that other.

(e) The
inestima-
ble ioy
which e-
uery of
the Blessed
haue in
behoul-
ding, and
treating
with the
all imma-
culate
Mother of
God.

But amongst all the (e) *Blessed*,
whether they be Angells, or meere
men and women, the creature, who
doth more enoble, and engrandize,
and delight, and make happy that
most glorious court of heauen, is the
most sacred *Virgin Mary*, that Lady,
that Queene, that most deerly diuinely sweet enamoured mother of the
all. For she is the true & naturall mother of him who created them all, &
who redeemed them all, and who
indued them all with that beatitude.
They all are great, they all are most
sublimely happy; but this Lady, is
more great, more happy, and more
glorious, then they all together. All
of them do ardetly loue one another,
and

and they all conuerſe, and behould
ech other with admirable ſweetenes;
and they are all a cauſe of exceſſiue
ioy and glory to one another. But (f)
this ſoueraign Queene loues them al,
and euery one of them as her deereſt
Children, and as her brethren and
companions, and as the louing members of *Ieſus Chriſt* our Lord, who is
her naturall ſonne. And ſhe behoulds
them all, with moſt gratious, & moſt
amorous eyes; and ſhe treates & communicates with them all, with a moſt
incomparable ſweetenes ; and by
that preſence, and communication of
hers, ſhe cauſeth in euery one of them
farre more ioy, and farre more glory,
then any other creature doth.

This bleſſed life, and this company of the *bleſſed* is deſcribed by the
Prophet *Iſay*, ſpeaking partly of the
militant Church, but principally of
the *triumphãt*, which is that celeſtial
Hieruſalem, in theſe wordes : *There*

N 3   *ſhall*

(f) And
woe will
be to thẽ,
who do
not loue
& honour
and ad-
mire, and
ſerue this
ſoueraign
Queene.

Iſa. 60.

shall neuer be in thee, O thou Soueraigne
Citty, and thou land of the liuing, any
sinne or punishement; nor any newes, or
noyse therof. Insteed of paine, thou shalt
haue perfect & eternal health; & insteed
of sinne, thou shalt haue the continuall
& euerlasting exercise of the loue of God.
Our Lord God shall be all in all to thee;
thy Sunne, and thy Moone, and thy
light and thy glory, and all thy good.
And all the elect are to make vppe, in
thee, a people, and a most glorious and
blessed commonwealth; to the end that all
together, may eternally enioy the inheritance of those celestiall benedictions.
And let vs see (since there are to be
so many inhabitants in that soueraigne
Citty, and since euery iust person
is to be a Cittizen therof) if there may
there be found, any one who is weake
or impotent, or who is subiect to the
least disgust. The Prophet doth instantly proceed, and say, *The least of
them al shalbe so full of power, as that he*
                                    may

may stand for a thowsand, of the stron-
gest men; and the little one shall stand
for a mighty Army. That is to say,
euery one of the *Blessed* shall participate so much of God, and shall finde
God to be so truely his, as that whatsoeuer he haue a mind to do, for
that he shall haue sufficient power.
And whatsoeuer felicity he shall desire, the same he shall possesse, for in
God he can do all, and he hath all.

These (g) benefites which we
haue heere recounted, & other which
be like to these, are possessed and
enioyed in that celestiall kingdome
which Christ our Lord, who is the
iudge both of the quicke and dead,
will impart to the iust, in reward of
their good life. And now let vs reach
towards the fruit which we must procure to gather, from the infallible
knowledge of this truth. Whereof
(h) the first is this : A very great
estimation, and profound internall

(g) The
fruites
which
grow from
the consi-
deration
of the
glory of
heauen.
(h) Great
estimatiō
of the be-
nefits ; &
great
thansgi-
uing to
the bene-
factour.

grati.

gratitude for this mercy, & vnspea-
ble grace of God ; that we being so
poore creatures , so weake , so igno-
rant , and who , by our owne fault ,
made our selues so miserable, so base,
so vnworthy of all good, and who so
well deserued the vttermost of all
paine , God would yet make choyce
of vs , from all eternity; and first create vs , and after that sinne was committed , redeeme vs ; to the end that
we might obteine that most sublyme,
and supernaturall end of beatitude;
which consisteth in seeing God , and
in enioying God, and in obteyning
and possessing that by grace, which
God himselfe doth possesse by nature, which is to loue & enioy himselfe . Againe, that he hath created ,
and ordayned, and called, and iustified vs, for the enabling vs to a dignity so sublime , as it is to be Kings
of heauen ; and to haue seates , and
thrones in that heauen which is called

led Empyreall, & that for euer. And
there to possesse the incomprehensible and eternall felicity of glory ; &
in this glory , to be companions of
the Angells, yea and of God himselfe
who is the Lord of the Angels . This
I say, is a grace , and mercy , which
we are to ponder, and most profoundly to esteeme in the very rootes of
our harts ; and to be gratefull to God
for it, withal the powers of our soule;
and with our tongue to blesse and
prayse him for it, with *S. Peter* saying;
Blessed and praysed be our God, and the
naturall fauour of *Iesus Christ* our
Lord , who through his great and
most aboundant mercy, hath engen-
dred vs anew (who were borne in
sinne , and were the Children of
wrath, by our descent from *Adam*) by
liuely *Fayth,* and by the *Sacraments* ;
making vs , by this spirituall generation to become the sonnes of God
himselfe, and giuing vs a certaine &

true

true hope of the true life , which is that blessed and euerlasting end. And this he wrought in vs ,by the *Resurre-ction* of Christ our Sauiour. For by his *Resurrection* , he procured that the world should beleeue in him , and should obey his ghospell ; and by me-anes of this faith, and obedience, the fruit of his life and passion might be communicated to it ; and by this liuely hope , he first enabled vs to ex-pect , and afterward to obteine, the inheritāce, which is due to the Sonns of God .

The (i) second thinge which we are to draw from hence, is a very great, and liuely , and efficatious de-sire of this kingdome of heauen ; and that once we may arriue to possesse and enioye that celestiall happines . A man desires , euen by the very ap-petit of nature , to be free from the affliction of paine , & other corporal miseries ; but this desire cannot be
ful-

(i) An in-satiable thirst after the ioyes of hea-uen.

fulfilled in this life. For all this life is full of affliction and sicknes, & paines of body, and sadnes and griefe of mind ; and difficulties, and troubles, and contradictions, by his kinfmen & friends, and of perfecution by iniustice, and oppreffions of enemies ; and of contrary and ill encounters in point of fortune ; and of temptations of deuils, and of the world ; and of their lawes and rights ; and of our owne corrupt nature, and al our euill inclinations. *A man*, faith *Iob*, *liues but a little tyme, and that little, is full of many miferies*. In heauen it is, where a man may haue this defire satisfied, becaufe there, as *S. Iohn* faith, *God will wipe away the teares from his frends eyes, & there fhall be no death, nor lamentation, nor any fad note, nor griefe*. For all this, had an end, in this life ; and therfore it is neceffary for a man to labour, with defire of the kingdome of heauen, where only

ly

Apoc. 21.

ly this defire can be accomplifhed.

　　A man (k) defires, by the appetite

(k) The
iuft reaſō
of this
thirſt,
drawne
from the
ſinnes
wherwith
the world
abounds.

of grace, to ſee himſelfe free from the ſins of his ſoule, which induce him to do ill. In this life, this delight cannot be accomplifhed; becauſe all this life is full of innumerable ſinns; and wherſoeuer thou goeſt, thou ſhal ſee ſinne, and plenty of wickednes. And althogh, in many places it aboundeth more, or leſſe, then in other; yet for the moſt part, euery one of them is corrupted & deſild with diuers kinds of vices; yea and euen the moſt iuſt and holy men, haue ſome veniall ſins, of which they cānot free themſelues; and the ſame men run hazard to fail into other which are greater. For as

ſ. Ioāu. 1. S. Iohn ſayth, *If we ſhall ſay that we haue no ſinne, we deceiue our ſelues therin, and we ſpeake not truth*. In heauen it is, where this deſire is fulfilled; for there, is neither fault, nether can there be any. For as the ſame Apoſtle ftle faith, *Into that celeſtiall Hieruſalem nothing can enter, which is ſpotted.* And therfore it is neceſſary, and moſt profitable, for a man to aſpire to that habitatiō of heauen, where his defire may be fatisfied.

Apoc. 21.

CHAP. XIX.

How all the things of this life which are good, and which giue delight, doe induce vs to a deſire of the kingdome of heauen.

NOT (ª) onely do the euills of ſinne, and puniſhment (wherof this life of ours is full) incline vs to defire the kingdome of heauē, which is free from al thoſe inconueniences; but ſo alſo do all good things, which giue vs in this life any contentment, or guſt either corporall or ſpirituall, perſwade and moue vs to the ſame. For they all diſcouer to vs, the im-

(a) We haue reaſon to thirſt af-ter the kingdom of heauen through the conſideration of earthly pleaſures, which are miſerable things, & yet they make a ſhift to pleaſe vs.

menſi-

menfity of that celeftiall happines;
and the greatnes of the appetite of
our foule, which cannot be fatiffied,
and put in quiet, by any thing,
which is leffe then that. For a man
who, by his fenfes, taketh experience of the fauour of his meat, and
drinke, and of the fweetenes of muficke, and of the contentment which
he hath in feeing thofe things which
are artificiall, gallant, and full of
beauty; by the light of reafon, and of
faith, will grow to make this confideration. If a creature (b) fo bafe and
of fo fmall importance, as a bird, a
liquor of milke, or wine, or any other
thing that concernes our food, being
toucht but by the courfe pallate of
a man, do yet caufe delight and guft;
and fuch guft, as that for it, fome
men do expofe themfelues to much
trouble and coft, yea and euen to the
very perdition of their foules; what
fauour, and what ioy fhall it giue the
foule

(b) A
moft cer-
tayne
truth, and
which en-
treth
fweetly
into the
foule.

foule, to be moſt profoundly inter-
nally with all the powers and forces
therof, vnited with God, and to taſt
God, he being that infinit good, and
that infinit ſweetnes and ioy; yea &
the infinit fountaine of all ioy and
ſweetnes. And with the ſame ſoule,
to ſwallow downe huge draughtes
of that riuer of delights, which is in
the houſe of God; and which, in
ſubſtance, is in euen God himſelfe,
and the infinit and inexhauſted ſea,
of all chaſt and pure delights.

If to ſee with theſe corporall
eyes of ours, the deſigne, the beauty,
and the grace of creatures (which
yet are but compounded of earth, &
water, and the other elements; and
framed by the will of man, out of
mettall, and wood, and other mate-
rialls of this world) do cauſe ſuch
contentment, and ioy, in the hart
of man, by the ſight therof, that for
this ſight, they endure, and ſuffer
much;

much ; and make long iourneys , and much expence ; what comfort , and ioy fhall it be , for the cleere eyes of the foule (being ftrengthned by fupernaturall force and light) to behould that beauty of the Angels , and bleffed fpirits ; yea and the beauty of God himfelfe.

It to heare with our corporall eares, that Muficke which is made by the voyce of a man , and of other inftrumēts of Muficke, doth impart fuch fweetnes , as that a man will remaine many houres as if his foule were euen fufpended; and he is content to loofe both his food and reft , for this earthly guft ; what fweetnes will it be , for thofe inhabitants of heauen , with the eares of their foule, to heare thofe conforts & melodious fonges , wherwith all the Quires of the Angells do praife and glorify Almighty God. And to heare that moft gratious voyce, wherwith the fame

God

God doth comfort , and recreate all
those blessed soules,& discouereth to
them his Loue , togeather with the
secrets of his very hart . And to heare
also euē with the ears of their bodies,
the sound of that praise,and thankgi-
uing , wherwith all those men who
are to be made happy after their Resurrection , shall glorify Almighty
God , & giue ioy to the whole court
of heauen.

A man(c) who considereth and
pondereth by these, and such other
discourses both of reason , and faith,
the greatenes of these celestiall blessings , and who findeth , that neither the naturall appetite of reason ,
and much lesse the supernaturall ,
which he hath , being caused in him
by grace , is satisfied or contented, or
quieted by al the benefits , and gusts,
and delights of the earth, but that e-
uen whilst he hath them he becometh
more hungry , more discontent ,and

(c) We
haue rea-
son to as-
pire to e-
ternall
glory,
since no-
thing of
this life
can quēc̄
our thirst

O   more

more vnquiet then he was before ; & that onely he can be satiſſied by the delights and guſts, which are in heauen , will be induced , vpon this motiue , to deſire the happines of heauen witha moſt vehement ardour of minde . And he is animated and encouraged to begge it of God , and to ſigh and grone for it continually;

Pſal. 41. and he ſayth with *Dauid: As the Hart with being chaſed and tired, and hauing deadly thirſt, deſires the waters and goes panting vp and downe in ſearch thereof; ſo my ſoule being ouerwrought by the miſeries of this life, deſireth thee o my God, & hath a mighty thirſt, and an vnſatiable appetit towards thee who art the fountaine of the liuing water both of grace & glory, which can only ſatiſſie and appeaſe my whole appetit. How longe o Lord am I to liue in this place of baniſhment!* When wil it be granted me that being freed from the miſeries of this exile, I may preſent my ſelfe before thee , and behould

behould thee face to face ; and enioy
thy presence , in the society of those
happy soules ! And as longe as this
sentence of banishement lies vpon
me , & that the sight of thy Diuinity
is deferred , I take contentment in
nothing, but spending of sighes and
shedding of teares , day and night ,
throgh the excessiue desire that I haue
to be with thee ; and by these teares
my soule is comforted & mantained.
Thus did *Dauid* , and all those holy
Patriarcks and Prophets , and great
seruants of God of the *old Testament*
aspire , sigh and groane , with vehement desire of this celestiall beatitude . And much more , and with more
reason , did the Saints of the *newe*
Testament performe the same , and
so should all true Christians do . First
because till the passion of Christ our
Lord was past, the Saints , how fully
soeuer they were purged from all
sinne and paine, went not yet to hea-

uen,

uen, but to the *Lymbus* of the holy
Fathers, where they staid frō entring
into heauē, till the redemption of the
world were accomplished by Christ
our Lord . But since his death , all
they , who are purified, either in this
life , or in the other , do instantly rise
vp, to the possessiō of euerlasting beatitude. And secondly now in tyme
of the *lawe of grace*, the guifts of the
holy Ghost are more aboundantly
communicated to the faithfull; & so
they receiue more consolations , and
spirituall ioy , and haue more gust , &
feeling, and experience of celestiall
graces; and do more perfectly vnderstand the height , the value , and
the maiesty therof, and consequently
they desire them more , & with more
ardour of affectiō then did the Saints
of the *old Testament* . It doth also increase this desire in the tyme of the
lawe of grace, to knowe that heauen is
full of blessed creatures , who are of
the

the race of mankinde, and who are
expecting vs there; and do greatly
desire our Society. For by the entry
which any one of the *elect* doth make
into heauen, the glory of God is
increased; who is far more beloued
and praised, and glorified by the iust
in heauen, then on earth; and so also
doth the accidentall ioy, and glory of
euery one of the *elect* increase, vpon
the arriuall of any other. But much
more then they altogether, doth (d)
Christ our Lord (who redeemed, &
saued vs by his death) desire to haue
vs there with him. Both because he
loueth vs much more then they all are
able to do, as also for that by the entry of the elect into heauen, and by
the possession which the is giuen the
of that kingdome, the whole fruit of
his passion, and death is gathered; &
all that is perfected and established,
which he did and suffred for vs heere;
that so he might make vs completely

(d) This reason would extremely oblige vs, though ther were no other.

O 3   happy

happy, & be like to himſelfe in glory;
& be partakers of his heauenly kingdome; and in fine, to make vs ſuch,
as that togeather with him, we may
perfectly prayſe, and glorify, and enioy his eternall Father . For theſe
reaſons doth he much deſire to ſee vs
in heauen; and when that deſire of
his is ſatisfyed by the aſcent which
any of the elect maketh thither; that
moſt ſacred ſoule of our Lord doth
receaue a new delight, & ioy, which
belongeth to his accidentall glory.
For as that kind of glory may increaſe in any of thoſe other Bleſſed
Spirits, ſo may it alſo do, in the moſt
glorious Humanity of Chriſt our
Lord.

CHAP.

CHAP. XX.

How from this knowledge, concerning the Kingdome of Heauen, which Christ our Lord will giue his seruāts, we are to gather a resolute purpose to fly from sinne, and to fullfill the Commandments of God, & to despise the commodityes of this life.

THE (a) third, and the principall vse which we are to make, of this our knowledge, and estimation, and desire of heauenly beatitude, is a stout and resolute minde, and a stiffe and effectuall purpose, to put in executiō all those meanes, which ar either necessary, or but euen conuenient, for the obteyning of this kingdome of heauen. Now, for the entring into heauen, it is necessary to cast sinne away. For Sinne giues impediment to al approach thither; and they who

(a) The consideration of eternall glory must awake vs to hate & fly from sinne.

O 4   haue

haue the soule loaden with any one
mortall sinne, cannot enter into the
kingdome of heauen. Let vs therfore
clense our soules from former sinne,
by penance; and let vs resist all temptations (least els we may returne to
fall againe) accordiug to the aduice
of the Apostle, who saith, *Houlding*
fast these promises of God, which are so
great, and so certaine, and do concerne
those sublyme guifts of grace and glory,
let vs, my brethren much beloued, clense
our selues from all spot of sinne; whether
it be interiour, or exteriour. He saith,
from all sinne, because it will behooue
vs to be clensed from al; and we must
fly with diligence from all. From
mortall sins, because they are against
Charity, & do separate vs from God;
and from *veniall sins,* because they are
contrary to the will of God, and they
weaken the soule; and dispose it to
commit mortall sinne, & consequently to forfaite the kingdome of heauen.

uen. So also, for entring into heauen,
it is necessary to do good works, &
such as are acceptable to God ; as
Christ our Lord affirmeth, saying, *Matt.* xix
If thou wilt enter into that eternall life,
which is true life, keepe the commaund-
ments . Complying (b) therefore (b) It
with this obligation , let vs per- must stir
forme holy workes, wherby we may vs vp to
fulfill the commaundement of God; & se of
and let vs put in execution the all vertue.
vertues of Humility , Chastity ,
Mercy, Iustice , Temperance , Forti-
tude , Religion , and Charity; by
which if they be wrought in state of
grace, and do growe out of Charity,
they will make vs worthy of eternall
life.

  Besides , (c) for the obteyning (c) It ex-
of this kingdome of heauen, it is ne- horteth vs
cessary that we continue in the good to perse-
begun , till we end in doeing well, uerance.
as our Lord did teach vs, saying, *He* *Matt.* 24.
that conty ... ueth to the end, shall be sa-
  O 5   *ued*

ued . Let vs therfore perseuere in good life; and although the deuills comber vs with their temptations, & though men do persecute vs with their iniuries, and though our Lord God do trye vs by many tribulatiõs, let vs not turne backe, nor be dismaied, nor suffer our selues to fall downe, to inordinate sorrow, nor impatience, nor disconfidence; but let vs continually make our recourse to God; and praying to him with humility, let vs beg strengh at his hands, wherwith to suffer, and constancy that we may perseuere, & confidence that we may not dispaire. So doth the *Apostle* aduise the *Galathians* saying : *We who are liuing well, and do exercise our selues in good workes,*

Galat. 6.

let vs not faint, nor giue ouer, no nor growe slacke in the good course begunne but let vs contynue, and grow therin, with great constancy . For in due tyme we shall gather the fruit, if we doe not faint.

faint . That is to fay , we fhall eat the fruit of glory, which fhall haue no end.

Moreouer (d) for the arriuing to enioy celeftial beatitude, we muft defpife the goodes, and pleafures of this world. And it is neceffary that we place not our hartes or endes in them ; nor that we feeke for comfort in them, as Chrift our Lord did fignify to vs by faying , *Woe be to you , who are the louers of riches , and who haue placed your comfort , in the comodityes of this life* . For this reafon it will be neceffary, in moft particuler manner, to contemne all the commoditºyes of this life; namely riches , honours, and pleafures, as poore things tranfitory, and bafe ; for by defpifing them we fhall not place our end, nor feeke for comfort in them .

This is therefore that fruit, which we are to gather from the knowledge, and defire of celeftiall be.

(d) We muft not thinke of finding our heauen in this life, if we meane to haue it in the next.

Luc. 6.

beatitude . For knowing the greatnes , and beauty, and valew of heauenly things, we grow quickly, and
clearely, to fee the vilenes, & poor-
nes of fuch as be earthly; and by defiring and tafting eternall things, we
grow inftantly to loofe the loue, and
taft of all thinges tranfitory . And
thus fhall we perfectly accomplifh
that which the Apoftle asketh at the
hands of all the faythfull , faying : *If
you be rayfed vp with Chrift , feeke the
things that are aboue* . That is (e) to
fay , *Since you are rifen vp in foule to a
fpirituall life of grace , with hope to be
rayfed vp , in due tyme , to an immortall
and glorious life both in body and foule ,
(in imitation of Chrift our Lord, who
rofe vp from the dead to an immortal and
glorious life) feek you with your thoghts,
with your defirs, with your good works ,
and with continuall prayer , the kingdom
of heauen* . *And fince Chrift our Lord
who is your head , is feated at the right
hand*

Colof. 3 .

(e) A place
of S. Paul
excellent-
ly ponde-
red .

hand of his Father, possessing and enioying even as man, the greatest authority and the greatest felicity of glory which
he did euer communicate in Tyme, or will
euer communicate for all Eternity, you
that are members of his, take gust and
sauour in heauenly thinges; and place not
your delight, and loue vpon those of the
earth, but desire those others so from the
hart, and with so great purity of life,
that you may, euen by experience, find
the gust and most pure sauour of them;
& addresse your life, in order to this end
of eterna'l glory, which you loue, and for
which you hope.

This efficacious purpose, &
determinate resolution to cleanse the
soule from all vice, to imploy it with
perseueranee in good workes ; and
cordially to despise earthly thinges,
is the vse which we are to make, of
the knowledg and desire of celestiall
beatitude, as hath beene sayd. And
it is most iust, & due, that so we do,
                                    and

and that, for the going through with this enterprize which we are to make, vpon heauen, we be content to vndertake all labour, and to encounter with any difficulty . All the things (f) of this life, which are of any valew , & are able to giue but the least cōtentment, do cost some trouble, and in all them some difficulty is to be endured. The husband-mā, for gathering in of a little corne, doth manure, and plough the ground before he ʃowes; and after he hath sowed, and that the blade is vp , and the corne is growne, is fayne first to cleanse it, and then to ʃheere it, with much labour. The Sheepheard for the breeding of his poore flocke, doth content himʃelfe to endure the heats, and coldes, and raines, and windes, and night-watches . All Marchants and Faʃtors, and all the Maryners & conductors who are of ʃeruice to thē in their negotiations, do, for the getting

(f) A plaine demonstration , and I am in good hope, that it will cōuince thee .

ting of a little money, passe through intollerable troubles, both by Sea & Land ; and do expose themselues to great danger of death. All kind of tradesmen, for the getting of a poore liuing, do labour and sweat both day and night, in their seuerall occupations. The souldier, for his miserable pay, and for a little fume of honour, is subiect to extreme inconueniences, and runs hazard of his life, at euery moment. The seruants and Courtiers of great Princes, for the obtayning of fauour, which yet doe passe, and change like any wind, depriue themselues of their owne gust, and deny their owne will, and are hanging day and night, vpon that of others ; and for the giuing of contentment to their Lords, they take an aboundance of discontentment & disgust to themselues. They who are enamoured of this world, the couetous, for money ; the intemperate,

for

for curious fare ; the dishonest , for
that filthy pleasure ; the proud , for
that vaine delight in honour , and
commaund ; and all of them in fine,
for the poore comodities of this life,
do suffer greiuous paines , and endure excessiue torments , and sick-
nesses , and other afflictions , which
vpon these occasions they incurre ;
as themselues do confesse when the
punishment of God shall haue laid
their errour before their face . And
then they will say , *We went astray*
Sap . 5. *from the way of truth and were estran-*
ged from that diuine light ; and did o-
uerworke and tyre our selues in the way
of sinne , and vice , and there we endured
many difficulties .

If then the men of this world ,
for the obteyning of most base and
transitory riches , and of certaine
pleasures , which are vaine and per-
nicious , both to body and soule; &
for the giuing of contentment to
mor-

mortall creatures; & for the yeilding
of obedience, to thofe infernall Diuels, who perfwade them to the loue
of earthly things, doe ingulfe themfelues into fuch a fea of troubles, and
breake through fuch a world of difficultyes; what, in the name of God,
will it not be fit for Chriftians and
the feruants of Chrift to do, for the
being faythfull; and loyall, to that
diuine Maiefty; and for the exact
complying, with that obedience, &
loue, which they owe him, both as
to a father, and as to a Lord; and for
the obtayning of the kingdome of
heauen, & the poffeffing of thofe immortall riches of the houfe of God; &
the honour & glory of being the fons
of God; and confequently the ioynt
heyres with Chrift our Lord, of his
patrimony Royall, and of his euerlafting entaile; and for the inioying,
and that for euer, of thofe incomprehenfible delights of his beatitude?

Certainly, it is moſt iuſt, it is
moſt due, that they ſhould vndergo
any trouble and ouercome any difficulty, and expoſe themſelues to any
temporall hazard, how great ſoeuer.
For as the Apoſtle ſayth, by way of
confirming this truth : *All (g) men
who ſtriue, and fight with others, in the
place deputed to that end (as the vſe of
the Romains was to do in their entertai-
nements and feaſts) do for the ouercom-
ming of their oppoſites, abſtaine from all
thoſe thinges of guſt, which may be of a-
ny impediment to them in their combat,
as namely from delicate meates, from
wine, from women, and the like, which
are wont to make men dull, and weake;
and they feed vpon groſſe meats, they
obſerue the rules of continency and temperance, and they prepare and accuſtome
themſelues before hand, to labour. And
all this they do, to obtayne the reward
of winning a corruptible crowne, which
might perhaps be ſome Iewell, or ſome*

(g) This truth con-firmed by S. Paul, moſt di-uinely, & excellent-ly ponde-red by our Author 1. Cor. 9.

suite of clothes, or some garland of bayes or flowres, or some vaine applause, and flying prayse of men. What then are we Christians obliged to do in this spirituall contention and strife which we are making against sinne, for the obtayning of that crovne of immortality, and glory; & of that celestiall kingdome? It is most certain, that if for the giuing of contentment to Almighty God, and for the obtayning of that eternall and immense beatitude, it were necessary to suffer all those pains put togeather which al the men of the world, from the beginning of it to the end, will haue beene to suffer; and which all the holy Martyrs haue endured; it were all reason, that we should willingly be content to endure them all. And if it were necessary, not only to suffer all the paines of this life, but to endure (yea and that for many ages) all the torments of hell, yea and of many hells; it (h) were most iust, &

(h) The ioyes of heauen are more to be desired, then euen the paines of hell to be auoyded,

fit

fit to endure them all, for the obtayning of the kingdome of heauen afterward . For greater is the good of
the glory of heauen , then the euill of
the paines of hell . And how much
then more iuſt, and more conuenient
will it be, to ſuffer the payne and difficulty which belongs to vertue, and
which accompanyeth the fullfilling
of Gods commandments. Which (¹)
difficultyes beſides that they are ſhort
(for as much as at the moſt, they laſt
no longer then this life) they are
with all both light and ſweet. For the
loue of God, and the heauenly conſo-
lations which he communicateth to
his ſeruants, doth make them ſweet;
and the helps and ſuccours of grace
which otherwiſe he giues the, make
them light . So doe iuſt perſons find
this to be by experience , as the Apoſtle confeſſeth, ſaying : *After the
rate of the tribulations and afflictions ,
which we ſuffer for Chriſt our Lord , and*
                                where-

(i) How
the diffi-
cultyes of
vertue
grow de-
lightfull
through
the good-
nes of
God, be-
ſides that
all tempo-
ral labour
is light,
ſince it is
ſo ſhort.

2. Cor, 1.

whereby we go in imitation of him, so do the consolations which are giuen by Almigh y God, through the vertue and merit of our B Sauiour, increase and copiously abound in vs.

If (ᵏ) then the labours & troubles of this life, be, on the one side, so momentany and so short; and on the other so sweet and light; and the reward of glory, and of that celestial kingdome, so eternal, and immense; and that as our good workes doe grow to be increased, so also doth the reward of glory go increasing; in such sort, as that to euery of our good workes, yea (ˡ) and to euery one of our desires, and euen to euery moment of a life which is lead in state of grace, there is a distinct degree of glory which correspondeth: what man is that, who will not labour for the leading of a vertuous life? Who will not be diligent, in making resistance to all temptations

(k) Consider seriously of the conclusion of this discourse.

(l) O infinite bounty of God! And are we then incurwits when we be either sinnefull, or euen but flouthfull in Gods seruice.

P 3   what-

whatfoeuer ? Who will not fuffer a-
ny iniury, or paine , for liuing wel! ;
And who will not refolue with
ftrength and courage , to perfeuere
in that good caufe which he hath begun ? Let vs all both heare, and with
great fidelity, obey the voyce of that
Prophet who fayth : *You who are the*
people of God, do you encourage, and ani-
mate your felues to ferue him, and to con-
tinue in that feruice of his without dif-
may ; for , in fine , your labours fhall e
anfwered with a great reward .

2. Paral.
25 .

CHAP. XXI.

How we are much to animate our felues,
to the exercife of good workes ; confi-
dering the great eftimation which
Chrift our Lord doth make of them at
the day of Iudgement ; and the re-
ward which he alfo imparteth to thē.

THERE is alfo another particular confideration , belonging to
this

this diuine *Iudgment*, and to the reward of good workes, which doth greately moue the foule, to labour hard in the feruice of God. And this is, the *Reafon*, and *Tytle* which Chrift our Lord alledgeth, in giuing his benediction, and reward to the iuft, when he faith; *Come yee bleffed of my Father poffeffe the kingdom which is prepared for you. For I was hungry, and you gaue me to eat, I was thirfty and you gaue me to drinke; I was a ftranger, & you receiued me into your howfe; I was ficke, and in prifon, and you came to vifit me.* For (a) by thefe words Chrift our Lord doth mightily difcouer the eftimation, and price which he hath ftamped vpon good workes, which are done in grace; and the great fauour and honor which they receiue in his diuine prefence; the much that they pleafe him, and the immenfe glory wherwith he rewardeth them; fince fo meane workes, &

Matt. 25.

(a) The great value which our Lord doth make, euen of our leaft good workes.

ſo very eaſy to be wrought, as it is to
giue a peece of bread to a poore hūgry
body ; or a cup of water to a thirſty;
or a ſhirt to couer the naked ; or a
nights lodging to a ſtranger ; or a
viſit to an impriſoned or ſick perſon;
though it be but to comfort him with
good words (for we ſee he doth not
ſay, *I was ſicke and you cured me; or I was
impriſoned and you freed me* ; but ſuch
eaſy workes, as are thoſe other, and
which put vs to ſo little coſt and
trouble;) that excellent Maieſty of
his, is pleaſed to publiſh & proclaime
in that great Theater, vpon the day
of *Iudgement* ; in the preſence of the
whole world, and he ſetteth out and
praiſeth them which his owne ſacred
mouth; & he ſublymes then ſo high,
as to take them for ſeruices and deare
fauours imparted to his owne perſõ,
which giue him great contenment &
guſt . And ſo much (b) account he
makes therof, as to eſteeme them for
merits

(b) That
which
maketh a
good
worke
meritori-
ous, is the
flowing of
it, from
the grace
of God in
Chriſt
our Lord,
and the
being ſe-
conded
by his
promiſe
of a re-
ward,
which
promiſe
makes the
reward
due.

merits which are worthy of eternall life; and he receaues them as a price of the kingdome of heauen; And he esteemeth them for meritorious; & that, not only, all together, but euery one of them a part; and a part he takes euery one of them for the price of glory, and of that kingdome which hath no end.

But (c) now, if Christ our Lord, who so highely esteemes, and vouchsafes the fauour of so great reward, to so light and easy workes as those, what will he do, to such workes of mercy as are great & hard; and which grow out of much Charity? As when a man doth giue all his goods, or a great part therof to the poore; or lodge Pilgrims for a long tyme; and serue them, and prouide them of all things necessary; & depriue himselfe of clothes to cloth the poore naked Christian; and to serue sicke persons day and night;

(c) What will not our Lord do to vs, for greater works since he doth so much for the lesse.

P 5 and

and that in the case of troublesome
and contagious diseases , as when
they may be strucké with the plague;
and to drawe with much trouble of
person and charge of purse , such as
are prisoners , or Captiues , out of
their chaines : How much , I say ,
will Christ our Lord esteeme such
works as these , which cost much labour and money ; and for the performing whereof a man endures much
incommodity , and imbraceth many
paineful things , and wrastling with
store of difficulties ; and mortifies
himselfe much , to comfort others ;
& renounces his owne will in many
things , that so others may be comforted and releeued ? There can no
doubt be made , but that much more
he will esteeme them, and will afford
them the fauour in that day of Iudgement of a reward so much higher,
as the works are more excellent, &
more acceptable in his eyes , for being

ing growne vp out of greater Charity.

And if the Corporall works of mercy, which are exercifed vpon the bodyes of men, which muſt quickly dy ; and for the maintenance and preferuation of this corporall life , which is foone to haue an end , be fo much eſteemed, and fauoured, and fo highly rewarded by Chriſt our Lord ; what will he be fure to do to the workes of ſpirituall mercy, wherby immortall foules are fuccoured, & redreſt ; and wherby they , being deliuered from the death of finne , and euerlaſting paine , there is imparted to them faluation , and a life of euerlaſting glory ? A plaine (d) cafe it is, that , the worke of mercy, wherby a foule is affiſted, is more excellēt, then that other wherby a body is releeued; & that thefe works of piety, wherby the ſpirituall and eternall life is holpen , is of much more valew , and

(d) How much therefore are we bound to ſuch as do affiſt our foules , though it be with hazard of theirliues.

merit

merit, then that other, wherby that corporall and fraile life is fuccoured. For as much, as according to S. *Tho-*

D. Thom. cont. Gen. l.4. cap.55.

mas, Amongst all thofe things which are created, no one is greater, then the faluation of a reafonable foule, which confifteth in the entoying of God: So alfo there is no other greater almes, then that, wherby this faluation, and this life of grace and glory is procured; & confequently a much greater benefit doth he impart to another, who remedieth the neceffityes of his foule, then if he had giuen him a great fume of money. And fince they who giue a little bread to the hungry, and a little water to the thirfty; and they who retyre a Pilgrime to their houfe, and apparel a naked perfon, with a peece of cloth; and vifit a man who is in prifon or ficke, giuing him a little temporall comfort, be fo efteemed and honoured by Almighty God, in the prefence both of heauen & earth,

in

in that terrible tribunall of his *Iudgment*; and are so enobled, and sublymed with the Crowne of celestiall glory, and with the dignity of the euerlasting kingdome; what will Christ do, that most iust and righteous Iudge, and that most liberal God with them who dispense the bread of heauenly doctrine to such as haue need, and are hungry after it; and who powre out the drink of spiritual comfort, and ease, to such as are afflicted, and deiected, that so they may beare their miseryes with patience; & who cloath their soules with vertues and celestiall guifts, who are naked & depriued of al spiritual graces, and who cure, and recouer, out of their miserable infirmityes, and who draw and deliuer out of that horrible captiuity, them who are sicke of sinne, and are taken prisoners, and made slaues by Sathan. Most certain it is, that although all they who ex-
                                                  presse

preſſe mercy towards their neighbours, ſhallbe eſteemed & honored
in that Tribunal; & ſhalbe ſublimed
with glory and royall dignity, yet
theſe others who haue imparted it towards the ſoules of mē, ſhalbe much
more eſteemed and honoured, by
Chriſt our Lord, and his Angels, &
ſhalbe raiſed to greater glory, & more
aduaūced in the kingdom of heauen.

It is alſo to be conſidered, that
although theſe works of mercy, whether they be corporall, or ſpirituall,
and which reſpect the ſpirituall or
corporall good of our neighbour, are
excellent and of great value, and merit, as we haue already ſayd; yet the
interiour, and exteriour workes of
Fayth, Hope, Charity, and Religion,
which haue (e) imediate relation to
Almighty God, and to the worſhip
& ſeruice which is due to him as our
God, and our Creatour, are more excellent, and of greater value, & merit,

(e) How
highly
gratefull
thoſe acts
of vertue
are,
which do
immedia-
tly reſpect
Almighty
God.

rit, then the workes of mercy, which
ayme but at the côfort of our neighbours . And so much more as any
vertue doth draw neere, & approach
to God, so much more is the vertue
more excellent . Now the vertues,
which are called Theological, which
are *Fayth, Hope, & Charity* , do looke
vp, and serue & immediatly honour
Almighty God, belieuing his truth,
and louing his goodnes, and hoping
in his mercy . And the vertue of Religion, doth respect, and exercise the
worship, and veneration, which is
due to God, as being soueraigne Authour and Lord of all thinges . And
these vertues being more excellent,
then that of *Mercy* towardes our
Neighbour, it is cleare, that those
faythfull Christians, who with firme
and liuely fayth, haue beleeued in
Christ our Lord, and who confessed
his fayth, in the face of Tyrants ; &
who placed all their confidence, &
loue

in Chrift, fearching, with care, after
his glory; and refigning themfelues
entirely to his moft holy will; and
honoring him, & reuering him with
true worfhip, & with pure prayers,
and with an exact performance of
their promifes, and the vowes which
they make to his diuine Maiefty; certaine I fay it is, that in the day of his
diuine *Iudgment*, they fhall be more
efteemed, and honoured by Chrift,
for hauing done and fuffered thefe
thinges, then either they, or any o-
thers fhallbe; for any other inferiour
works which they may haue wroght
towardes their Neighbours. And
therefore, the reward of glory being
fo illuftrious and fo high, which for
the workes of fpirituall and corporall mercy they fhall receaue; & confidering that yet, the reward which
thefe others fhall obtayne, is to be
much more eminent and great; and
fince, notwithftading that the kingdome

dome which is to be giuen in reward
of thefe workes of mercy, is celeftiall
& eternall; yet for thefe acts of *faith*,
and *Charity*, and *Religion*, a greater,
and a better portion fhall be allotted,
and fet out in the fame kingdome;
let vs be moft diligent in the leading
of a good life;in cõferuing our foules
pure and cleane; in exercyfing our
felues in the acquifitiõ of vertue. And
let vs be full of feruour towards the
works of mercy, whether they be fpirituall or corporall, euery one according to his Tallent.

O *happy* (f) and for euer moft (f) Con-
happy they, who fhall thus imploy clufion.
themfelues. *Happy*, becaufe they were
elected from all *eternity*, by almighty
God ; *Happy* becaufe they were called in *Tyme* to his faith, and Religion,
and were inftructed therin; *Happy*,
becaufe they did correfpond to that
vocation of God, and did begin to
lead a good life ; *Happy*, becaufe they
Q   did

did contynue therin ; *Happy* , becauſe
if they fell, they quickly roſe againe,
by penance, and were conſtant therin ; And *Happy* beyond all *happies* , becauſe, when our Lord came to call
them to accompt , at the houre of
their death, he found them imployed
in a good life , and watchfull in the
exerciſe of good workes , expecting
the tyme of his comming, to receaue
the reward of their labours , at his
mercifull, and moſt liberall handes .
For it is ſayd , by no leſſe then Truth

Luc. 12. it ſelfe , *Happy is that ſeruant , whome
his Lord , when he commeth , ſhall find
watching , and imployed in the diſchar-
ge of his duety , with fidelity and pru-
dence , and complying with his obligations , whether they be common to all
Chriſtians , or particulerly belonging
to his ſtate . I tell you as an vndoubted
truth, that to ſuch a ſeruant as this, his
Lord ſhall deliuer vp the poſſeſſion of all
his goods* . That is , Chriſt our moſt
merci-

mercifull Lord, and our God, will rayfe him vp from the bleſſinges of grace in this life, to the bleſſinges of glory in the next; and from the ba-ſenes of this earth, to raigne eter-nally, together with himſelfe, in heauen. Amen.

Q 2   THE

THE

CONCLVSION

TO THE READER.

MAKE accompt, good Reader,
that this difcourfe is a Letter, &
this which now thou art reading , is
the Poftfcript of it. Thou haft feene
the torments of Hell, and the ioyes
which are imparted to the elect in
heauen. Thou haft feene that if thou
dye in mortall finne, thou wilt for
euer be chayned in thofe torments;
& for euer be depriued of thofe ioyes.

Q 3   Take

Take heed therefore of all finne; and
efpecially take heed of the finne either of *Schifme* or *Herefy* , which are
of the greateft that can be comitted.
The nature of *Herefy* , confifteth in
this , That a man will make election
of fome one doctrine, or more, which
is contrary to the beleefe of that true
Church , which is celebrated in the
Creed of the firft Councell of *Nice*; to
be *One*, to be *Holy*, to be *Catholike*, &
to be *Apoftolike*. Be fure thou be of
that one true *Church* , which foeuer
that be (for thogh myfelf be refolued,
yet I will not heere handle that queftion, by way of Controuerfy;) but
there is but one wherin a Chriftian
can be faued , one in the faith which
it profeffeth , howfoeuer it may be
accounted many, in refpect of the infinite perfons which it conteyneth ,
and confequently of the particular
Churches which it imbraceth . The
nature (a) therfore of *herefy*, doth not
consist

(a) Wher in the na- ture of herefy , doth in- deed con- sift .

confift in the multitude or quality
of the Articles of Religion, which
are held, in difference from the do-
trine and direction of the holy Catholike Church ; but it confifteth
properly, in the pride and prefump-
tion of that hart, which dares pre-
ferre a priuate opinion, of any one,
or feuerall Countries, or any interpretation of holy Scripture (which
interpretation, is alfo no more then *(b)* **For he**
a(b) meere opinion) before the Iud- will make
gement of that *Church*, which is, & the fcrip-
is ftill to be inftructed and taught by tur affirm
the holy Ghoft. And this finne, is of will.
fo high a nature, as that vnleffe it be
remoued by pennance, the man in
whome it liues, fhall (c) dye a double *(c)* No
death, and neuer behould the face of heretike
God; howfoeuer he may, otherwife, repentan-
feeme to be a perfon of moft holy life, ce can be
& fo ful of Charity, as to fell his ftate, faued,
and giue it all to the poore; and of fo
valiant and Chriftian a hart, as,

Q 4 amongft

amongſt Infidels , to ſuffer death, &
torments for the name of Chriſt. For
to proue that euen this will not ſerue
the turne of an Heretike towards ſaluation, ſee heere the authority of the
greateſt Fathers of the church cōcerning this point. Who(d) (beſids, that
in the way of practice, the Church of
their tyme , did cōdemne many men
for *Hereſy*, who held, though it were
but one point of doctrine, in contra-
riety to the Catholike Church (and
ſomtymes of ſome ſuch doctrine , as
in it ſelfe, did not ſeeme to be of moſt
importance) they do alſo declare,
and that in moſt cleere and conſtant
words , in what certainty of damnation they are , who dy in any Hereſy
at all. *Whoſoeuer*, ſaith S. Cyprian *&
what kinde of perſon ſoeuer, a man be ,
a* (e)*Chriſtian he is not , vnles he be in the
Church of Chriſt* . And againe : *He belongs not to the rewrd of Chriſt , who
forſakes the Church of Chriſt ; ſuch a one*

(d) The
practiſe
of the pri-
mitiue
Church
in this
point .
See S.
*Aug . ad
Quod-vult
Deum* , &
the Cata-
logues of
S . Irenæ-
us, and S,
Epiphani-
us *,
D. Cypr.
epiſt. in
Anton.*

(e)No he-
retike is a
Chriſtian
any more
then only
in name.
*Idem de v-
nit. Eccleſ.*

is

is an alien, he is a prophane person, he is an enemy. And to this effect, he also sayth, if such an one should euen giue his life for the confession of the name of Christ, he should yet (by the Iudgement of this holy Father) be condemned to the flames of Hell for his Herely, and not be receiued to the ioyes of heauen for his constancy; & he expresseth himself in these words, *Non esset illi corona fidei, sed pœna perfidiæ.* S. *Hierome,* in like manner, speaking of the Church of *Rome* affirmeth it to be, *The true house of Christ ; and* *D. Hier.* *that whosoeuer eateth the lambe, out of* *epist. ad* *that house, is a prophane person, and that* *Dam. l. 2.* *vnles he be found, in that Arke of Noe, he shallbe ouerwhelmed , and perish in the floud.*

S. *Augustine* doth also abound *D. Aug.* euery where, in the profession of this *tom. 7. su-* truth. *A man,* sayth he *cannot obtaine* *ter gest.* *saluation, but in the Catholike Church:* *cum Emer.* *he may haue all except saluation ; he may* *vlt. med.*

Q 5   haue

haue honour, he may haue the facram̅ets, he may fing *Alleluia*, he may anfwere *Amen*, he may belieue the Ghoſpell, he may be baptized in the name of the Father, & of the Sonne, and of the holy Ghoſt, but no where can he haue faluatiō, but in the Catholike Church. No man cometh, faith he, to faluation, and life eternall, but he that hath Chriſt for his head; and no man can haue Chriſt for his head, who is not in his body, which is the Church. Heretikes by belieuing falfely of God, do violate the faith; and Schifmatikes by their wicked diſſentions, flye of from fraternall charity, although they belieue as we do. And therefore neither doth the Heretike belonge to the catholike Church becaufe he belieueth not God; nor the Schifmatike, becaufe he loueth not his Neighbour.

Let (f) vs fuppofe that a man were chaft, and contynent; not couetous, no worſhiper of Idolls, but full of hofpitality; no enemy to any man, nor contentious,

D. Augu. tom. 7. de vnit. Eccl. vlt. med.

Idem. tom. 3. de fide & fymb.
(f) The fchifmatik hath no Charity, and the Heretike hath neither Charity, nor Fayth.
Idem. tom 7. de Bapt. cont. Don. l. 4. c. 18.

ous, but patient & quiet ; not emulating or enuying any body, but sober and fru- gall; but yet withall, that he were an he- retike, and there can no doubt be made , but (g) *that for this only,* That he is an Heretike, he shall not possesse the kingdome of heauen.

(g) No Heretike can be sa- ued, though he be neuer so virtu- ous other- wise.

It is not sayd alone , Blessed are they who suffer persecution, *but these words are added,* for iustice sake . *Now where* (h) *true* Fayth *is not , there can be no* Iustice, *because the* iust *man liues in* Fayth . *Neither yet let* Schismatikes *promise themselues any thing thereby, be- cause where there is no* Charity, *neither can there be any* Iustice. *For* Charity *to- wards ones Neighbour , doth worke no euill ; which* Charity *if they did possesse , they would not teare the body of Christ, Which is his Church .*

Idem. tom. 4. l. 1. de serm. Do. in monte c. 9.
(h) No heretike , or schi- matike can be a Martyr .
Tom 1. de fide ad Pe- trum. c. 39.

Belieue (i) *most firmely, and haue no manner of doubt, but that euery He- retike and Schismatike, though baptized in the name of the Father, and of the Sonne,*

(i) Some doubt , whether this book be of S. Augustin, or of S. Fulgenti- us, who

liued within 40 . yeares after S. Augustine.

Sonne, and of the holy Ghost, if he re-
turne not to the Catholike Church, how
(k) Euen *great (* k *) Almes soeuer he distribute,*
the giuing *yea and though he shed his bloud for the*
al in alms
and suffe- *name of Christ, he can by no meanes be*
ringdeath *saued. For neither Baptisme, nor most*
for the *liberall almes, nor death endured for the*
name of *name of Christ, can auaile any man to*
Christ, wil
not deli- *saluation, who holdeth not fast the vnity*
uer an *of the* Catholike Church *; and so long*
heretique *as any (* l *) hereticall, or schismaticall ini-*
from dam
nation. *quity (which leadeth men to destruction)*
(l) How *remayneth in him.*
small soe-
uer that   These are they, amongst many
be.   others, whome God hath giuen to his
        Church, as lightes whereby all good
        Christians may be guided towardes
        their saluation ; and take heed thou
        be not so miserable, as to follow a-
        ny *ignis fatuus*, insteed of them ; for
        thy error in this life, will import thee
        no lesse then thy eternall damnati-
        on in the next.

FAVLTS

FAVLTS

escaped in the Printing.

Page	Line	Fault	Correction.
10.	10.	intention	attention
20.	*vlt.*	fo	of
35.	1.	interiourly	exteriourly
36.	12.	he is to make	*deleatur* he
49.	16	vnanſwerable	vnanſwerably
50.	3.	to friend	to that friend
55.	13.	and for zeale	and zeale of
63.	1.	whither	wither
65.	7.	for thus	for this
78.	13.	infinity	infinite
79.	13.	guifts	gufts
81.	14.	Sathan that	*deleatur* that
90.	16.	is infinite	is an infinite
101.	10.	is hauing	is their hauing
Ibid	11.	then being	their being
110.	7.	by all	by ill
113.	17.	my pennance	*deleatur* my which

Page	Line	Fault	Correction.
118.	8.	which	with
122.	18.	ſtrike into him	ſtrike him into
143.	22.	for his mercy	of his mercy
154.	5.	when themſelues	where themſelues
174.	6.	containe	containes
175.	16.	to be of	are to be of
187.	17.	niuite	inuite
201.	15.	fauour	father
216.	1.	the ſoule	their ſoule
223.	14.	yet doe	yet doth
230.	5.	cauſe	courſe
232.	19.	them	them

FINIS.

JOHN HEIGHAM
The Gagge of the Reformed Gospell
1623

THE
GAGGE

OF THE REFORMED
GOSPELL.

BRIEFLY
Diſcouering the errors of
our time.

WITH
The Refutation by expreſſe textes
of their owne approoued
Engliſh Bible.

THE SECOND EDITION;
Augmented thoroughout the whole, by the
Author of the firſt.

By thine oͮwne mouth I iudge thee, naughᵗ
tie ſeruant. Luc. 19. 22.
With permiſſion. Anno 1263.

TO THE CATHOLIQVE
READER, HEALTH AND
encouragement in his
holy Faith.

Vrteous Reader, before thou peruse this litle Treatise, haue (I pray thee) so much patience, as to permit me to giue thee myne aduise, concerning some certaine points, very necessarie for thee, the better to serue thy selfe therof with fruit and profit.

1. The first point is, that in the inscription therof, it doth not tell thee, out of which English Bible, the alledged passages are extracted, for as much as this were meerely in vaine, sith England hath brought forth within these few yeares past, a great number of seue-

A 2   rall

rall forts of Bibles, far different one
from another; So that our aduerfaries
(to whom I wish from my very hart,
as I doe to thee, that this little booke
may prooue profitable) haue not all one
fort of Bible. Notwithstanding know
for certaine, that they are faithfully
taken forth of the Bible in quarto, printed at London by Thomas Barker,
anno 1615. But if any one shall shew
vnto thee some other Bible, wherin
they are not so written, worde for
worde as here they are, yet rest affu-
red, and out of dout, that thoushalt
finde them written as they ar here alleadged, in this edition of Robert
Barkers.

2. The second point is, that thou
admire the splendor of the truth, the
which is such and so passing bright,
that notwithstanding they haue endea-
uoured to obscure the same by so many
varieties of translations, and by such a
number of grosse corruptions and falsi-
fications yet neuertheles their condemnation is so expresly set downe in their

owne

owne Bible, and is so cleare to all the
world, that nothing more is needfull
hereto, but that thou know to reade,
and haue thine eyes in thy head to behould the same, at the opening of this
their booke. This can not choose but
be, an exceeding comfort vnto a Catholique, concerning the vprightnes of
his cause, to offer to be tried, and to
confound them by their owne Bible, the
translation wherof, doth in a number
of places, and particularly of those that
are most in question, swarue and differ notoriously from the authenticall
Latin, and that to the incredible
disparagement, darkning and obf-
curing of the Catholique cause. Neuer did, nor neuer dare our aduersaries, offer themselues, to giue the like
aduantage vnto vs, as to stand to be
tried, by our translation, and
that in fiftie and od maine points of
controuersie.

3. The third point is, that when
thou shalt vrge or alleadge any passage,
in fauor of thine owne faith, if anie

A 3

one returne ther change , be it ether in
vsing recrimination and blaming of the
Roman Church, or be it in alleadging
some obscure textes and ill vnderstood,
to counterpoint those alleadged by thee;
Shew then the partie amiably, that this
is not to proceed in due order, nor dea-
les not with thee as he ought, in oppo-
sing a passage darke and obscure , to
confound a passage that is most cleare.
For example, when we set before their
eies these few wordes (much more clea-
rer then the Sunne it self at noone day)
Take eate, this is my body, this
is my blood which shal be shed. &c.
Marc. 14. 25. they suppose to haue
found forth an important place , yea
and to haue giuen vnto vs a great
ouerthrowe , if they presently reply,
that our Sauiour saith in S. Iohn 6.
63. The flesh profiteth nothing,
the wordes that I speake vnto you,
they are spirit, and they are life; *a*
passage far more obscure, then that
which is in question , & which affir-
meth nothing lesse, then that which
they

they pretend to prooue thereby; for
how absurd were it to say, that
the flesh of Christ profiteth nothing?
And if (as they themselues say) we
must interpret one passage by another,
then doutles, it is better to explicate an
obscure passage, by one that is cleare,
then one that is cleare, by a passage
obscure: and that one text giue place
to many, rather then many to giue place
to one, or to fewer.

4. The fourth point is, that if
they reiect some of the passages which
thou producest, pretending it to be Apocripha; know that to preuent this obiection, no such scriptures as they call
Apocripha are here produced, but allwayes there goe accompanied with
them, others also that are canonicall
by their owne confession: and so far
forth as Apocripha, shall and doe agree
with Canonicall, they themselues by
their owne rule, are bound to receiue
them. Which will also fully stop the
Reformers mouthes, in their common
pretence of conferences of places; for

rare-

rarely hast thou lesse, then three or four seuerall passages cited at large (besides references) for the proofe of euerie seuerall point; All the pack of them put together, being neuer able in their defence to doe the like, that is, to produce so many in number, so expresse & cleare, and for so great a quantitie of controuersies, as are here disputed and couched in so litle a roome.

5. The fift point is, *that if they shall contend with thee, not about the wordes themselues, as being cleare, but about the sence and meaning of them; for such places, I say, as may be subiect to this cauill, thou shalt forthwith haue recourse and fly to that,* which the scriptures call, the Rule of faith, *to wit, to the euer constant and vniforme iudgement of the Church and Fathers, who in euery age since Christ our Lord vnto this present, haue vnderstood the point in question, in the selfe same sence that Catholiques doe, an example wherof thou maist lay before him, or them, out of that learned*

trea-

treatise, intituled The Summarie of Controuersies, *debating the question of the blessed Sacrament :* Which hauing *done, then bid thine aduersarie to doe the like, and thou* wilt instantly *yeld vnto him (a thinge* which he can *neuer doe in his defence.*) Which being *so,* what man of reason will reiect this Rule, *grounded so clearly in holy scripture, to prefer the priuat interpretation of some sillie* Cobler, before Sainct Chrisostome, *of a* Baker, before S. Basill, *of some* Tinkar before Tertullian, *or of any* Nouellist whatsoeuer, *before the iudgement of the* Church , *and the* whole streame of the *holie* Fathers? *This point therfore being so important, shall be the* very first, which I wil *fortifie and proue by the* word of God *in this present* Treatise , *I meane this* Rule , *and therfore in no* wise for- *get ,* allwayes *to rap thine* aduersaries with *this* Rule , *as often as they shall proue vntruly , and thou shalt be sure to get the* victorie, *although there be thousandes of them* against
thee

thee alone.

The fixt and laft point is , *that I here proteft in the prefence of God (whom I call vpon in this behalfe, and pray thee alfo to call vpon, for the faluation and reduction of all thofe that goe a ftray) that it is not in the power of all our aduerfaries that are in England, to finde in their owne Bible, one only expreffe text, I fay one only, I fay in their owne Bible , by the which they can pofsibly proue, one only point of their falfe doctrine , without their vfuall art of adding , diminishing, or changing it by interpretation : which yet should be to alter the text , and to employ mans wifdome , infteed of the pure word, a thinge by their owne confeffion, flatly forbidden them : they protefting, that the word of God, doth in fuch fort containe all that which is neceffarie to faluation, that it is not lawfull for men , nor yet for Angells, to adde, diminish, or alter ought ther-of; and command their followers and adherents, vtterly to renounce all an-*

tiqui-

tiquitie, cuftomes, multitude, human
wifdome, iudgement, decrees, edicts,
counfailes, vifions, and miracles themfelues: defending obftinatly (but without foundation) that the fcripture con-
taines all that is neceffarie for the feruice of God, and our faluation. Far-
well, my deare Reader, feing I haue
now faid vnto thee, all that which
I defired.

A 6   THE

THE
GAGGE OF THE
REFORMED GOSPEL.

BRIEFLY
Discouering the errours of our time.

WITH
The Refutation, by expreſſe textes, of
their owne approued English
Bible.

They mayntaine in the firſt place.

I.

*That there is not in the Church, one,
and that an infallible Rule, for
vnderſtanding the holie ſcriptures,
and conſeruing of vnitie in matters
of faith.*

Ontrary to the expreſſe
wordes of their owne Bi-
ble, Rom. 12. 16. *Hauing
then giftes, differing according to the
grace*

grace that is giuen to vs, whether pro-phecie (that is interpretaion) *let vs prophecie* (that is interpret) *according to the proportion* , or Rule, *of faith.* Whence we gather, that pro-phecie according to the Rule of faith, is one of the giftes which God bestoweth on his Church. Therfore there is in the Church, one, and that an infallible Rule for vnderstanding the holy scriptures.

Philippians 3. 16. *Neuertheles, wherto we haue attained, let vs walke by the same Rule, let vs minde the same thinge.* Loe how plainly the Apost-le speaketh in this second place, of a certaine Rule to be walked by: clearly presupposing , that in mat-ters of faith, we can neuer be of the same minde , vnles we walke by the same *Rule*, Therfore &c.

Gal. 6. 16. And *as many as walke according to this Rule, peace be on the, and mercie.* And 2. Cor. 10 15. *Hauing hope when your faith is increased, that we shall be enlarged by you, according to our Rule, abundantly, to preach the gospell in the regions beyond you, and not to boast in another mans line.* Loe here againe, because that euery man is to direct and order his beleefe, according to the doctrine of the Church, therfore it is called by S. Paul, both the *Rule,* and *Line* of our holy faith. Therfore &c.

1. *Cor.* 11. 16. *But if any man seemi to be contentious, We haue no such custome, nor the Church of God.* Loe how S. Paul still pleadeth the *Rule* and *Custome* of the Church, against the contentious : which if it could then, by the sole prescription of twentie or thirtie yeares, and by the authoritie of so few pastors, stop the mouthes of new sect-masters, what ought not the custome of sixteene hundred yeares, and the decrees of so many hundred pastors gayne, of reasonable, modest and humble men? Therfore &c.

And here I would haue it to be noted, that this Analogie, or *Rule of*
faith,

faith, (befides the titles already recited) the holie fcripture in other places, calleth by the name of *forme of doctrine,* as Rom. 6. 17. *A thinge made* readie to our hande, as 2. Cor. 10. 16. the *Depofitum,* or Treafure, *committed to the Churches truft,* and euer moft carefully to be kept by her, as 1. Tim. 6. 20. And with al in the very felfe fame places, alwayes ftileth that which is contrary to this Rule, by the name of *Difunion, Difcord, Difobedience, forfaking, of our firft vocation, Diuifion, Contention, Prophane and vaine balbinges, Oppofition of fciences &c.* Whence plainly appeareth, how great the neceffitie is for euery Chriftian, to keepe this *Rule,* the leaft breach or crack wherof, doth prefently crack his Chriftiã credit with the Church of God, and with all good Chriftians.

See more Rom. 6. 17. Gal. 1. 6. Rom. 16. 17. Actes 15. 2. 1. Tim. 6. 20. Rom. 12. 16.

See therfore according to this
very

very Rule, Fathers who affirme the
fame, S. Ireneus l. 4. cap. 45. Tertul. de præfcrip. cap. 19. Vincent.
Lyr. in fuo Commonitorio, faying.
It is very needfull in regard of fo many
errors proceeding from the mifinter-
pretation of fcriptures, that the line of
propheticall and Apoftolicall expofi-
tion, should be directed according to
the Rule, of the Ecclefiaft.call and Ca-
tholique fenfe: h is writeth this moft
worthie witneffe. Tertul. prefcrip.
heref. cap. 15. & ibid. cap. 19. faith.
We doe not admit our aduerfaries to
difpute out of fcripture, till they can
shew who their anceftors were, & frō
whom they receiued the fcriptures. For
the orderly courfe of doctrin requires,
that the first queftion be, whofe the
fcriptures are by right, from whom,
and by whom, and to whom, the forme
of Chriftian religion was deliuered.
Otherwife prefcribing against him as
as a ftranger &c. Thus he.

Loe how thefe two ancient Fathers, lay hou d of, and vrge thefe
two

two very termes, *Rule,* and *Forme,*
of faith and religion, euen as before
the holy scripture aid, from whence
doutles they tooke the phrase. And
with very great reason, for the
knowledg of Tradition (which is
this Forme or Rule) goes before the
knowlege of the scripture : for the
Rule must be first knowen, before
the thinge Ruled can be assuredly
knowen: as the Carpenter cannot
know certainly, that he hath measured his timber aright, nor the
Taylor, that he hath measured his
cloth aright, except he first assuredly know that his measure be
both true and right: but the Rule
of faith, to wit, the summe of all
those points, that euery Christians
is bound expresly know, as deliuered to them from hande to hande,
is the knowledg of Tradition.
Therfore &c.

II. *That*

I I.

*That in matters of faith, we must not
not relie vpon the iudgment of the
Church and of her Pastors,
but only vpon the writ-
ten worde.*

Ontrarie to the expresse wordes of their owne Bible. Mat.
23. 2. *The Scribes and the Pharises sit
in Moyses seat, all therfore whatsoeuer they bid you obserue, that obserue
and doe.* In which wordes, Christ
not only commãdeth vs in matters
of faith, to haue recourse to som-
what else besides the only written
word (to wit, to the pastors of the
Church) but moreouer, biddeth vs
to obey them: and that not only in
some principall matters, but in all
whatsoeuer, without distinction or
limitation. Therfore in matters of
faith, we are not tyed to rely, only
vpon the written word.

Luc.

Luc. 10. 16. He that *heareth you,* *heareth me, and he that despiseth you,* *despiseth me: and he that despiseth me,* *despiseth him that sent me.* Heare a-gaine Chrit our Lord honoreth, and giueth as much authority to the preachers of the word, as he can possibly doe to the word it self, saying. *He that heareth you &c.* Therfore.

Mat. 16. 19. *Whatsoeuer thou* *shalt binde on earth, shall be bound in* *heauen: Whatsoeuer thou shalt loose in* *earth, shal be loosed in heauen.* Where is to be noted, that he doth not say, *Whomsoeuer,* but *Whatsoeuer;* giuing vs therby to vnderstand, that not only the bondes of sinnes, but as well all other knotts and difficul-ties in matters of faith, are to be loosed by S. Peter, and by the pa-stors that succeed him in the Church. Therfore &c.

See more Deut. 17. 8. Aggeus 2. 11. 2. Chron. 19. 8. vnto the end. 2. Thef. 2. 15.

See

See Fathers that affirme the same.
S. Greg. Naz in orat. excusat. Ter-
tull. l. de prescrip. hæret. S. Cyprian l. 1. epist. 3. S. Aug. l. 1. con.
Crel. cap. 33. & l. cont. epist. fund.
cap. 5. Vincent. Lyr. in suo com-
monit. S. Anselme l. de Incar. cap. 1.
who writing to Pope Vrban, saith
vnto him. *Vnto no other is more right-*
ly referred to be corrected, whatsoeuer
ariseth in the Church against the Ca-
tholique faith. S. Augull. cont. epist.
fund. cap. 4. the place beginneth.
Quibus ego obtemperaui dicentibus.

I I I.

That the Scriptures are easie to be vn-
derstood, and that therfore none
ought to be restrayned from
reading of them.

Ontrary to the expresse wordes of their owne Bible 2. Pet.
3. 16. where S. Peter speaking of S.
Paules epistles saith. *In which are*
some

some thinges hard to be vnderstood,
which they that are vnlearned and vn-
stable wrest, as they doe also the other
scriptures, vnto the.r owne destruct.õ.
But all vnlearned Reformers, both
reade, and are allowed to reade
those hard thinges (yea the Reuelations also, harder then those)
without restraint of man or woma,
which yet they vnderstand not:
therfore they wrest them, as also
other scriptures, to their owne
destruction.

Actes 8. 30. *And Phillip said. Vn-*
derstandest thou what thou readest?
And he said. How can I, except some
man should guide me? Where first
may be noted, that this noble
Enuch freely confest, he could not
vnderstand the scriptures, without
an interpreter to expound them,
albeit he was a great & serious stu-
dier of them, and with all a ho'y
and an humble man, as S. Hierom
noteth of him. Epist. ad Paulin. de
stud. scrip. And next that he saith,
Except

Except some man guide me : and fled not to his priuat spirit, nor yet to conferring of place with place , as these men doe. Therfore the scriptures are not easie &c.

Luc. 24. 25. Christ called two of his owne Disciples *fooles , and beginning at Moyses, and all the Prophets, he expounded vnto them in all the scriptures, the thinges concerning him selfe* . How then are the scriptures so easilie to be vnderstood of the vnlearned, when the Disciples them selues vnderstood them not, till first they were expounded to them?

Reuelations 5. 1. &c. The Angel speaking of *the booke, sealed with seauen seales, wept much , because no man in heaue nor in earth, was able to open the booke, nether to looke theron.* A strange case , to reade in scripture it selfe, that the booke of scripture should be shut with so many seales: but much more strange, that euen in S. Iohn and the Apostles time,
none

none could be found , nether in heauen nor earth, able to open the same, nor to looke theron , which euery prentice now a dayes, without any difficultie will vndertake to doe. Therfore &c.

See more 2.Pet.1.20. Mat.13.11. & 36. Luc.24.45. 1.Cor. 12.10.Luc 8.10.& 54. Luc. 2. 50. 2. Tim. 3.7. 1.Iohn 4. 6. Iohn 5.35. Pſal. 119.18. & 34. Reue. 5. 1. &c.

Our next recourſe ſhal be to our former Rule, for which ſee S. Ireneus l. 2. cap. 47. Origen. l. cont. Celſ. S. Amb.epiſt.44. ad Conſtât, calleth it *a ſea, and depth of propheticall riddles.* S. Hier. in præfat.comment. in Epheſ. 5.S.Aug.epiſt.119. cap. 21. ſaith . *The thinges of holy ſcripture that I know not , are many more then thoſe that I knowe.* S.Greg. hom. 6. in Ezech. and many other fathers confeſſe the ſame. S. Denis Biſhop of Corinth , cited by Euſebius lib. 7. hiſt. Eccleſ. 20. *Of this booke, this is my opinion , that*

the

*the matter thereof is far more profound
then my wit can reach vnto.*

III.

*That Apostolicall Traditions, and an-
cient customes of the Church, (not
found in the Written Word) are not
to be receiued, nor due oblige vs.*

Contrary to the expresse wordes of their owne Bible. 2.
Thes. 2. 15. *Therefore brethren stand
fast, and hold the Traditions, which
yee haue bene taught, whether by word,
or by our epistle.* Hence it is as cleare
as the Sunne that shines, that some
Traditions were deliuered to the
Thessalonians by word of mouth,
and those of equall authoritie with
what was written, if not of more,
for the holy Ghost doth name them
first (as they were indeed the first
in being:) yea it is certaine, that
before the new Testament was
written, the Apostles deliuered all
by

by Tradition and word of mouth.
Therfore Apoftolicall Traditions are
to be receiued and doe oblige vs.

2. Thef. 3. 6. *Now I command you
bretheren, in the name of our Lord Ie-
fus-Chrift , that yee withdraw your
felues from euery brother that walketh
diforderly , and not after the Tradition
which he receiued of vs.* Lo, He faith
not, I *councell you*, but, I *commaund
you*; But thefe men reiecting al Traditions, walke diforderly : therfore
they breake the Apoftles commandment: Yea, they *ftand* not, but are
fallen: they let goe , what the word
it felfe, doth will them to *hould*: and
therfore in the name of our Lord
Iefus Chrift, let all good men withdraw them from them.

1. Cor. 11. 2. *Now I praife you
bretheren, that you remember me in all
thinges, and keepe the Traditions , as I
haue deliuered them vnto you.* But thefe
reiect al Traditions, therfore needes
muft S. Paul fpeake thus vnto them.
Now (none of my bretheren) I dif-

praife you, for that you forget me in
all thinges, and keepe not the Traditions, as I haue deliuered them
vnto you.

Laftly, If nothing at all be to be
beleeued, but only that which is left
vs written , wherein fhould the
Church haue exerçifed her felfe frō
Adam to Moyfes, the fpace of two
thoufand fix hundred yeares? Therfore &c.

See more 1. Tim. 6. 3. 20. & 2. Tim.
1. 13. 2. Tim. 2. 2. Iohn. 20. 30. & 21.
25. & 16. 12. 1. Cor. 11. 16. 34. 2. ep.
Iohn 12. 3. ep. of. S. Iohn 13. Actes 16.
4. & 15. 28.

See fathers that affirme the fame.
S. Ireneus l. 3. c. 4. Origen in cap. 6.
ad Rom. S. Damaf. l. 4. c. 17. S. Chrifoft. in 2. Thef. 2. S. Bafil l. de Spiritu
fan&to faith. *Some thinges we haue
from fcripture , other thinges from the
Apoftles , both which haue like force
vnto godlines.* S. Chrifoft. hom. 4. in
2. Thef. faith. *It is a Tradition , feeke
thou no further.*

V. *That*

V.

That a man by his owne vnderstanding
or priuat spirit, may rightly iudge
and interpret scripture.

Ontrary to the expresse wordes of their owne Bible 1. Cor. 12. 8. &c. *To one is giuen by the spirit, the word of wisdome : to another the word of knowledg by the same spirit : to another the working of miracles:to another prophecie: to another discerning of spirits: to another kindes of tongues:to another the interpretation of tongues, diuiding to euery man seuerally, as he will* . Where the Apostle in expresse words, opposeth & refelleth this vnsauory doctrine, teaching that the gifte of prophecying, or truly to interpret the holy scripture, is not giuen to all the faithfull, but to some only in particular: yea he presupposeth that one may haue the gift, euen to worke miracles, & yet may want the gift, truly to interpret

B 2   the

the word of God. Therfore a man
by his owne priuat spirit cannot &c.

2. Pet. 1.20. *Knowing this first, that
no prophecie of the scripture is of any priuat interpretation*, *for the prophecie came not in old time* (margent, or at any
time) *by the will of man*, *but holy men
of God*, *spake as they were moued by the
holy Ghost* . Loe how clearly the A-
postle taketh this facultie and authoritie, from a priuat and prophane
man, restrayning the same to a companie and societie of men, and those
also of some especiall note for their
sanctitie and holines, assuring vs that
such spake as they were moued by
the holy Ghost. Therfore &c.

1. Iohn. 4. 1. *Beloued*, *beleeue not
euery spirit*, *but try the spirits*, *whether
they are of God.* By which wordes we
are taught, that the spirit of others
are to be examined, whether they
proceed from God or not, but this
caueat cannot be vnderstood of the
spirit of the whole Church, sith then
it would follow, that there should
be

be none left to try the said spirit of the Church (euery particular man being included therin.) If then it be to be ment of priuat men (as needes it muft)it followeth, that a priuat spirit cannot be this iudge, sith it selfe is to vndergoe the iudgment and examination of some other. Therfore &c.

See fathers that affirme the same, S. Aug. epift. 162. & l. de Baptifmo. cap. 18. ad Epictetum. S. Bafil. epift. 78. S. Amb. epift. 32. S. Leo epift. 53. S. Hier. lib. cont. Luciferanos. Vincent Lir. cont. prophan. heref. nouitates. And laftly Luther him felfe faith lib. de poteftate Papæ. *We are not certaine of any priuat person, whether he hath the reuelation of the father or no, but that the Church hath it, we ought not to dout.*

VI.

That S. Peters faith hath fayled.

COntrary to the expreffe wordes of their owne bible. Luc. 22. 31. *Simon behould Satan hath defired to*

B 3 *haue*

haue you, that he may sift you as wheate: but I haue praid for thee , that thy faith fayle not . Loe Satan required to sift them all , but our Lord here prayed for Peter only, that his faith principally might not fayle . Therfore S. Peters faith hath not fayled.

Mat. 16.18. And I say vnto thee, that thou art Peter, and vpon this rock I will build my church, and the gates of hell shall not preuayle against it. But had S. Peters faith fayled, the gates of hell had preuailed. Therfore &c.

Mat. 23. 2. The Scribes and the Pharises sit in Moyses seat, al therfore whatsoeuer they bid you obserue, that obserue and doe. How could Christ bid the people of the old law, doe all whatsoeuer he should bid them, by those that sate in Moyses chaire , if they could erre ? But God hath no lesse preserued the truth of christian religion, in the chaire of S. Peter, which is in the new law , answerable to that of Moyses in the old . Therfore &c.

Iohn

Iohn 11.49.51. speaking of Cay-
phas, saith. *And this he spake not of him*
selfe, but being high priest that yeare,
he prophecied that Iesus should die for
that nation. Loe how in this most
wicked time of the sinagogue, at the
very dregges, and last cast of that
disobedient people, yet speaking
forth of that chaire, which Christ
had commanded to be heard and o-
beyed, touching matter of faith, they
answer truly, and their bishop pro-
phecieth: therfore S. Peters faith nor
chaire hath not fayled.

See Fathers that affirme the same.
S. Leo ser. 3. de assump. sua. *The dan-*
ger was common to all the Apostles, but
our Lord tooke speciall care of Peter, that
the state of all the rest might be more
sure, if the head were inuincible.

VII.

That the Church can erre, and
hath erred.

Ontrary to the expresse wordes
of their owne Bible. Isay. 49.
21. *As for me, this is my couenant with*

B 4 *them*

*them, saith the Lord . My spirit that is
vpon thee, and my wordes which I haue
put into thy mouth, shall not depart out
of thy mouth, nor out of the mouth of thy
seede , nor out of the mouth of thy seedes
seede, saith the Lord , from hence forth,
and for euer .* Therfore the Church
cannot erre &c.

Iohn 14. 16. *I will pray the father,
and he shall giue you another comfor-
ter, that he may abide with you for euer,
euen the spirit of truth.* But the Apoſtles them ſelues aboade not for e-
uer, therfore this is to be vnderſtood
of the perpetuall aboade of the ſpirit of truth with their ſucceſſors.
Therfore &c.

Mat. 18.17. *If he neglect to heare the
Church, let him be vnto thee as an heathen man and a publican.* Whence is
clearely to be gathered , that the
Church in her cenſure cannot erre.

Iſay 9.7. *And a high way shal be there,
and away, and it shall be called the way
of holines, the vncleanne shall not paſſe
ouer it, but it shall be for thoſe: the way-
faring*

faring men though fooles, shall not erre therin. How far deceiued then are many fimple foules, who doe affirme, that all the whole Church and all holy men that euer haue bene therein for thefe thoufand yeares, (how wife foeuer) haue all erred?

Ephef. 5. 27. *That he might prefent it to him felfe a glorious Church, not hauing fpot or wrincle, or any fuch thinge, but that it should be holy and without blemish .* Note well thefe wordes, *without fpot , wrincle, or any blemish:* Tel me now it is poffible, that reading this, thou canft euer beleeue, that fhe hath taught fuch horrible blafphemies & abhominations as fhe at this day is charged with? Therfore &c.

See more Iohn 16. 13. Ephef. 5.27. Efay 9. 7. Ezech. 37. 26. Luc. 22. 32. Mat. 23. 3. 1. Pet. 2. 9. Iohn. 17.17. 1. Cor. 11. 25. Pfal. 101. 23. 29. Ephef. 2. 10. Iohn 10. 16. Acts. 4. 32. Ephef. 4. 5. 11. Luc. 10. 16. Deut. 17.8. Ieremie 3. 15. Malac. 2. 7. Mat. 16. 18. Acts 15. 28. 2. Cor. 13. 8. 1. Tim. 3. 15.

See Fathers that affirme the same.
S. Aug. cont. Crescon. lib. 1. cap. 3.
Also vpon the 118. Psal. the place
beginneth. *Ne auferas de ore meo ver-*
bum veritatis vsquequaque. S. Cypr.
epist. 55. ad Cornel. num. 3. S. Ireneus lib. 3. cap. 4. with manye
others.

VIII.

That the Church hath bene hidden
and inuisible.

COntrary to the expresse wordes
of their owne Bible, Mat. 5. 14.
Yee are the light of the world , a cittie
that is set on a hill, cannot be hid . Ne-
ther doe men light a candle , and put it
vnder a bushell, but on a candlestick,
and it giueth light to all that are in the
house . But the Catholique Church
is such a light, such a candle, and
such a cittie, built vpon Christ as
vpon a mountaine , therfore hath
not, nor cannot be hidden, nor inuisible.

Mat. 18. 17. *Tell the Church, if he ne-*
glect

glect to heare the Church, *let him be vnto thee as a heathen man*. But it were a very hard cafe to be condemned for a heathen, for ether not telling, or hearing a Church which hath fo clofely lyen hid, that no man could heare, fee, feele or vnderftand it, for a thoufand yeare. Therfore &c.

2. Cor. 4. 3. *If our gofpel be hid*, *it is hid to them that are loft*. Loe the cenfure of S. Paul vpon all fuch, as affirme that the Church, or her gofpell, can be hid.

Ifay 2. 2. *And it shall come to paffe in the laft dayes*, *that the mountaine of the Lords houfe*, *shall be eftablished in the top of the mountaines*, *and shall be exalted aboue the hilles*, *and all nations shall flow vnto it*. In a thoufand places doe the prophecies fpeake of this kingdome of Chrift as Dan. 7. 14. Mich. 4. 7. which fhould be all in vaine, if this his kingdome could be inuifible; for a prophecie muft be of thinges, which may be feene and

B 6 per-

perceiued by our senses ; otherwise
euery man might be a prophet, and
fortell of thinges to come, which if
they should not come to passe, he
might answere, that they had come
to passe in very deed as he had prophecied, but that it was inuisible to
the world. Loe the visible absurdi-
ties of this inuisible Church.

See more. Psal. 27. 8. Rom. 10.
14. 1. Cor. 11. 19. Psalm. 19. 3. 4.
Isay. 60. 20. Acts. 20. 28. Isay.
61. 9.

See Fathers that affirme the same.
Origen. hom. 30. in Mat. *The Church*
is full of light , euen from the east to
the west. S. Chrysostom. hom. 4.
in 6. of Isay . *It is easier for the*
sunne to be extinguished , then the
Church to be darkned . S. Aug. tract.
in Ioan, calleth those *blinde, that doe*
not see so great a mountaine. S. Cypr.
de vnitate ecclesiæ.

IX. *That*

IX.

That the Church was not alwayes to
remaine Catholique or vniuersall, &
that the Church of Rome is not
such a Church.

COntrary to the expresse wordes
of their owne Bible, Psalm. 2.8.
*Aske of me, and I shall giue thee the
heathen for thine inheritance, and
the vttermost parts of the earth for
thy possession.* And Luc. 1. 33. *He
shall raigne ouer the house of Iacob for
euer, and of his kingdome there shall
no end.* But none of these promises
haue bene so much verefied as they
haue bene in the Church of Rome;
therfore both the Church hath bene
alwayes vniuersall, and Church of
Rome only such a Church.

Colos. 1.3. &c. W*e giue thankes to
God for you &c. since we heard your faith
&c. for the hope which is laid vp for you
heauen, wherof yee heard before in the
word of the truth of the gospell, which
is come vnto you, as it is in al the world,
and bringeth forth fruit, as it doth*
also

*also in you, since the day you heard of it,
and knewe the grace of God in truth.*
But no faith or gospell hath, or is,
so dilated in all the world, nor hath
fructified and growen (for so we
reade) as the faith of the Roman
Church hath done. Therfore &c. but
all this shall appeare much more
plainly by that which followeth.

Rom. 1. 8. *First I thanke my God
thorough Iesus Christ for you all , that
your faith is spoken of thoroughout the
whole world.* Where in expresse tear-
mes, S. Paul calleth the faith of the
whole world (or Catholique faith)
the faith of the Romans , that is to
say, of the Church of Rome . Therfore the Church of Rome , and no
other , is truly and in deed such a
Church.

See more Colof. 1. 23. Gen. 22. 18.
Mat. 24. 46: Acts 1.8. Dan. 2. 35. Luc.
24. 47. psal. 46. 9. psal. 72. 8. (we 71.)
Marc. 16. 20. Ezech. 13. 3. Mat. 28.
19. Actes 1. 8.

All which places are to be vnderstood,

ſtood, not that the whole world
ſhould be Catholique at one and the
ſame time, but that the whole ſhould
be conuerted to Chriſt at ſundrie times, and that it ſhould comprehend
a greater part of the world, then any
ſect of hereticks ſhould euer doe: and
this is the true ſence of being Catholique or vniuerſall.

To follow ſtill our former Rule,
ſee Fathers that affirme the ſame. S.
Cypr. ep. 57. writing to Cornelius
pope of Rome, ſayeth. *Whilſt with
you there is one minde and one voice, the
whole Church is confeſſed the Roman
Church.* S. Aug. de vnitat. eccleſ. cap.
4. ſaith. *Who ſo diſſente from the bodie of Chriſt, which is the Church, that
they doe not communicate with all the
whole corps of Chriſtendome, certaine it
is, that they are not in the Catholique
Church.* S. Hierom in his Apologie
againſt Ruffinus, and in other places, ſaith, that it is all one to ſay the
Roman faith, and *the Catholique faith.*
Againe S. Aug. vpon the pſal. 45. 16.
(we

(we 44.) But much more excellent-
lie the same holy Doctor ad Hono-
rar. epist. 161. The place beginneth.
Dignare ergo rescribere nobis. As also
cont. lit. Petil. l.2.cap. 16. The place
beginneth. *Si queras.*

X.

That the Churches vnitie is not ne-cessarie in all pointes of faith.

COntrary to the expresse wordes
of their owne Bible, Ephes. 4.
5. *One Lord , one Faith, one Baptisme.*
Therfore vnitie is necessarie in all
points of faith . The reason is, the
Church being a congregation of the
faithfull , one faith is necessarie to
make one Church; but our aduersaries differ in matters of faith, therfore they haue not the vnitie requisite to one Church.

Iames 2. 10. *Whosoeuer shall keepe*
the whole law , and yet offend in one
point, he is guiltie of all . And euen so
is it in our faith, for who denieth one
article, denieth all.

Acts

Acts 4.32. *And the multitude of them that beleeued, were of one hart, and of one soule.* And againe 2. Cor. 1. 10. *Now I beseeche you bretheren, by the name of our Lord Iesus Christ, that yee all speake the same thinge, and that there be no diuisions among you, but that yee be perfectly ioyned together in the same minde, and in the same iudgement.* But our aduersaries will needes ioyne with vs in vnity of Church (yea and with others also) who differ frō them in matters of faith. But this as you see, cannot be. Therfore &c.

See more Ierem. 32. 39. Can. 2. 6. psal. 67. 7. Mat. 12. 25. Marc. 3. 24. Luc. 11. 17. Mat. 18. 19. Ephes. 2. 14. 15. 16. 8. 2:. Ephes. 5. 27. Phillip. 3. 16. Phillip. 1. 26. 27. Galat. 5. 9. & 1. 8. Colol. 3. 15. Iohn 17. 11. 2. Cor. 3. 11. psal 121. 3.

And now to Rule with our commō Rule, the breakers of vnitie & of Rule. *In cathedra vnitatis, posuit Deus doctrinam veritatis,* faith S. Aug. (cited by the Manuduc. p. 134) In the chaire

of

of vnitie, God hath placed the doctrine of veritie. And cont. ep. Par. l.
3. cap. 5. The place beginneth. *Qui
non vult federe.* S. Cyprian lib. de vnitate ecclef. num. 3. faith. *This vnitie
of the Church, he that holdeth not, doth
he thinke he holdeth the faith?* Laftly S.
Hillarie lib. ad Conftantium Augu-
ftum, with many more.

XI.

*That S. Peter was not ordained by Chrift
the Firft, Head, or Chiefe amongft
the Apoftles, and that amongft the
twelue, none was greater, or leffer
then other.*

C
Ontrary to the expreffe wordes
of their owne Bible. Mat. 10. 2.
Now *the names of the twelue Apoftles
are thefe. The firft Simon, who is called
Peter.* All the Euangelifts doe put
bleffed Peter in the firft place, and
wicked Iudas in the laft : and wherfore this ? but becaufe the one was
Firft in dignitie and worthieft of the
reft; and contrariwife, the other laft,
worft, and vnworthieft of all his fellowes.

lowes. Againe, why as Peter is called *First*, are not the rest called, *Second, Third &c*? But to shew therby,
that they did not therfore call Peter
First, because he occurred first to be
named, but because he was the First,
both in dignitie & authoritie, whom
therfore they all number First, and
call the *First*.

Mat. 16.18. *And I say also vnto thee,
that thou art Peter, and vpon this rock I
will build my church, and the gates of
hell shal not preuaile against it.* Wordes
clearly insinuating S. Peters supremacie in the Church of God; for according to the Greeke and Syriack
text (as our doctors note) these wordes; *Thou art Peter,* found thus. *Thou
art a rock, and vpon this rock I will
build my church.* So that to say, that
Peter is the rock of the church, is all
one in sense, as to call him chiefe or
head of the Church.

Nether without especiall myste-
rie, did our Lord impose vpon him
this new name, the name of Peter (a
Rock

Rock or Stone)being one of the moſt excellent names of Ieſus Chriſt, who is many times in holy ſcripture, tearmed by the name of a Rock, or Stone: as Pſal. 117. 22. Iſay 28. 6. Dan. 2. 34. Mat. 21. 42. Rom. 9. 33. So that this foueraigne and abſolut paſtor of the Church, did communicate this new name vnto his vicar, to repreſent the more liuely, the ſupreame authoritie, which he would giue vnto him ouer his troupe.

And note, Chriſt ſaith not, *I haue built*, or, *I doe build*, but, *I will build*; the Church being built vpon Chriſt from his Incarnation : ſo that theſe wordes referred to Chriſt (as our Reformers vſe to doe) doe not well agree to build the Church on Chriſt as head therof for time to come: but doe well agree to S. Peter, as head therof for time to come . Therefore &c.

Mat. 16. 19. *And I will giue vnto thee, the keyes of the kingdome of heauen, &c.* by theſe wordes alſo, no leſſe

lesse then by the former, is clearly
signified S. Peters supremacie ; For
none hath the gouernment or commandement of the keyes of any
towne or cittie, but the Prince or
Gouernor of the same. And that soueraigne power is signified by the
keyes, is likewise proued by that of
our Sauiour Christ. *I haue the keyes
of hell and of death. Reuelat. 1. 18.*
Againe. *He that hath the keye o f Dauid,
he that openeth, and no man shutteth,
shutteth and no man openeth.*

Now adde to this that hath bene
saide, the correspondence of the
wordes of our Sauiour to S. Peter, with the wordes of S. Peter a-
gaine to him, and how cleare will
this doctrine appeare to all ? For
when our Lord asked his disciples.
Mat. 16. 15. W*hom say yee that I am?*
he demanded not how they called
his name, which was Iesus (for that
they knew full well before) but what
his qualitie, office, and dignitie was.
And S. Peter answering. *Thou art
Christ*

*Chriſt the Sone of the liuing God.*Chriſt
tould him not his name (which was
Simon) but gaue him another name,
and ſuch an one, as likewiſe ſignified
the office, qualitie and dignitie that
he beſtowed vpon him, ſaying. Thou
art *Cephas* or *Petrus*, that is to ſay, a
Rock or Peter. Therfore &c.

1. Cor. 3. 4. 22. *One ſaith I am of
Paul, I am of Apollo, I of Cephas, I of
Chriſt .* Loe how from thoſe he
would haue eſteemed leſſer, he aſ-
cendeth to thoſe whom he would
haue eſteemed greater, and placeth
Peter next to Chriſt. Therfore &c.

Luc. 22. 31. *And the Lord ſaid, Simon , &c. when thou art conuerted
ſtrengthen*(we reade,*confirme*)*thy bretheren.* Now what other thinge is it
for Peter, to ſtrengthen or confirme
his brethren, but to practiſe and exerciſe his greatnes ouer them ? for
he that doth ſtrengthen or confirme
others, is the greater : and they who
are ſtrengthned or confirmed, are
made therby inferiors to him , who
doth

doth ftrengthen or confirme them.

Luc. 22. 26. *He that is greateft a-mongſt you, let him be as the younger, & he that is chiefe, as he that doth ſerue.* Where the wordes, *is greateſt*, *is chiefe*, doe euidently fhew, that a-mongft the twelue, one was greater then another, and was fo accounted euen by Chriſt him felfe.

Iohn 21. 15. *Ieſus ſaid to Simon Pe-ter : Simon loueſt thou me more then theſe? Feede my lambes, feeede my sheepe.* (Where the Greeke hath in the fecōd place for *feede, gouerne* or *rule*.) Hence it followeth, that either the Apoſtles were not cenfured to be in the flock of Chriſt, or elſe they were fubiect to S. Peter as to their head, when Chriſt commanded him to feede or gouerne, not only his lambes (to wit, the lay people) but his fheepe alſo, to wit, the Apoſtles and paſtors them felues: for befides lam-bes and fheepe, there is nothing in the Church of God : Againe, if S. Peter loued our Lord more then all
his

his fellowes did, it followeth neceffarily, that he receiued more power
to feede then all his fellowes did;
For it cannot be conceiued that he
is willed to loue, more then to feede:
but he loueth more thē others, therfore he is willed to feede more then
the others; and confequently, is head
of the others.

Mat. 12. 25. 26. *Euery kingdom di-*
uided againſt it felfe, is brought to de-
folation &c. And if Satan caſt out Sa-
tan. Sathan therfore hath a kingdome, wherof he is the chiefe kinge.
If then there be, not only a vifible
head of the Church triumphant in
heauen, but alfo a vifible head euen
in hell, why not a vifible head alfo
in earth ? Therfore &c. But here I
craue pardon, for hauing far excee-
ded my pretended breuitie, though
as much no more might be faid,
ether vpon this, or vpon any other
point, as hath bene of this.

See more pfal. 18. 43. pfal. 45.
16. (we, 46.) Marc. 2. 16. Actes 1. 3.
                                    Luc.

Luc. 1. 33. 2. Cor. 11. 5.

See fathers that affirme the fame.
Theophilact in 22. Luc. calleth Peter, Prince of the Difciples. Eufebius
in Chron; Firft bifhop of Chriftians.
S. Cyril of Hier. cat. 2. Prince , and
moft excellent of all the Apoftles. S.
Chryfoft . Hom. 55. in Mat. Paftor
and head of the church. Euthym. in
cap. vlt. Ioan , Mafter of the whole
world. S. Leo epift. 89. Head and
chiefe of the Apoftles.

XII.

That a woman may be head or fupreame
gouerneße of the Church in all cau-
fes , as Queene Elizabeth
lately was.

C Ontrary to the expreffe wordes
of their owne Bible. 1. Tim. 2.
11. *Let the woman learne in filence, with*
all fubiection. But I fuffer not a woman
to teache, nor to vfurpe authoritie ouer
the man . Therfore a woman cannot
be head or fupreame &c.

1. Cor. 14. 34. *Let women hould*
their peace in the Churches, for it is not

permitted them to speake, but to be sub-
iect, as also the law saith. Therfore &c.

I produce no fathers for disproofe
of this point, for neuer was any woman so presumptuous in our forefa-
thers dayes, but will content my selfe
to refute this folly, with an euident
and conuincing reason, the which is
this.

Whatsoeuer power an inferior
minister of the Church hath, that
the head of the same Church hath
(at the least) if not much more. But
euerye inferior minister of their
Church, hath power to Baptise, to
giue the Communion, to marrie, to
burie, and to preache in pulpit: therfore the Queene could Baptise, giue
the Communion, marrie, burie, and
preach in pulpit. And who now is
so simple as sees not the ridiculous
sequel of this doctrine? for the which
notwithstanding, hundreds of ours
haue bene hanged, cut vp, and quar-
tered aliue, as most wicked traitors.

But that no secular Kinge can be
this

this head, an infinitie of Fathers doe
affirme. S. Iohn Damafcen . fer. 1.
The place beginneth . *Tibi ô Rex.*
And againe. *Non affentior.* I *confent*
not that the Church of God, be gouerned
by kinges . Theodoret. hift. ecclef. l.
4. c. 28, recounteth of one Eulogius
that he anfwered to an officer of the
Emperor Valens (telling him the
Emperor would haue it fo) with this
prettie quippe, faying . What, was
he made a Bifhop, that day that he
was crowned Emperor ? The place
beginneth. *Tum ille.*S. Ignatius epift.
ad Philadelph, willeth all men without exception , euen the Emperor
him felfe, to be obedient to the Bifhop: the place beginneth. *Principes o-*
bedite Cafari. S. Chrifoft. hom. 5. de
verbis Ifaiæ , calleth the Bifhop a
prince as well as the Kinge, yea and
that a greater alfo . And hom. 38. in
Mat, 21. The place beginneth. *Quia*
in rebus fpiritualibus.

C 2   XIII.

XIII.

That Antechrist shall not be a particular man; and that the Pope is Antechrist.

COntrary to the expresse wordes of their own Bible. 2. Thes. 2. 3. *Let no man deceaue you by anie meanes, for that day shall not come, except there come a falling away first, and that man of sinne be reuealed, the sonne of perdition* . Where these wordes, *man of sinne*, and, *sonne of perdition*, doe plainly prooue, that a succession of men (as the Popes are) cannot be this man of sinne: for so S. Peter also should be Antechrist, for he was Pope, and the very first of all the Popes. Therfore Antechrist shall be a particular man &c.

Reuelations 13. 18. *Let him that hath vnderstanding* , *count the number of a man* . Therfore the great Antechrist, that egregious Apostata, or notable enimie of Iesus Christ, shall be a particular man.

1. Iohn 2. 22. *Who is a lier, but he that*

that denieth that Iesus is Christ? This is Antechrist, which denieth the Father & the Sonne. But the Pope denyeth nether of both; Therfore the Pope is not Antechrist.

Againe in the 2. Thef. before alleadged 2. 4. the scripture saith, that Antechrist shal be extolled aboue al that is called God: and verfe 8. that our Lord Iesus shal kil him with the spirit of his mouth, at his coming: but none of al these agree to the Pope, no more then that our Lord Iesus is come the secod time. Therfor &c.

Iohn 5. 43. *I am come in my Fathers name, and yee receaue me not: if another shall come in his owne name, him yee will receiue.* He meaneth specially the wicked Antechrist: how then can the Pope be he, feeing the Iewes receiue him not?

See more Dan. 7. 7. & cap. 12. 11. Reuel. 13. 17. & cap. 17. 8. 11. Luc. 13. 14. Mat. 24. 15.

To follow our Rule, fee Fathers that affirme the fame. And firft S.

Chrisostom and S. Cyril. doe both
thus vnderstand this very place last
alleadged. S. Amb. vpon the 2. Thes.
2. Hierom in ep. ad Algasia quæst. 11.
S. Aug. in 29. tract. in Ioan. S. Ireneus l. 5. cont. heres. Valentin. Theodoret. in the epitome of the diuine
decrees cap. de Antichristo.

XIV.

That no man , nor none but God , can
forgiue or retaine sinnes.

Ontrary to the expresse wordes
of their owne Bible Iohn 20.
21. *As my Father hath sent me, euen so*
send I you . Now Christ was sent by
his Father, not only to teache, preache, administer sacraments , and to
worke miracles, but also to forgiue
sinnes: but the Disciples were sent
with power to teache, preache, administer sacraments , and to worke
miracles: therfore also to forgiue
sinnes.

Ibid. v. 22. 23. *When he had said*
this , he breathed on them , and saith
vnto them . Receiue yee the holy Ghost:
Whose

*Whose soeuer sinnes yee remit , they are
remitted vnto them, and whosoeuer sinnes yee retaine, they are retained.* Chrift
hauing firft fhewed his owne com-
miffion , which was to pardon finnes , prefently giueth his Apoftles
power to doe the fame, breathing on
them the holy Ghoft . He therfore
that denieth man to haue this power,
ether denyeth that the holy Ghoft
can forgiue finne, or that Chrift gaue
not his Difciples the holy Ghoft to
this end and purpofe : both which
are clearely falfe , and againft the
fcripture. Therfore &c.

Mat.9.3.8. *But when the multitude saw it, they maruelled and glorified God , which had giuen such power
vnto men,*as to forgiue finnes. Which
though they knew to appertaine to
God only by nature , yet they perceiued that it might be done by mãs
miniftrie in earth, to the glorie of
God . Yea thofe , who affirme
God only fo to remitt finnes, that
the minifteriall power therof cannot

be communicated to men, deny the
one part of Christes distinct, or double maner of remittinge sinnes, to
wit, only in heauen, and not in earth.
Therfore &c.

See more Mat. 16. 19. & Mat. 18.
18. 1. Cor. 5. 5. 1. Tim. 1. 20. 2. Cor. 2.
10. 2. Cor. 5. 19. Num. 5. 6.

Alwayes to comply with our
common Rule see, Fathers which affirme the same. S. Aug. tract. 49. in
Ioan. And in his booke of fiftie ho-
milies hom. 9. S. Chrisost. de sacer-
dotio l. 3. S. Amb. l. 3. de pœnitentia . S. Cyrill. l. 12. cap. 50. or 56. in
Ioan saith. *It is not absurd, that they*
should remit mans sinnes , who haue in
them the holie Ghost. S. Basil. l. 5. cont,
Euuomius proueth the holy Ghost
to be God (which that detestable
heretique did deny) because he for-
giueth sinnes by the Apostles. S. Ireneus l. 5. cap. 13. S. Greg. hom. 6. in
Euang.

XV.

X V.

*That we ought not to confesse our sinnes,
to any man, but to God only.*

C Ontrary to the expresse wordes
of their owne Bible, Mat. 3.5. 6.
Then went out to him (to wit, to Iohn)
*all Hierusalem, and were baptised of him
in Iordan, confessing their sinnes.* Not
by acknowledging them selues in
generall to be sinners, but euery man
to vtter and tell his particular sinnes. Therfore we may confesse our
sinnes, not only to God, but also
to man.

Actes 19. 18. *And many that beleeued, came and confessed and shewed
their deedes* (behould Confession) *Manie also of them which vsed curious
artes, brought their bookes together,
and burned them before all men: and
they counted the price of them, and
found it fiue thousand peeces of siluer* (behould Satisfaction.) Therfore &c.

Num. 5. 6. *When a man or woman
shall, commit any sinne &c. then they*
C 5 *shall*

shall *confeſſe their ſinne which they haue done.* And that this is not vnderſtood to God in heauen, but alſo to his Prieſt in earth, the whole chapter, from verſe 12. vnto the end, doth clearly teſtifie. Adde, that he ſaith not, they ſhall confeſſe their *ſinnes* (to wit, in generall) but their *ſinne,* to wit, in particular. Therfore &c.

See more Marc. 1. 4. Iames. 5. 16. Mat. 18. 18. Mat. 17. 14.

To bring vnruly people to Confeſſion by the helpe of our holeſome Rule, ſee Fathers that affirme the ſame. S. Ireneus l. 1. cap. 9. Tertulian l. de pœnitentia, where he reprehendeth ſome, who for human ſhamfaſtnes, neglected to goe to Confeſſion. It is written of S. Ambroſe, that he him ſelfe ſate in Confeſſion, Amb. ex Paulino. S. Clement S. Peters ſucceſſor, ſpeakes wonderfull pithylie to this purpoſe. Epiſt. ad frat. Dom. But of all others, Origen is moſt plaine for this point. l. 3. Periorchon: S. Chriſoſt. l. 3. de ſacerd.

&

& hom. 85. in Ioan . S. Aug. cited a litle before and others. S. Amb. orat. in muliere pecatrice, faith . *Confesse freely to the priest, the hidden secrets of thy soule.*

XVI.

That Pardons and Indulgences, were not in the Apostles times.

COntrary to the expresse wordes of their owne Bible. 2. Cor. 2. 10. *To whom yee forgiue any thinge, I forgiue also: for if I forgiue any thinge, to whom I forgaue it, for your sake forgaue I it, in the person of Christ.* The Corinthian aforsaid, was excommunicated, and put to penance by the Apostle, as plainly appeareth 1. Cor. 5. 3. and in the 2. Corinthians last cited, he giueth order for his pardon. A plaine proofe of the Apostles power, there of binding, here of loosing: there of punishing, here of pardoning. Therfore pardons were in vse in the Apostles times.

2. Cor. 2. 6. *Sufficient to such a*
C 6   *man,*

man, *is this punishment*. Whence it
is cleare, that it lyeth in the handes of the spirituall magistrates,
to measure the time of such punishment, or penance imposed. Therfore &c.

See more Mat. 18. 18. & Mat. 16. 19

See Fathers that affirme the same. Tertul. l. ad Mart. cap. 1. 5.
S. Cyp. l. 3. ep. 15. & sermo de lap-
fis. Concil. Lateran. Can. 62. The
decrees of Innocentius 3. & 4. de
pœnitent. & remis. cap. quod autem. S. Amb. l. 1. de pœnit. cap.
2. the place beginneth, *Dominus par
ius*. S. Aug. ep. 75. ad Auxilium
Episcop. The place beginneth, *Spi-
ritalis pœna*. S. Chrisost l. 3. de sa-
cerdot: the place beginneth. *Si rex
aliquis*. Lastly, Pope Vrban the 2.
granted a plenarie Indulgence to
such as would goe to the holy
warre.

XVII.

XVII.

That the actions & passions of the Sain-
tes, doe serue for nothing to
the Church.

COntrary to the expresse wordes
of their owne Bible, Colos. 1.
24. *I reioyce in my sufferinges for you,*
and fill vp that which is behinde (we
reade wanting) *of the afflictions of*
Christ in my flesh, for his bodies sake,
which is the Church . Hence hath
the ground bene alwayes taken , of
Indulgences (but much more principally , from the superaboundant
merits of Iesus Christ.) Therfore the
actions and passions of the Saintes,
doe serue for somethinge to the
Church &c.

Phillip. 2. 30. *Becausè for the*
worke of Christ , he was nigh vnto
death , not regarding his life, to supply
your lack. Therfore &c.

Contrary also to an article of our
Creed , *I beleeue the communion of*
Saintes. But to what purpose beleeue
we this, if their actions and passions,

may

may not be imparted to vs, nor serue to no purpose to the Church. Therfore &c.

See more pſal. 119.63.(we 118.)1. Cor. 12.12.2. Cor. 11.28.pſal.53. (we 52.) 9.2. Mac.15.16. Mat. 17.3. Luc.9. 30.31. Mat.27.52. Apoc. 5.8. Gen.26. 5.& 48.16. Exod.32.13.Iob.5.1.Hier. 15.1. Iſay.37.35. Marc. 14.36. Luc. 8. 44. Acts 5.15. All theſe paſſages con- tayning actions or prayers, of the Church triumphant, for the militant or patient, or for both, I care not which they grant, and yet one they muſt needes confeſſe. Therfore &c.

See Fathers that affirme the ſame, S. Aug. lib. de cura pro mort. cap. 1. The place beginneth, *Etſi nuſquam.* And againe the ſame Saint in the ſame booke, the place beginneth, *Prouiſus ſepeliendis.* S. Maximus ſer. de ſanctis Octauio, Aduentio, the place beginneth, *Cuncti martyres.* S. Bede hiſt. eccleſ. Angliæ l. 3.cap. 19. the place beginneth, *Furſeus.* S. Auguſt. in Pſal. 61. the place begin- neth,

neth, *Vnus enim homo* : as alſo S. An-
ſelme vpon the ſame.

XVIII.

That no man can doe workes of
ſupererogation.

Contrary to the expreſſe wordes
of their owne Bible. Mat. 19.
21. *If thou will be perfect, goe and ſell
that thou haſt, and giue to the poore, and
thou ſhalt haue treaſure in heauen, and
come and follow me.* Hence it plainly
appeareth, that man by the aſiſtance
of Gods grace, may doe ſome thinges councelled, which are of more
perfection then the thinges commā-
ded: and theſe we call workes of
ſupererogation.

1. Cor. 7. 25. 38. *Now concerning
virgins, I haue no commandement of
the Lord, yet I giue my iudgment* (we
read councell) *as one that hath obtained mercie of the Lord to be faithful:
he that giueth her in marriage doth wel,
but he that giueth her not in mariage,
doth better.* To doe that which is
councelled is not neceſſarie, becauſe
one

one may be saued notwithstanding, but he who omitteth what is commanded (vnles he doe penance) can not escape eternall paines . Therfore. &c.

Mat. 19. 12. *There be Eunuches which haue made them selues Eunuches for the kingdome of heauen, he that is able to receiue it* (we reade, *take it*) *let him receiue it.* But this cannot properlie be said of precepts, as S. Aug. noteth vpon this place, ser. 61. de temp. for of precepts it is not said , keepe them who is able , but absolutly. Therfore &c.

See more Luc. 10. 25. 1. Cor. 7. 1. Reuel. 4. 3. Actes 2. 44. Actes 4. 34. See Fathers that affirme the same. S. Amb. l. de viduis. Origen in c. 15. ad Rom. *Those thinges which wee doe ouer and aboue our dutie.* Euseb 1. Demonstrat. cap. 8. S. Chrysost. hom. 8. de act. poenit. *Blame not our Lord , he commandeth nothing impossible, yea manie doe more then they are commanded.* S. Greg. Nicen. 15, Moral. cap. 5.

XIX,

*That by the fall of Adam, we haue all
lost our free will: and that it is not
in our owne power to choose
good, but only euill.*

C Ontrary to the expresse wordes of their owne Bible 1.
Cor. 37. *He that standeth stedfast in his
hart, hauing no necessitie, but hath
power ouer his owne will, and hath so
decreed in his hart, that he will keepe
his virgin, doth well.* But if a man
haue not freedome of will, as well
to the one, as to the other, why
doth the holy Ghost (Prou. 23. 26.)
require of vs to giue him our hart, if
we cannot consent but vnto euill?
Therfore it is in our power to choose
good, or euill.

Iohn 1. 11. 12. *He came vnto his
owne, and his owne receiued him not:
but as many as receiued him, to them
gaue he power to become the sonnes of
God.* Wordes which plainly imply a
libertie of will; For when he saith
some receiued him, & some not, who
lees

fees not the libertie both of the one,
& of the other: for thefe would not
receiue him , and thefe would.
Therfore &c.

Deut.30.19. *I call heauen and earth
to record this day againft you , that I
haue fet before you life and death,blef-
fing and curfing , therfore choofe life,
that both thou and thy feede may liue.*
And rightly may we call heauen and
earth to witnes againft them , who
commit the fame fault touching
grace, which the Turkes doe touching nature ; For the Turkes beleeue that the fire burnes not , nor
water wetts not , but God by the
fire and the water:fo they,that a man
defireth no good , nor dooth no
good, but only that God dooth all
by man : but this is falfe . Therfore. &c.

Luc. 13. 34. *O Hierufalem, Hierufalem &c. how often would I haue gathered thy children together, as a henne
doth gather her brood vnder her winges,
and yee would not.* I would, and yee
would

would not; what for Gods fake can be fpoke more plainly?

See more Luc. 10. 42. Acts 5. 4. Ad Philemon v.14. 1.Cor.7.37.& 9. 1.14. 2.Cor.9.7. Ofe. 3. 9. Num. 30. 14. Iofua 14.13. 2.Reg.24.12. 3.Reg. 3.5. Ecclef. 15. 15. Mat. 19. 17. Iofue 24.15.2. Samuel 12. Pro. 11. 24. Reuel.3.20. Ifay 1.19.20.

For further proofe we will fly to our Rule. Eufeb. Cefar. de prep. l.1.cap.7.faith,that thofe who hould this opinion, doe peruert and ouer-throw, *Vniuerfam vitam humanam, all the life of man.* And in very deed his reafon is good, for vpon this confi-deration of mans free wil,are groun-ded all politicall lawes, precepts and prohibitions, paines and rewardes, which elfe were meerely fuperfluous and againft reafon. S. Hilarie l. 1. de Trinitate, faith. *He would not there should be a necefsitie for men to be the fonnes of God, but a power.* S. Aug. l. 1. ad Simp. q. 4. faith. *To confent,or not to confent vnto Gods vocation, lyeth*

in

in a mans owne will. So teacheth S.
Amb. in Luc. cap. 12. S. Chrisost.
hom. 19. in Genes. S. Ireneus l. 4.
cap. 72. S. Cyrill. lib. 4. in Ioan.
cap. 7. W e *cannot in any wise deny
freedome of will in man.* And S. Aug.
afore recited saith, lib. 2. cap. 4. de
act. cum Felic. Manich. *How should
our Sauiour reward euerie one according to their workes, if there were no
free will?*

XX.

*That it is impossible to keepe the Com-
mandements of God, though assisted
with his grace, & the holy Ghost.*

Ontrary to the expresse words
of their owne bible. Philip. 4.
13. *I can doe all thinges, thorough
Christ which stregthneth me.* Therfore
it is possible to keepe the commandements, or else it is false, that he
could doe all thinges.

Luc. 1. 5. 6. The scripture speaking of Zacharie & Elizabeth, saith.
*And they were both righteous before
God, walking in all the commandements
and*

and ordinances of the Lord, blameles.
Yet they vſuallie ſay, that none are ſo
righteous as that they can keepe any
of them: but theſe two were ſo righteous as they kept all of them : now
whither of theſe wilt thou beleue?

Luc. 11.27. 28. *Bleſſed is the wombe
that bare thee, and the papes which thou
haſt ſucked . But he ſaid; Yea rather,
bleſſed are they that heare the word of
God, and keepe it .* Chriſt pronounceth them bleſſed, who heare the
word of God and keepe it : but the
commandements are the word of
God (which they affirme no man can
keepe) therfore they affirme that no
man can be bleſſed . And like vnto
this is that of Iohn 13.17. Mat. 12.50.
Iohn. 14..23. with an infinit number
of ſuch like places, al which this lew-
ed doctrine, doth plainly dally with
all, as it doth with this.

Luc. 11.2. *Thy wil be done as in heauē
ſo in earth .* In making this demand,
ether we demād a thinge impoſſible,
or the Saints in heauen fulfill not the
will,

will of God in all thinges, or it may
be fulfilled alſo by vs on earth (one
of the three:) But the two firſt are ful
of abſurdities : therfore the later is
to be granted.

1. Iohn 5. 3. *For this is the loue of*
God, that we keepe his commandements,
and his commãdcments are not greeuous.
If the cõmandements were impoſſible, they could binde no man: for
it is not to be conceiued how one
ſhould ſinne in a thinge, which he
could not poſſibly auoide. And Chriſt
ſaying to the young man ; If thou
wilt enter into heauen, keepe the
commandements, is as if he had ſaid ;
If thou wilt enter into heauen, take
hould of the Moone betwixt thy
teeth.

See more Ezech. 36. 27. Mat. 11.
30. & 19. 17. Eccleſ. 15. 15. Rom. 13. 8.
10. & 7. 3. Ioſua 11. 15. & 22. 5. pſal. 17.
3. Deut. 30. 11. 1. Iohn 2 4. Iob. 27.
6. & 1. 22. Rom. 2. 27. Luc. 10. 28.
&c. 15. 7. 3. Reg. 14. 8. & 15. 5, Epheſ.
1. 4. Galat. 5. 14. Gen. 6. 9.

But

But to rectifie them herein by our
common Rule, fee Origen hom. 9.
in Iofue. S. Cyril. l. 4. cont. Iulian.
S. Hillar. in pfal. 118. S. Hier. l. 3.
cont. Pelag. S. Bafil, who faith. It
is an impious thinge to fay, that the
commandements of God are impoffible.

XXI.

That only faith iuftifieth; And that good
workes are not abfolutely neceffary
to faluation.

C Ontrary to the expreffe wordes
of their owne Bible 1. Cor. 13.
2. *And though I haue the gift of prophe-*
cie, and vnderftand all myfteries, and all
knowledge; and though I haue all faith
fo that I could remoue mountaines, and
haue no charitie, I am nothing. Therfore faith only doth not iuftifie: yea
this plainlie proueth, that faith is nothing to faluation, without good
workes.

Iames 2.24. *Yee fee therfor, how that*
by workes a man is iuftified, and not by
faith only. S. Aug. lib. de fide & operibus

ribus cap. 14. writeth, that this heresie, was an old heresie, euen in the
Apostles times. And in the preface
of his comment.vpon the 32.psal. he
warneth all men, that this deduction
vpon S. Paules speeche, *Abraham was
iustified by faith, therfore workes be not
necessarie to saluation,* is the right way
to hell and damnation. See the Rhe.
Test. vpon this place.

Iac. 2. 14. W*hat doth it profit my
bretheren, though a man say he hath
faith, and haue not workes? Can faith
saue him?* This proposition (but espe-
cially the former) is directly opposite
to that which our aduersaries hould.
Neuer can they pretend, that there
is the like opposition or contradiction, betwixt S. Iames speeches and
S. Pauls: for though S. Paul say,
Man is iustified by faith, yet he neuer
sayeth, by faith only.

Gal. 5. 6. *For in Iesus Christ, nether
circumcision auaileth any thinge, nor vn-
circumcision, but faith which worketh
by loue.* Note well this place; for if
                                    our

our aduerfaries, who pretend confe-
rence of places, to be the only rule
to explicate the hard paffages of holy
fcripture, had followed but this their
owne Rule, this one text would haue
cleared vnto them all other, wherin
iuftice and faluation might feeme to
be attributed to faith alone.

See more Mat. 7.21.22. Mat. 5. 21
Mat. 19. 17. & 11. 26. Mat. 12.33.
Mat. 16. 16. Gal. 3.12.1. Tim. 5.8. 1.
Ioan. 2. 4.1. Ioan. 3. 22. Rom. 3. 31.
Phillip. 2. 12.

See Fathers that affirme the fame.
Origen in 5. Rom. S. Hillar. cap. 7.
in Mat. S. Amb. in 4. ad Heb. faith.
faith alone fufficeth not. S. Aug. de
fide & operibus cap. 15. faith. *I fee
not, why Chrift should fay*. If thou
wilt haue life euerlafting keepe the
commandements, *if without obfer-
uing of them, by only faith, one might
be faued.*

D   XXII.

XXII.

That no good workes are meritorious.

COntrary to the expreſſe wordes of their owne Bible. Mat. 16.27. *For the Sonne of man shall come in the glorie of his Father, with his Angells, and then he shall reward euerie man according to this workes.* He ſaith not, that he ſhall reward euery man according to his mercie, or their faith, but according to their workes. So S. Aug. de verbis Apoſt. ſer. 35. Therfore &c.

Mat. 5. 12. *Reioyce and be glad, for great is your reward in heauen.* The word Reward, in latin & greeke, ſignifieth very wages, and hyre, due for workes, and ſo preſuppoſeth a meritorious deed, as the Rhe. Teſt. noteth vpon this place. Therfore &c.

The like of this place, is that of S. Mat. 10. 42. *And whoſoeuer shall giue to drinke, a cup of cold water only, in the name of a Diſciple, verely I ſay vnto you, he shall in no wiſe looſe his*

his reward. Therfore.

1. Cor. 5. 10. For *we must all appeare before the iudgment seate of Christ, that euery one may receiue the thinges in his body, according to that he hath done, whether it be good or bad.* Wordes most cleare, that heauen is as wel the reward of good workes, as hell is the stipend of euill workes, howsoeuer the aduersaries of good life and workes, doe teache the contrarie.

See more 1. Cor. 9. 17. & 18. 25. Heb. 11. 26. Psal. 18. 20. 1. Cor. 4. 5. & 3. 8. 2. Esdras 15. 19. Apoc. 22. 12. Apoc. 16. 6. Apoc. 3. 4. & 22. 12. Rom. 2. 6. Ecclel. 12. 2. Colos. 3. 23. Luc. 16. 9. & 6. 38. Gen. 15. 1. Ierem. 31. 16. Sap. 5. 16. 1. Tim. 4. 8. 2. Thes. 1. 6. Rom. 11. 21.

See Fathers that affirme the same. S. Amb. de apolog. Dauid cap. 6. S. Hier. l. 3. cont. Pelag. S. Aug. de spiritu & lit. cap. vlt.

D 2   XXIII.

XXIII.
That faith once had, cannot be lost.

COntrary to the expresse wordes of their owne Bible. Luc. 8. 13. *They on the rock, are they, which when they heare, receiue the word with ioy, which for a while beleeue, and in time of tentation fall away.* Therfore faith once had, yet afterwards may be lost.

1. Tim. 1. 18.19. *This charge I commit vnto thee, sonne Timothie, according to the prophecies which went before on thee, that thou by them, mightest warre a good warfare, houlding faith and a good conscience, which some hauing put away, concerning faith, haue made shipwrack.* Both which places doe plainlie reproue this false doctrine, that no man can fall from the faith, which he once truly had.

2. Tim. 16. &c. *Shun prophane and vaine bablinges, for they will increase vnto more vngodlines, and their word will eate as doth a canker, of whom is Hymeneus and Philetus, who concerning the*

the truth haue erred, saying, that the resurrection is past already, and ouerthrow the faith of some. If faith once had, could not be lost, this saying of the Apostle should be false. Therfore &c.

See more 1. Tim. 6. 20. Reuelations 2. 5. Luc. 19. 24. Mat. 25. 8. &c. Rom. 11. 20.

See Fathers that affirme the same. S. Augult. de gratia & lib. arbit. De correp. & gratia & ad articulos falso impositas. Concil. Trid. sess. 6. cap. 9. 12. 13.

XXIIII.

That God by his will and ineuitable decree, hath ordained from all eternitie, who shall be damned, and who saued.

COntrary to the expresse wordes of their owne Bible. 1. Tim. 2. 3. 4. *God our Sauiour, who will haue all men to be saued, and to come to the knowledge of the truth.* Meaning, by his conditionall will, that is to say, if men wil themselues, by accepting,

D 3 dooing,

dooing, or hauing done vnto them,
all thinges requisite by Gods law:
for God vseth not his absolute will
or power towards vs in this case.
Therfore he hath not willed , and
ineuitably decreed , any at all to be
damned.

2. Pet. 3. 9. *The Lord is not slack
concerning his promise &c. not willing
that any should perish , but that all
should come to repentance .* Therfore
far off from euer making anie such
decree.

Wisdome 1. 13. *For God made not
death , nether hath he pleasure in the
destruction of the liuing .* The reasons
which conclude this truth, are very
manifest: for we must assure nothing
of those thinges, which depend vpon the only will of God (without
cleare and euident reuelation) but
predestination is such. Therfore.

See more. Ose 13. 9. Ezech. 18.
32. Wis. 11.24. Ioan. 3.16. Rom. 11.
20. 32. Pro. 20. 9. & 28. 14. Phil. 2. 12.
1. Cor. 4. 4. & 9. 27. & 10. 12. Eccles.
5. 5.

5. 5. Iob. 9. 21. Ioel 2. 14. Ionas 3. 9.
Acts 8. 20. Ierem. 17. 9. 2. Ioan 1. 8.

See Fathers that affirme the same.
S. Aug. l. 1. ciuit. Tertul. orat. cap. 8.
S. Cyp. l. 4. ep. 2. S. Amb. lib. 2. de
Cain & Abel, will not that we refer
vnto God, the preuarication of Adā,
or the treason of Iudas, though he
knew the sinne before it was committed.

XXV.

That euery one ought infallibly to assure
him selfe of his saluation, and to
beleeue that he is of the num-
ber of the predestinat.

Contrary to the expresse wordes
of their owne Bible. 1. Cor. 9.
27. *I keepe vnder my body, and bringe*
it into subiectiō, least that by any meanes,
when I haue preached to others, I my
selfe should be a cast-way. A mā would
thinke that S. Paul might be as sure
and as confident of Gods grace and
saluation, as any one of our aduersaries be, and yet you see he durst
not adhere vnto their presumptuous

D 4   and

& vnhappie securitie. Therfore &c.

Rom. 11. 20. *Thou standest by faith, be not high minded, but feare, for if God spared not the naturall branches, take heede least he also spare not thee: behould therfore the goodnes and seueritie of God; on them which fell, seueritie; but towards thee goodnes, if thou continue in his goodnes, otherwise, thou also shalt be cut off.* Therfore &c.

Philippians 2. 12. *Worke out your owne saluation, with feare and trembling.* A plaine and forcible place, against the vaine securitie of saluatiō.

See more. Pro. 28. 14. Ecclef. 9. 1. 2. 2. Tim. 2. 15. 2. Pet. 1. 10. Toby 12. 2. 13. Pro. 20. 9. Ecclef. 5. 5. Iob. 9. 20. Psal. 18, 13. 1. Cor, 4. 4. Deut. 4. 29. 2. Cor. 10. 18. 1. Pet. 1. 17.

To let nothing slip without our Rule, see S. Amb. fer. 5. in psal. 118. S. Basil in constit. monast. cap. 2. S. Ierom l. 2. aduers. Pelagianos, & l. 3. in Ierem. cap. 13. S. Chrysost. hom. 87. in Ioan. S. Aug. in Psal. 40. *I know that the instice of my God remaineth,*
Whe-

whether my iuſtice remayne or no, I *know not, for the Apoſtle terrifieth me ſaying.* He that thinketh him ſelfe to *ſtand, let him take heede leaſt he fall.* S. Bernard. ſer. 3. de Aduent. & ſer. 1. de Septuageſ. Who can ſay I am one of the elect? &c To conclude, it is none of the articles of our Creed. Therfore &c.

XXVI.

That euery one hath not his Angell keeper.

C Ontrary to the expreſſe wordes of their own Bible. Mat. 18. 10. *Take heede that yee deſpice not one of theſe litle ones, for I ſay vnto you, that in heauen, their Angells doe allwayes behould the face of my Father which is in heauen* . Therfore they haue their Angell keeper. A thinge ſo plaine, that Caluin dares not to deny it, and yet he will needes doubt of it. l. 1. Inſt. cap. 14. ſect. 7.

Pſal 91. (we 90.) 11. 12. *He ſhal giue his Angels charge ouer thee, to keepe thee in all thy wayes, they ſhall beare thee*

D 5 *vp*

vp in their handes , least thou dashe thy
foote against a stone . This very paffage S. Cyrill of Alexandria lib. 4.
cont. Iulian, applyeth to our Angel
keeper. Therfore &c.

Acts 12.13. &c. Peter knocking at
the doore, they said; *It is his Angel.*
Loe how apparantly the faith of the
primitiue Church appeareth concerning this point.

See more, 1. Cor. 11. 10. Zacharie 3.10. Luc. 15. 10. Luc. 16.22. Tob.
5. 15. 20. Tob. 12. 12. Tob. 5. 27.
Exod. 23.23. Iosue 5. 13. Num. 22.22.
31. Gen. 24. 40. Dan. 6.22.

To measure this doctrine by our
Line or Rule, see S. Greg. dial. l. 4.
cap. 58. S. Athanas. de communi es-
sentia. S. Chrisost. hom. 3. in ep. ad
Colos. lib. 6. de sacerd. Greg. Turo-
nens. lib. de gloria mart. S. Aug. ep.
ad Probam cap. 9. & epist. 69. ad
fratres in eremo. lib. 11. cap. 31. ciuit. S. Hiero. vpon these wordes,
Their Angels &c. Mat. 18. 10. teacheth,
that it is a great dignitie and mar-
 ueleous

uelous benefit, that euery one hath from his natiuitie, an Angell for his cuftodie and patronage.

XXVII.

That the holie Angells pray not for vs, nor knowe the thoughts and defires of vs on earth.

COntrary to the expreffe wordes of their owne Bible Zacharie 1. 9. 10. 11. 12. *Then the Angell of the Lord answered and faid. O Lord of boftes, how longe wilt thou not haue mercie on Hierufalem, and on the citties of Iuda, againft which thou haft had indignation, thefe threefcore and ten yeares?* And what I pray you, is a prayer, if this be not? Therfore the holie Angells pray for vs.

Toby 12. 12. *Now therfore, when thou didft pray, and Sara thy daughter in law, I did bringe the remembrance of your prayers, before the holy one.* He which pleafeth to reade the whole chapter, fhall clearly fee the manifould benefits befides this one, which men receiue at the handes of

D 6 Angels:

Angels : for which see the annotations of the Catholique Bible vpon
this place. Therfore &c.

Reuelations 8. 4. *And the smoke of
the incenses of the prayers of the Saints,
ascended from the hand of the Angell before God.* What can be possibly spoken
more plaine, to proue that Angells
offer vp our prayers before God?
yea this very place is so vnderstood
by S. Ireneus l. 4. cap. 34. towards the end.

See more Gen. 19. 18. 19. 20. Dan.
8. 15. Dan. 9. 20. Acts 5. 19.

According to our Rule, these fathers following affirme the same. S.
Hillarie in psal. 129. saith. *The inter-
cession of Angels, Gods nature needeth
not, but our infirmitie doth.* S. Amb.
lib. de viduis. victor Vtic. lib. 3. de
persecut. Vandal.

XXVIII.

That we may not pray to them.

COntrary to the expresse wordes
of their owne Bible. Gen. 48.
16. *The Angel which redeemed me* (we,
read

read *deliuered*) *from me all euill* , *blesse the laddes* . But some perhappes will here say , that this was Christ. But this is but a sorry shift, for Christ had not then redeemed man, but long after: yea this very passage is appropriated by S. Chrisoft. to our Angel gardian hom. 3. vpon the 1. of the Colos. And by S. Hierom vpon the 66. of Isay. Also S. Basil.l. 3.cont.Eunom, affirmeth that this was spoken of a true Angel , and not of Christ: which being so , who can with reason say, he praied not to him?

Tobie.5. 16. *And when his sonne had prepared all thinges for the iorney, his father said* . *Goe thou with this man, and God which dwelleth in heauen* , *prosper your iorney, and the Angell of God keepe you companie* . Loe, both God is here prayed vnto , and his Angell also is praied vnto at the same preset, saying. God prosper you in your iornie, and the Angel of God keepe you copany. Both therfore doe very well cosist together, and be both aggreable to the word of God.   Osee

Ofee 12. 4. *Yea, he had power ouer the Angell, and preuailed, he wept, and made supplication vnto him.* Loe, what is plaine, if this be not, for proofe of prayer to the blessed Angels?

But some perhaps will here say; I could be perswaded to pray to Angells, if I could assure my selfe that they could heare me, and knew what passeth here on earth. Wherto I reply, that we in earth, know that the Angells are in heauen, and often also with vs in earth: that they are in full ioy and felicitie: and finally, that they see God &c. Now if they know not what we doe in earth (hauing much more perfect knowledge then we haue) we attribute to our selues more knowledge in earth, then we doe to them who are in heauen: the which, were blasphemie to affirme. Therfore we may pray vnto them.

See more, Ofee 12. 4. Song of the three children verfe 36. Pfal. 148. Num. 22. 34. Gen. 19. 18. 19. 20. Pfal. 148. 2.

And

And now to confirme what hath bene said by our Line or Rule. Iob. 19. 21. we reade as followeth . *Haue pittie vpon me , haue pittie vpon me, o yee my friendes for the hande of God hath touched me:* which wordes (as S. Aug. him selfe expoundeth) holy Iob addressed to the Angells. 'Iob. 5. 1. *Call now &c.* the same. S. Aug. expoundeth of praying to Angels in his annot. vpon Iob.

XXIX.

That the Angells cannot helpe vs.

COntrary to the expresse wordes of their owne Bible. Dan. 10. 13. *Michael one of the chiefe princes came to helpe me.* Which is further verefied Reuel: 12. 7. 10. where the selfe same Angell , with his fellow Angells, fought a battell with the dragon, and with his Angells. Therfore they can helpe vs.

The same chapter, verse 21. *And there is none that houldeth with me in these thinges , but Michael your prince.* Therfore &c.

Acts

Acts 12. from verſe 7. to verſe 12. *Now I know of a ſuretie, that the Lord hath ſent his Angell, and hath deliuered me.* Therfore &c.

See more, Mat. 2. 13. Mat. 4. 6. Pſal. 91. (we 90.) 11. 12. Acts 5. 19. Acts 27. 23. pſal. 104. (we. 103.) 4. Heb. 1. 7. Luc. 16. 22. Gen. 19. 10. 15. 16. Gen. 2. 117. Iſay. 63. 9.

See Fathers that affirme the ſame. S. Iuſtin. Apol. 2. S. Amb. l. de viduis. Victor Vticenſ. l. 3. de perſec. Vand. S. Aug. de Ciuit. l. 12. cap. 31. ſaith. *The holy Angels doe helpe vs without all difficultie, becauſe with their ſpiritual motions (pure and free) they labour or trauel not.* And in pſal. 62. he ſaith, The Angells waite vpõ vs pilgrimes, and by the commandment of God, do helpe vs: the place beginneth, *Attendunt nos peregrinos.*

X X X.

That no Saint deceaſed, hath afterwards appeared to any vpon earth.

Contrary to the expreſſe wordes of their owne Bible, Mat.
17. 3.

17. 3. *And behould there appeared vnto them, Moyses and Elias talkinge with them.* Therfore Saints deceased, haue afterwards appeared to some in earth.

Mat. **27..52.** *And the graues were opened, and many bodies of Saints which slept, arose; and came out of the graues after his resurrection, and went into the holy cittie , and appeared vnto many.* Therfore &c.

2. Mac.15.12. Onias the high priest after he was dead, appeared to Iudas Machabeus being aliue. The like did Samuel vnto Saul. What shall we say then to those, that will deny a truth so cleare? for some such my selfe haue met with.

See more Luc. 16.27.28. Ioan. 11. 44. Luc. 7.15.& 23.Mat. 9.25.Marc. 5. 42.

Conforme to our Rule, see S.Bed. l. 5. cap. 13. historie of England . S. Gregorie in his booke of Moralls, in sundry places.

XXXI,

XXXI.

That the Saints deceased, know not
what passeth here in earth.

Ontrary to the expresse wordes
of their owne Bible Luc. 16.
29. Where Abraham knewe, that
there were Moyses and the prophets
bookes here in earth, which he him
selfe had neuer seene when he was
aliue: as S. Aug. witnesseth *l. de cura*
pro mortuis. cap. 14. Therfore the
Saints deceased, know what passeth
here in earth.

Iohn 5. 45. *Doe not thinke that I*
will accuse you to the Father , there is
one that accuseth you , euen Moyses in
whom yee trust. But how could Moyses (dead two thousand yeares before) accuse those that were then liuing, if the Saints deceased , know
not what passeth here in earth? Therfore &c.

Like vnto this, is that Reuel. 12.
10. *And I heard a loud voice saying in*
heauen &c. the accuser of our bretheren
is cast downe , which accused them be-
fore

fore our God day and night. Now the
diuells cannot accuse men day and
night before God, but they must first
know wherof: who then may for
shame deny that to Saints and Angells, which must needes be granted
to the very deuills? Therfore &c.

2. Kinges 6. 12. (we 4. Kinges)
*O kinge, Elisem the prophet, that is in
Israel, telleth the kinge of Israel, the
wordes that thou speakest in thy bed
chamber.* Hence I thus argue; If the
light of prophecie, could extend it
selfe so far, as to make knowen, see,
and vnderstand thinges so secret yea
euen to inward thoughtes: who can
with reason deny, that the light of
glorie can doe the same in the soules
of the blessed?

The like is proued out of many
other places of holy scripture, as 2.
Kinges 5. 26. where the prophet Elizeus, being a far off, saw all that passed betwix Naaman, and Giesi his
seruant. S. Paul was rapt in to the
third heauen, and saw that which
                                    was

was not to be tould to man 1. Cor.
12. S. Stephen faw from earth, Chrift
fitting at the right hand of his father,
Acts 7. Diues faw from hell to heauen (as Proteftants fay) how then fay
they, that the Saints cannot know or
fee from heauen to earth?

To conclude; without fome reci-
procall knowledg, there could be no
communion at all, betwixt the Saints
in heauen, and the faithfull in earth;
which who fo denieth, denieth a
part of our common creede: which
yet the continuall paffage of foules
thither, doth conuince. Therfore &c.

See more Mat 19. 28. Reuel. 2. 26.
Luc. 22. 30. Acts 5. 3. 1. Kinges 28. 14.
Ecclef. 4. 6. 23.

See Fathers that affirme the fame.
Eufebius ferm. de Annunc. S. Hierom in epitaph. Paulæ. S. Maximus
ferm. de S. Agnete.

XXXII.

That they pray not for vs.

C Ontrary to the expreffe wordes
of their owne Bible. Reuelat. 5.

8. *The*

8. *The four and twentie elders fell downe before the Lambe, hauing euery one of them harpes, and golden vialls, ful of odors, which are the prayers of Saints.* Loe, how among so many diuine and vnsearchable mysteries set downe in scripture without exposition, it pleased God, that the Apostle himselfe should clearly open this point vnto vs, saying: *which* (odors) *are the prayers of Saints,* that so our aduersaries may haue no excuse of their error. Therfore they pray for vs.

2. Machabees 15. 14. Then Onias answered saying. *This is a louer of the bretheren, who prayeth much for the people, and for the holie cittie, to wit, Ieremias the prophet of God.* Ancient Origen tom. 18. in Ioan saith. It appeareth that Saints departed from this life haue care of the people, as it is written in the acts of the Machabes, many yeares after the death of Ieremie. Therfore &c.

Ieremie 15. 1. *Though Moyses and Samuel stood before me, yet my minde could*

could not be towards this people. Hence
S. Ierom in his commentaries, and S.
Greg. the 9.of his Morales cap. 12.
doe gather, that Moyſes and Samuel after their death, both could,
and did, ſomtimes pray for the ſame
people: for otherwiſe, it ſhould be
as fooliſh, and abſurd to ſay. *Though*
Moyſes and Samuel ſtood before me, as
if one ſaid; If an Horſe or an Aſſe
ſhould pray. Therfore &c.

Baruch 3. 4. *O Lord almightie, thou*
God of Iſrael, heare now the prayers of
the dead Iſraelites (we reade, *of the*
dead of Iſrael.) And Theodoret para-
praſing vpon the prophet Baruch,
interpreteth this place as Catholiques doe. Therfore the dead of
Iſrael, prayed for the liuing.

Reuel. 2. 2. 26. 27. *And he that ouer-*
commeth, and keepeth my workes vnto
the end, to him will I giue power ouer
the nations, and he ſhall rule them with
a rod of iron. Sith Ieſus Chriſt therfore imparteth his power vnto them
vpon natiõs, therfore they may with
Ieſus

Iesus Chriſt and by Ieſus Chriſt, pray
for thoſe ouer whom they are thus
eſtabliſhed. So S. Auguſt. expoundeth the ſame , writing vpon the
2. Pſalme.

To conclude this queſtion , we
reade in the 16. of S. Luc. that Diues
in hell, prayed for his brethren that
were in earth; If therfore the Saints
in heauen pray not for vs their bretheren on earth, then let vs ſay, that
greater is the charitie of the damned
then of the ſaued. But this were abſurd to ſay. Therfore &c. A conclu-
ſion which S. Aug. draweth from
this very place.

See more, Reuelat. 6. 9. Reuelat.
6. 26. 27.

See Fathers that affirme the ſame.
S. Aug. ſerm. 15. de verbis Apoſt. S.
Hillar. in pſalm. 129. S. Damaſcen
lib. 4. de fide cap. 16, with many
others.

XXXIII.

XXXIII.

That we ought not to beseeche God, to graunt our prayers in fauor of the Saints or of their merits, nor doe receiue no benefitt by them.

TWo wayes there are, of praying by the mediation of the the blessed Saints. The one, by beseeching God, to grant our desires in fauor of them, and of their merits. The other, by expresly praying thē, to intercede and pray to God for vs: both being impugned by Reformers, we will proue them both out of their owne Bible. The proofe of the first.

Contrary to the expresse wordes of their owne Bible. Exod. 32. 13. *Remember Abraham, Isaac, and Israell thy seruants, to whom thou swarest by thine owne selfe, and saidst vnto them. I will multiplie your seede, as the starres of heauen &c. And our Lord repented (we reade, was pacified) of the euill which he thought to doe vnto his people.*

Loe

Loe, how plainly Moyſes prayed to
God, by the mediation of the holie
Patriarches;a forme of praier ſo plea-
ſing to him, as hauing ſaid a litle before, that for their ſinne of idolatrie,
he would conſume them, the memo-
rie of his holy ſeruants being but laid
before him, he preſently pardoned
them . Therfore we may beſeech
God to grant our prayers in fauor of
them. Theodoret queſt. 67. in Exod.
writeth , that Moyſes not thinking
him ſelfe ſufficient , to appeaſe God
by him ſelfe, added the interceſſion
of the holie patriarkes : and the like
doth S. Aug. queſt. 149. in Exod.

2. Chronicles 6.16. *Now therfore,*
o Lord God of Iſrael, keepe with thy ſer-
uant Dauid , that which thou haſt pro-
miſed him . And pſal. 132. (we 131.)
Lord remember Dauid, and all his afflic-
tions . Loe againe , the faith of the
ancient Church of God, before the
coming of Ieſus Chriſt, and how
feruent they were in this deuotion,
ſtill alleadging the memories and

me-

merits of their Saints deceafed, therby to moue Gods mercie towards
them. So praied Salomon 2. Chron.
1.9. So praied Ifay 63. 17. So praied
Hefter 13. 14. So praied Dauid, 1.
Chron. 29. 18. naming Abraham,
Ifaac, and Iacob for his intercef-
fors. Who euer heard a Proteftant
make the like prayer? faying, Lord
remember thine owne mother, and
all her afflictions, or Peter and Paul
and their perfecutions? They defire
the Papifts to hould them blameles
for feare (for footh) leaft they fhould
blafpheme.

Exod. 20. 5. *I the Lord thy God, am
a iealous God, vifiting the iniquitie of the
fathers, vpon the children, vnto the
third and fourth generation of them that
hate me, and shewing mercie vnto thou-
fands, of them that loue me, and keepe
my commandements.* Here againe God
threatneth to punifh the demerits of
wicked mé deceafed, vnto the fourth
generation of their children aliue:
and to reward the merits of good
men

men deceafed, vnto the thoufand generation of their children aliue.
Therfore, we aliue at this very day,
receiue benefitte by meanes of our
godly anceftors, which are deceafed
fince a thoufand generations. Thus
much for the proofe of the firſt point,
and now to paffe vnto the fecond.

XXXIIII.

That we ought not exprefly to pray to
them, to pray or intercede to
God for vs.

COntrary to the expreffe wordes
of their owne Bible, Luc. 16.24.
Father Abraham, haue mercie on me
and fend Lazarus, that he may dip the
tip of his fingar in water, and coole my
tongue, for I am tormented in this flame.
Loe, two Saints are here prayed and
befought in one verfe, and yet they
vfually bid vs fhew them, fo much
as one place in all the Bible for proofe
hereof. Where for Gods fake, are
their eies?

But they reply that this is a parable: which we deny, offering to be

E 2   tryed

tryed by our common Rule, hauing on our fide, ten renowmed and ancient fathers, all affirming this to be a true hiftorie, and not a parable, as Theophila&t, Tertullian, Clemens of Alexandria, S. Chryfoftome, S. Ireneus, S. Ambrofe, S. Auguftine, S. Gregorie, Euthymius, and our owne contryman Venerable Bede.

But granting it to be a parable, what I pray doth this make, ether for them, or againft vs? For euery parable, is ether true in it felfe, and in the perfons named, or at leaft, is, or may be true in fome other, elfe were it a flat lye, or at leaft a fiction or a fable. If they grant this, then are they gone, and we haue gayned what we defire.

Where vpon I thus conclude, as S. Aug. did a litle before vpon the felfe fame hiftory: If Diues in hel, prayd to Abraham who (as Reformers fay) was in heauen, why may not we, who are in earth, pray to them who are in heauen?

Iob.

Iob. 5. 1. *Call now, if there be any that will answer thee, and to which of the Saints wilt thou turne?* we reade, *and turne to some of the Saints.* Now, if it had not bene the custome in the time of Iob, to inuocate the holy Saints, it had bene friuolous for Eliphas, to haue asked Iob, to which of the Saints he would turne him: no, such an error can not iustly be supposed, in so sensible a man as Eliphas was. Wherto I add, that S. Aug. expoundeth this very place in his annotations vpon Iob, in the same sence that Catholiques doe; yea and long before him the seauenty interpreters.

Contrary to the expresse wordes of their owne Bible, appointed to be publikely read at morning prayer, in the Canticle, *O all yee workes of the Lord, blesse yee the Lord, praise him, and magnifie him for euer*, and with vs is found in the 3. of Daniel, where thus they say. *O Ananias, Azarias, and Misael, blesse yee the Lord, praise him, and magnifie him for euer*. Now,

if

if the vocatiue cafe be knowen by calling or fpeaking to (as euery gramarian wil côfes) ether this is plaine calling vpon, and fpeaking to thefe three Saints, or I will begin my gramar againe. But perhaps they will reply, that in this Canticle of the three children, brute beaftes, and other dead and infenfible thinges, are likewife inuited to prayfe God, or inuoked, as well as the Saints aforenamed: the fcripture faith fo, it muft needes be granted. If therfore beaftes, and other dead and infenfible creatures, may be inuited, or inuoked, to praife God in their kinde, why not Saints alfo in theirs? Or who will fhew him felfe fo fenfles, as to fay, that the liuing Saints(being capable of Inuocation, as hath bene proued, which the others ar not) are no otherwife to be inuited or inuoked, then plants and trees, hilles, and mountaines, and other dead and infenfible thinges? Therfore Saints may be paayed vnto.

See

See more 2. Pet. 1. 15. Dan. 3. 28.
Heſter. 13. 14. 1. Chron. 29. 18. Luc.
16. 9. & 15. 10.

See Fathers that affirme the ſame.
Dioniſ. cap. 7. eccleſ. Hier. S. Athanaſius ſerm. de Annunt. S. Baſil orat.
in 44. martyrs. S. Chriſoſt. hom. 66.
ad popul. Finally, S. Hierom prayed
to S. Paula, in epitap. S. Paulæ, S.
Maximus to S. Agnes, ſerm. de S.
Agnete. S. Bernard to our bleſſed
Lady, and the like.

XXXV.

That the bones or Reliques of Saints,
are not to be kept or reſerued: no ver-
tue proceeding from them, after
they be once dead.

COntrary to the expreſſe wordes
of their owne Bible, 2. Kinges
(we 4.) 13. 22. Where it is written,
that the bones of Elizeus, being touched by one that was dead, they did
reuiue him. But this could not be,
had not ſome vertue proceeded from
them: therfore &c.

Acts 15. 14. 15. *And beleeuers were*
E 4 *the*

the more added to the Lord, multitudes,
both of men and women: in so much that
they brought forth the sick into the stree-
tes, and laid them on beds and couches,
that at the least the shadow of Peter pas-
sing by, might overshadow some of them.
It followeth in ours , *and they all*
might be deliuered from their infirmi-
ties : quite left out in the Englifh
Bible. S. Aug. fer. 39. de Sanctis faith.
If the shadow of his body could helpe
then , how much more now , the fulnes
of his power ? Wherin he fuppofeth
two thinges; The one; that the fhadow of his body being here in earth,
did both helpe and heale infirmities
(which the Englifh Bible feaueth
out.) The other, that being in heauen, he can fti'l helpe vs by his power. Therfore &c.

Acts 19. 11. 12. *And God wrought*
speciall miracles by the handes of Paul,
so that from his body were brought vnto
the sick hand kerchiefes or aprons, and
the diseases departed from them, and the
euill spirits went out of them. S. Chry-
fostome

foſtome tom. 5. cont. Gentiles *quod Chriſtus ſit Deus*, in a whole booke proueth hereby, and by the like virtue of other Saints, and their Reliques, that Chriſt their Lord and maſter is God, whoſe ſeruants ſhadowes and napkins, could doe ſuch wonders. Therfore &c.

See more Exod.13.19.2.Kinges 2. 8.14. Iohn. 1. 27. Where S. Iohn. had a reuerend eſteeme of the very latchet of our Sauiours ſhoe, as of a Relique he was not worthie to vnbuckle, or touch wi h his hande: and the woman with the bloody flux, of the hemme of his holy garment.

Se Fathers that affirme the ſame. Euſeb.lib.7. hiſt. cap. 15. S. Athanaſius in vita S. Antonij.S. Baſil in pſal. 115. S. Chryſoſt. ſerm. de ſanctis Iuuentio & Maximo . Laſtly, S. Ambroſe ſaith ; But if you aske me, what I honor in fleſh diſſolued, I honor in the martyrs fleſh, his woundes receiued for Chriſts name

&c. I honor his ashes, made holy by confession of Christ.

XXXVI.

That creatures cannot be sanctified, or made more holy, then they are alrea-die of their owne nature.

Ontrary to the expresse wordes of their owne Bible. 1. Tim. 4. 4. *For euery creature of God, is good, & nothing to be refused, if it be receiued with thanksgiuing, for it is sanctified by the word of God, and prayer.* Yea it was a common vse in the primitiue church, to bringe breads to the priests to be hallowed, auth. op. imp. hom. 14. in Mat. and being blessed, to send them for sacred tokens from one Christian to another, as S. Aug. witnesseth. ep. 31. 34. 35. 36.

Mat. 23. 17. *Yee fooles and blinde, whither is greater, the gold, or the temple that sanctifieth the gold?* Therfore &c.

Mat. 23. 19. *Yee fooles and blinde, whither is greater, the gift, or the Altar that sanctifieth the gift?* Loe how
plainly

plainly our Lord affirmeth in both
these places, that the temple sanctifieth the gold, and the Altar the gift:
and generally all creatures, feuered
from comon and profane vse, to religion and worship of God, are therby made facred and holy. Are not
they therfore much to blame, who
keepe fuch a howting at holy water,
holy ashes, & the like? Therfore &c.

See more 2. Kinges (we, 4. 2.) where
the Prophet Elifeus applyed falt, to
the healing and purifying of the waters. Toby 6. 8. where the Angell
Raphaell vfed the liuer of the fifh,
to driue away the diuel. 1. Samuel
(we 1. Kinges) 16. Where Dauids
Harpe and pfalmodie, kept the euil
fpirit away from Saul.

See other Fathers that affirme the
fame, S. Greg. l. 1. dial. cap. 4. S.
Aug. lib. 18. de ciuit. Dei. S. Hierom
in the life of Hilarion, poft medium.
S. Bede lib. 1. cap. 30. hift. Angliæ.

E 6   XXXVII

XXXVII.

*That children may be saued by their pa-
rents faith, without the Sacrament
of holie Baptifme.*

COntrary to the expreffe wordes, both of truth it felfe, and
alfo of their owne Bible. Iohn 3. 5.
*Verely verely I say vnto thee, except a
man be borne of water, and of the spirit,
he cannot enter into the kingdome of
God.* Therfore they cannot be faued
without Baptifme.

Titus 3. 5. *Not by workes of righte-
ousnes which we haue done, but according to his mercie he faued vs, by
the washing of regeneration, and re-
newing of the holy Ghoft.* Therfore &c.

Marc. 16. 16. *He that beleeueth, and
is baptifed, shall be faued: but he
that beleeueth not, shall be damned.* Seing infants therefore cannot beleeue, therfore at the left they
muft be baptifed, or cannot be
faued.

But they obiect againft vs, that of
S. Paul

S. Paul 1. Cor. 7. 14. That the children of the faithful, are fanctified.
But if they vnderstand by their fan-
ctification , that they are borne
without finne, they doe directly re-
pugne S. Paul, who affirmeth (Ephes.
1.) that we are all borne the fonnes
of wrath. Yea S. Paul in the felfe
fame place, faith, that the vnbeleeuing woman, is fanctified by the beleeuing man: and yet I hope they
will not fay, that fhe obtaines therby, the full remiffion of her finne.
Therfore &c.

Gen 17. 14. *The vncircumcifed
man-childe , whofe flesh of his fore-
skine, is not circumcifed, that foule shal
be cut off from his people* . But cir-
cumcifion , was not more neceffarie to the Ifraelites , then Baptifme to the Chriftians . Therefore &c.

See Fathers that affirme the fame.
S. Aug. lib. 1.de peccat.merit.& re-
miff. cap. 30. & epift.90. 92. S. Leo
epift. 80. ad epifcop. Campaniæ.
S.Ire=

S. Ireneus lib. 3. cap. 19. S. Cyp. lib.
3. ep. 8. ad Fidum.

XXXVIII.

That impoſition of handes vpon the peo-
ple (called by Catholiques Confir-
mation) is not neceſſary, nor
to be vſed.

Ontrary to the expreſſe wordes
of their owne Bible, Acts 8. 14.
Peter and Iohn prayed for them, that they
might receiue the holy Ghoſt (for as yet
he was fallen vpon none of them, only
they were baptized in the name of the
Lord Ieſus.) Then laid they their handes
on them, and they receiued the holy Ghoſt.
Loe the holy Ghoſt is giuen in Confirmation, which was not giuen in
Baptiſme, how then not neceſſarie,
nor to be vſed?

Heb. 6. 1. *Therfore leauing the prin-*
ciples of the doctrine of Chriſt, let vs goe
on vnto perfection, not laying againe the
foundation of repentance from dead wor-
kes, and of faith towards God, of the
doctrine of Baptiſme, and of laying on of
handes. Loe, Confirmation is here
called

called, one of the principles of the doctrine of Christ, and a foundation of repentance, how then not necessarie nor to be vsed?

See Fathers that affirme the same. Tertul. lib. de resurrec. carnis. S. Pacianus lib. de baptismo. S. Amb. lib. 3. de Sacram. S. Hierom cont. Lucifer. Lastly, S. Cyprian lib. 2. epist. 1. speakinge both of Baptisme and Confirmation, saith. Then they may be sanctified, and be the sonnes of God, if they be borne in both Sacraments.

XXXIX.

That the bread of the supper, is but a figure or remembrance of the body of Christ receiued by faith, and not his true and very body.

Ontrary both to the expresse wordes and truth of their owne Bible, Luc. 22. 15. With *desire I haue desired, to eate this passeouer with you before I suffer.* Now to refer these wordes, to a figuratiue eating only
by

by faith, were moſt abſurd, for we
cannot ſay, that Ieſus Chriſt could
receiue or eate him ſelfe in this ſence,
ſith all diuinitie forbids vs, to admit
faith in the Sonne of God; Therfore
that paſche, which he ſo greatly deſired to eate with his Diſciples before he ſuffered, was the paſche of
his owne body.

Luc. 22. 16. *For I ſay vnto you, I will
not any more drinke of the fruite of the
vine, vntill it be fulfilled in the kingdome
of God.* Wordes of wonderfull force,
and which cannot be vnderſtood fi-
guratiuely, no more then the former;
it being a thinge as cleare as the Sunne, that of material bread and drinke,
there is no vſe at all aboue in heauen. Therfore &c.

Iohn. 6. 51. *I am the liuinge bread,
which came downe from heauen, if any
man eate of this bread, he shall liue foreuer. And the bread that I wil giue is my
flesh, which I will giue for the life of the
world.* Beza is very angrie, when we
ask him, if the bread that came down

from

from heauen, be liuing or life giuing?
He willingly gráteth vs the later, but
cannot endure to heare tel of the former, and therfore tranſlateth life-giuing, inſteed of liuing. But this is abſurd, for the Sunne is life-giuing, but
is not liuing: and being granted to be
liuing, what elſe is it then his body?

And note withall, that thus our
Lord ſpake of this bleſſed bread, before he gaue it.

Mat. 26. 26. *Take eate this is my bodie* . And Luc. 22. 19. *This is my body,
which is giuen for you* . What I pray
can be ſpoke more plaine? Notwith-
ſtanding, they wil needes ſinge theire
old ſong, that what he gaue, and they
receiued, was nothing elſe but his
bare body. Well, this alſo being granted to them, let vs ſee what they get
therby . That which Chriſt gaue to
eate, was nothing elſe but bare bread:
but that which he gaue to eate, was
that which he would giue for the life
of the world: therfore that which he
gaue for the life of the world, was nothing elſe but bare bread.   Note

Note next, that thus our Lord spake, at the very giuing of it.

1. Cor. 10. 16. *The cup of blessing which we blesse, is it not the communion of the blood of Christ? The bread which we breake, is it not the communion of the body of Christ?* And 1. 11. he addeth. *He that eateth and drinketh vnworthely, eateth and drinketh damuation to him selfe, not discerninge the Lords bodie.* Loe both *before* our Lord gaue it: *at* the very giuing of it: and his owne Disciples *after* he him selfe had giuen it them, and they to others, all of them, call it our Lords body. Poore reformer, whither now is thy figure fled?

Finally, against their true and reall receiuing of Christ by faith; Ether the soule ascendeth to heauen, there to feede on Christ by faith (which Caluin confesseth:) or Christ descendeth in to earth to feede the same. Not the first, for so the vnglorified soule, should be in two places at once, which they deny to the glorified

rified body of Iesus Christ. Not the
second, for so Christ should be in
two places at once : whom yet they
say, that the heauens must contayne
till the day of iudgment. Acts 3. Therfore &c.

See Fathers that affirme the same.
S. Ignat. in ep. ad Smyr. S. Iustin
Apol. 2. ad Antoninum. S. Cyprian
serm. 4. de lapsis. S. Amb. lib. 4. de
Sacram, saith. It is bread before the
words of the Sacrament , but after
&c. of bread it is made the flesh of
Christ. S. Remigius saith. The flesh
which the word of God tooke in the
virgins wombe , and the bread con-
secrated in the Church, are one body.

XL.

That we ought to receiue vnder both
kindes: and that one alone
sufficeth not.

C Ontrary to the expresse wordes
of their owne Bible , Iohn 6.
51. *If any man eate of this bread , he*
shall liue for euer, and the bread which

I

I will giue, is my flesh. Loe, euerlasting life, attributed by our Lord him selfe, to eating only vnder one kinde. Therfore one alone doth suffice.

Luc. 24. 30. 8. 35. Christ at Emaus, communicated his two Disciples vnder one kinde. Both S. Aug. and Theophilact expound this place of the B. Sacrament. lib. de consens. euang. cap. 35. S. Chrysost. hom. 17. operis imperfecti. S. Thomas of Aquin cited in the Sauegard, and many others.

Against that of S. Iohn, *vnles you eate the flesh of the Sonne of man, and drinke his blood, you shall not haue life in you.* The answere hereto, is very easie, which is, that the coniunction *and*, is there taken disiunctiuely insteed of *or*, as is learnedly obserued by Doctor Kellison, in his Reply to Suctliffe pag. 189. Againe, Christ in those wordes, teacheth vs the precept, and not the maner of the precept; that is to say, he commandeth vs to receiue his body and his blood,

with-

without determining whither vnder one kinde or vnder both , as the Councell of Trent declareth. For he that said ; *vnles you eate the flesh of the Sonne of man, and drinke his blood, you shall not haue life in you* ; hath also said . *If any one eate of this bread , he shall liue foreuer.* He that said; He that eateth my flesh, and drinketh my blood, hath life euerlasting: hath also said; The bread which I will giue, is my flesh for the life of the world. He that said; Who so eateth my flesh, and drinketh my blood, dwelleth in me, and I in him: hath likewise said; He that eateth this bread , shall liue foreuer. Therfore &c.

See more Acts 2. 42. And as for Fathers , they haue before bene al-leadged.

XLI.

That there is not in the Church , a true and proper Sacrifice: and that the Masse is not this Sacrifice.

Contrary to the expresse wordes of their owne Bible. Malachie

1. 11.

1. 11. *From the rising of the sunne, euen to the going aowne of the same, my name shall be great among the Gentils, and in euery place incense shall be offered to my name, and a pure offering.* But this facrifice or pure offering, cannot be vnderftood of Chrift vpō the Croffe, which was offered only once, and in one place, and then alfo not among the Gentils, nor yet can be euer iterated: therfore nether is, nor can be other, then the daylie facrifice of the Maffe.

Pfal. 110. (we 109.) 4. *The Lord hath sworne, and will not repent, thou art a prieft foreuer, after the order of Melchifedech.* But Melchifedechs facrifice was made in bread and wine: therfore it muft ether be granted, that our Sauiour doth now facrifice (yea and euer fhall) in bread and wine aboue in heauen (which were abfurd to fay:) or that this is ment of the facrifice of the Maffe, wheron the eternitie of his priefthood doth depend in earth. Nor can this be in a
spi-

ſpirituall ſort only, for that would
not make him a prieſt of any certaine
order. Therfore &c.

Luc. 22. 19. *This is my body, which
is giuen for you.* Which wordes doe
plainly proue, not only that Chriſts
body is truly preſent, but withall ſo
preſent, as that it is giuen, offered, or
ſacrificed for vs. For Chriſt ſaith not,
*which is giuen to you, broken to you, or
ſhed to you,* but, *for you;* Which clearly
ſheweth it to be a ſacrifice, it being e-
uidēt, that on would neuer ſay of the
Sacrament (in the qualitie of a Sacrament) that it is giuen for man, but
to man: that is to ſay, that a man re-
ceiueth it: and contrary wiſe of a Sacrifice, that it is offered, not to man,
but for man. Therfore &c.

See more Heb. 7. 15. 16. 17. Heb.
8. 1. 3. Heb. 9. 11.

See Fathers that affirme the ſame.
S. Clement Apoſt. conſt. lib. 6. cap.
23. calleth it, a reaſonable, vnbloody,
and myſticall ſacrifice. S. Aug. a ſin-
gular, or moſt excellent ſacrifice. lib.
1, cont.

1. cont. aduerſ. leg. & prophet. cap.
18, 19. S. Chryſoſt. hom. in pſal. 95.
The myſticall table, a pure and vnbloody hoſt, a heauenly and moſt re-
uereũd ſacrifice. Iſichius in Leuit. cap.
4. ſaith, that Chriſt preuenting his
enimies, firſt ſacrificed him ſelfe in
his myſticall ſupper, and afterwards
on the Croſſe. S. Greg. Niſſen orat.
4. de Reſurrectione, prouing that
our Sauiour gaue his body and blood
in ſacrifice for vs in his laſt ſupper,
ſayeth excellently, that a man cannot eate the ſheepe, vnles the ſlaugh-
ter goe before, and yet auerreth this
to haue bene done by Chriſt in his
laſt ſupper.

XLII.

That ſacramentall vnction, is not to
be vſed to the ſick.

COntrary to the expreſſe wordes
of their owne Bible. Iames 5.14.
Is any ſick among you? Let him call for
the elders of the Church, and let them
pray ouer him, anointing him with oyle
in the name of the Lord: and the prayer
of

of faith shall saue the sick, and the Lord shall raise him vp, and if he haue committed sinnes, they shall be forgiuen him. Hardlye is there any Sacrament, wherof the matter, the minifter, and the effect, are more exprefly fpecified in all the fcripture, then of this. The forme is the praier, *Let them pray ouer him.* The matter, the oyle, *Anointing him with oyle.* The minifter, a Prieft or Elder of the Church, *Let him cal for the Elders of the church.* The primarie effect is, the forgiuenes of finnes, & the fecodary, the eafing of the fick in body, faying. *And the Lord shall raise him vp, & if he haue committed sinnes, they shalbe forgiue him.* Therfore facramétal vnctió, is to be vfed to the fick.

Marc. 6. 13. *And they anointed with oyle, many that were sick, & healed them.* Where it is cleare, that the Apoftles them felues, put in practife this holy vnction; Which Beza cófeffeth in his Annotatiós, faying that it was a Simbole of admirable & fupernatural virtu. And had he not reafó fo to fay? for

F　　　oyle of

of it felfe, could not be naturally the
Antidote of all difeafes: and albeit it
were, yet the Apoftles were not fent
to practife phifick, but to preache the
gofpell; Yea it were a thinge too ridiculous, to make them Triaclers,
carriars of Drogues, or Paracelfians.
Therfore &c.

Marc. 16. 18. *They shall lay handes
on the fick, and they shall recouer.* But
firft, the Reformers are no Priefts. Secondly, they lay not their handes
vpon the fick. Thirdly, they anoint
them not with oyle in the name of
the Lord, as S. Iames willeth: fay
the truth then, and fhame the diuell,
are not they fick in their witts, which
will oppofe fo plaine fcriptures?

See Fathers that affirme the fame
Origen. hom. 2. in Leuit. S. Chrifoft.
lib. 3. de facerd. S. Aug. in Speculo.
& ferm. 215. de temp. Venerable
Bede in 6. Marci, & 5. Iacobi: with
many others.

XLIII.

XLIII.

That no interior grace is giuen by the im-
position of handes, in holy Orders; And
that ordinarie Vocation and Mission
of pastors, is not necessarie in the
Church?

Ontrary to the expresse wordes of their owne Bible, 1. Tim.
4. 14. *Neglect not the gift* (we reade
grace) *that is in thee, which was giuen*
thee by prophecie, with the laying on the
handes of the presbitery. Loe how plaine it is, that holy orders doe giue
grace. Doctor Kellison handling this
question touching the mission of the
Reformers, proueth most learnedly,
as his maner is, that this foundation
being disproued, the whole frame of
their Church and Religion falleth:
yea that they haue nether true faith,
nor worship of God, & his reason is
this. If faith depend of hearing, hearing of preaching, preaching & admi-
nistration of Sacraméts, of ministers
and preachers, and preachers & ministers of their mission, where there

is

is no miſſion (as they haue none)
there can be no true faith, nor lawfull adminiſtration of Sacraments,
and conſequently no religion. Reply
pag. 7. & 44. Therfore vocation is
neceſſarie in the Church.

1. Tim. 1. 6. *Wherfore I put thee in*
remembrance , that thou ſtir vp the gift
of God which is in thee, by the putting on
of my handes. Loe how plaine the holie ſcripture is againſt them; But they
reply, that laying on of handes is not
needfull to them, who haue already
in them the ſpirit of God, and inward anointing of the holy Ghoſt.
To which very queſtion Theodoret
makes anſwer, that God commanded Moyſes (Numb. 27.) to lay his
handes vpon Ioſue, wheras by the
teſtimony of God him ſelfe, Ioſue
had already in him the ſpirit of God.
S. Paul, although he were called immediatly from heauen, yet was after
ſent with laying on of handes. Acts.
13. 3. Therfore &c.

Heb. 5. 4. *And no mã taketh this honor*
vnto

vnto himselfe,but he that is called of God as was *Aarō.*But here our aduersaries reply againe,that Aarō had no external vocatiō. But this is very easily solued, for Aaron was the first of his order, and therfore could not haue his calling by succeſsiō. Whose caſe therfore is far vnlike to our Reformers, vnles they wil alſo cōſes that they are the firſt of their order : wherin they ſhal be eaſily beleeued. Therfore &c.

See more Acts 13. 2. Tim. 1. 6. 1. Tim. 5. 22. 2. Tim.1.8. Numb. 27. 23.

See Fathers that affirme the ſame. S. Aug. lib. 4. queſt ſuper Num. S. Cyprian epiſt. ad Magnum. Optatus Meleuir, the place beginneth. *Nequis miretur.* Tertulian in preſcript. The place beginneth, *Æant origines.*

XLIIII.

That Prieſts and other Religious perſons who haue vowed their chaſtitie vnto God,may freelie marrie, notwith-ſtanding their vowes.

Ontrary to the expreſſe words of their own Bible,Deut.23.22.Whē *thou shalt vow a vow vnto the Lord thy God, thou shalt not slack to pay it, for the Lord thy God, will surely require it of thee, and it would be sinne in thee: but if thou shalt forbeare to vow, it shall be no sinne in thee.* Out of which wordes, two thinges are clearly proued. The one, that it is both lawfull, and laudable to make vowes. The other, that vowes being once made, they doe binde, where otherwise there was no obligation. Therfore such as haue vowed the vow of chastitie, may not, nor ought not afterwards, attempt to marrie, which if they doe, they breake their vow.

1. Tim. 5. 11. 12. *But the younger widdowes refuse, for when they haue begun to wax wanton against Christ, they will marry, hauing damnation, because they haue cast off their first faith.* All the auncient fathers that euer wrote vpon this place, expound the Apostles wordes of the vow of chastitie, or the faith and promise made to Christ, to liue continently ; as is

abun-

abundantly proued in the Rhemes Teſtament vpon this place . Ther-fore &c.

1. Tim. 5. 15. *For ſome are already turned aſide after Sathan*. Loe , to marrie after the vow of chaſtitie once made, is here termed by the Apoſtle him ſelfe ; *turning aſide after Sathan* ; And herupon it is , that we call the Religious, that after marry, (as Luther, Bucer, Peter Martyr and the reſt of that laſciuious rable) Apo-ſtataes, Gods adulterers, inceſtuous, ſacrilegious, and like.

See more pſal. 66. 16. Numb. 6. 2. 18. Ioſue 2. 26. Ieremie 35, 18. Eccleſ. 5. 3. Actes 21. 23.

See Fathers that affirme the ſame. S. Aug. lib. de bono viduit. cap. 9. S. Athanaſius lib. de virginitat . S. Epiphanius heref. 48. S. Hier. cont. Iouin. lib. 1. cap. 7. W*hat is to breake their firſt faith* (ſaith S. Aug?)*they vow-ed and performed not.* In pſal 75. The place beginneth. *Quid eſt, primam fi-dem &c.*

F 4   XLV.

XLV.

That fasting and abstinence from cer-
taine meates, is not grounded on holy
scripture, nor causeth any spi-
rituall good.

COntrary to the expresse wordes
of their owne Bible, Ieremy 35.
5. *And I set before the sonnes of the house*
of the Rechabits, pots full of wine, and
wine cups, and I said vnto them, drinke
yee wine. But they said, we will drink no
wine, for Ionadab the sunne of Rechab
our father, commãded vs saying; Yee shall
drink no wine, nether yee, nor your sonnes
foreuer. Thus haue we obeyed Ionadab
our father, in al that he hath charged vs.
Therfore fasting is grounded in holie scripture.

Luc. 1.15. *For he shall be great in the*
sight of the Lord, and shall drinke nether
wine nor stronge drinke. Loe abstinéce
not only foretould, but also preſcri-
ded by the Angel; which plainly proueth that it is both a worthie thinge,
and also an act of religion in S. Iohn,
as it was in the Nazarits, and Rechabits afore-mentioned.

Actes 13. 3. *And when they had fasted and prayed, and laid their handes on them, they sent them away.* Hence the Church of God, hath sufficient ground and warrant, for the vsing and prescribing of publique fastes. Which was not fasting from sinne, as our Reformers pretend (for such fasting they were bound euer to keepe:)& that at such time or season as the church pleased to determine (as in Lent, or the like)& not when euery man list, or the toye takes him, as Ærius and the like hereticks did teache, testified by S. Aug. heref. 53. Therfore &c.

Mat. 17. 21. *Howbeit, this kind of deuill, goeth not out, but by prayer and fasting.* Loe the great force of prayer and fasting, able to expell the very deuil. Therfore it causeth great spirituall good.

See more. Ioel 2. 12. Mat. 6. 16. Mat. 9. 15. 29. Toby 12. 8. Luc. 2. 37. Acts 14. 22. 2. Cor. 11. 27. 2. Cor. 6. 5. Numb. 30. 14. 1. Tim. 4. 3.

See

See Fathers that affirme the same,
S. Ignat. ad Phillip. S. Basil orat. de
Ieiunio. S. Chrysost. orat. in sanct.
Lauacrum . & hom. 1. in Gen. S.
Amb. fer. 4. S. Hierom in cap. 18.
Isaij, and many others.

XLVI.

That Iesus Christ descended not into
hell, nor deliuered thence the soules
of the Fathers.

COntrary to the expresse wordes of their owne Bible . 1. E-
phes.4.8. *When he ascended vp on high,*
he led captiuitie captiue (margent, *or*
a multitude of captiues) and gaue gifts
vnto men. Now that he ascended, what
is it, but that he also descended first, into
the lower parts of the earth . These
freed captiues, cannot be the soules
of the glorified, which no man in his
right witts can call captiues; Nor of
the damned, for so the deuills should
be brought againe into heauen; therfore they were the soules of the Fathers, which Christ deliuered forth
of Limbo.

Actes

Actes 2. 27. *Becaufe thou wilt not
leaue my foule in hell, nether wilt thou
fuffer thine holy one, to fee corruption.*
Thefe very wordes S. Aug. applieth
to the proofe of a third place, and
addeth. W*ho but an Infidelle, wil deny
Chrift to haue defcended into hel.*Epift.
99. ad Euodium.

1.Pet. 3. 18. 19. *Being put to death
in the flesh, but quickned by the fpirit,
by which alfo he went and preached
vnto the fpirits in prifon.* To interpret by the word *prifon,* heauen,
there is no fence, fith it is called the
feate of God, and not the prifon of
God. To vnderftand it of the wicked, Caluin him felfe oppofeth this
opinion, and maintayneth, that S.
Peter fpeaketh of the good, which
were knowen from the dayes of
Noe. Add, that this doctrine def-
troyeth an article of our Creed, and
maketh the twelue, to be but ele-
uen. Therfore &c.

Heb. 11. 38. 39. 40. *And thefe all
hauing obtained a good teftimonie, tho-*
rough

rough faith, receiued not the promise (to wit, of heauen) *God hauing prouided some better thinge for vs, that they without vs, should not be made perfect* : to wit, in their perfect and complete glory. Whence it followeth neceffarily, that they muft needes grant another place, diftinct as well frō the heauen of the faued, as from the hell of the damned, wherin thefe holy foules were cōferued. Therfore &c.

Mat. 12. 40. *For as Ionas was three dayes and three nights in the* Whales *belly, fo shall the Sonne of man be three dayes and three nightes , in the hart of the earth.* But how I pray , is this figure fulfilled , if Chrift were not as many dayes and nightes in the heart of the earth, as Ionas was, who was not in the whales belly in body only, but alfo in foule? Whence it followeth , that ether Chrifts holye foule, was three dayes, and three nights in the hart of the earth, as wel as his body, or that this place of fcripture, is ether falfe, or vnfulfilled,

led. But this were moſt abſurd to
ſay. Therfore &c.

Mat. 27. 52. 53. *And the graues were
opened , and many bodies of Saints
which ſlept, aroſe , and came out of the
graues after his reſurrection , and
went into the holy cittie , and appeared
vnto many.* Vnderſtood by S. Ignatius
biſhop of Antioch , of Limbus Patrum , writing theſe wordes to the
cittizens of Trallis . *Manie aroſe
with our Lord , for the ſcripture ſaith,
that many of the bodies that ſlept , a-
roſe with our Lord. He deſcended a-
lone, but returned with a multitude.*
Therfore &c.

Zacharie 9. 11. *As for thee alſo, by
the blood of thy couenant , I haue ſent*
(we reade, *let*) *forth thy priſoners, out
of the pit, wherin is no water.* Both S.
Hierom and S. Cyril, vnderſtand
this pit, to be ment of Limbus Patrum. And with very great reaſon, for
how abſurd were it to ſay , that the
damned haue their ſhare *in the blood
of the couenant?* Or that they are *let*
                                      forth,

forth, of their infernall pit ? Or that
they may be said to be, *thy prisoners,*
(that is Chrifts) but rather the prifoners of the diuell? Yea, where I
pray (to speake properly) hath
Chrift had any prifoners at al(which
he hath let forth) if not out of this
place? Therfore, ether Chrift let
forth prisoners out of Limbo Patrum, or this place likewise as the
former, is ether falfe, or yet vnfulfilled.

1. Samuel 2. 6. Like vnto this place, is that of the Kinges, *The Lord
killeth, and maketh aliue, he bringeth
downe to the graue* (we read, *hell*) *and
bringeth vp,* we reade, *back againe.*
Loe, how plaine and conforme, the
faith of that old church, was and is to
this of ours, *bringeth downe to hell,
and bringeth backe againe,* which
hardly in any cleare senfe can be auerred, if Limbus Patrū be denved.
As for the word *graue,* which they
erroniously haue added, insteed of
hell, to diminifh the force of so plaine
a place,

a place , bid them but to repeate
their Creede, and there to foiſt in &
ingraft the word *graue* , inſteed of
hell, as here they haue done , and
then muſt they ſay . W*as crucified
dead and buried , he deſcended into the
graue.* And who for Gods ſake ſees
not the groſſe abſurditie of this in-
grafting ?

See more. Oſee 6.3. Pſal. 16. 10.
2. Pet.3. 19. Zach. 9.11. Rom. 10.6.
Eccleſ. 24. 45. Pſal. 23. 7. Geneſ.
37. 35.

See Fathers that affirme the ſame.
S. Hier. in 4. ad Epheſ. S. Greg. lib.
13. Moral. cap. 20. S. Aug. in Pſal.
37. v. 1. The place beginneth. *Futu-
rum eſt enim.*

XLVII.

*That there is no purgatorie fire, or other
priſon, wherin ſinnes may be ſa-
tisfied for after this life.*

COntrary to the expreſſe wordes
of their owne Bible , 1. Cor.
3: 12. 15 *The fire ſhall try euery mans
worke, of what ſort it is. If any mans
worke*

worke shal be burnt, he shall suffer losse, but he himselfe shall be saued, yet so as by fire. S. Aug. writing vpon the 37. psalme, and drawing these very wordes of the Apostle into his discourse, saith. Because it is said, *He him selfe shall be safe,* that fire is contemned. Yea verely, though safe by fire, yet that fire shal be more greuous, then whatsoeuer a man can suffer in this life. Thus he ; Therfore there is a purgatorie fire, wherein sinnes may be satisfied for after this life.

Iohn. 11. 22. *But I know, that euen now, whatsoeuer thou wilt aske of God, God will giue it thee.* S. Martha , sister to Marie Magdalen beleeued, that our Lord (whom then she only held for a holie man , but not for the Sonne of God) could obtaine of God, somthinge profitable to her brother Lazarus , who was deceased: For hauing said . *Lord if thou hadst bene here , my brother had not bene dead .* She presently added. *But I knowe , that euen now whatsoeuer*

soeuer thou wilt aske of God , God will giue it thee . Which fpeeches fhe could neuer haue vfed in anie good fence, if fhe had not learned this doctrine of the Sinagogue, who offered facrifices, almes and prayers for the departed : and vnles fhe had knowen and beleeued, that the dead might be holpen by the pietie of the liuing ; as Cardinall Allen learned concludeth. Therfore &c.

Actes 2. 14. *Whom God hath raifed vp, loofing the forrowes of hell .* In which wordes two thinges are to be noted, which clearly make for the proofe of Purgatorie. The one, that in this place , there were certaine forrowes and paines , where Chrift was. The other, that fome there were inflicted for finne , vpon whom he beftowed that gratious benefit, as to difcharge and loofe them of thofe paines. For as the Rhemes Teftamét very well noteth, Chrift was not in paines him felfe , but loofed other men of their paines.

1. Cor.

1. Cor. 15.29. *Otherwise what shall they doe, that are baptised for the dead?* From this place an euident proofe is drawen, touching the helpe which the soules departed out of thisworld, may receiue by the Church in earth, and consequently proueth purgatorie: vnderstanding the paines and afflictions which voluntarily we doe inflict vpon our selues, to exempt those that are therein: for to baptise, signifieth to afflict ones selfe, to doe penance, to suffer death &c.as Luc. 12.30. *But I haue a baptisme to be baptised with.* And Marc. 10.38.

Luc. 16. 9. *And I say vnto you, make to your selues friendes of the mamon of vnrighteousnes, that when yee faile, they may receiue you into euerlasting habitations.* S. Ambrose vpon this place; and S. Aug. lib. 21. de Ciuit. cap. 27. say, that it is to receiue succour after death, according as the word *faile*, enforceth. Therfore &c.

Luc. 23. 42. *Lord remember me, when thou comest into thy kingdome.* S. Aug.

Aug. saith in his fift booke againſt
Iulian (about the middeſt) that the
good thiefe in this prayer, preſuppo-
ſed, that (according to the common
opinion) ſoules might be holpen after death. Therfore &c.

2. Mac. 12. 44. 45. *For if he had
not hoped, that they that were ſlaine ,
ſhould haue riſen againe, it had bene ſuperfluous and vaine, to pray for the dead.*
And a litle after, concludeth ſaying.
It was an holy and good thought. This
place of holy ſcripture, is moſt cleare
for praying for the dead , for had it
not bene , the continuall doctrine
and practiſe of the Church to pray
for the dead, nether could Iudas Machabeus (who was himſelfe a prieſt)
haue euer thought of any ſuch re-
medie, as to gather twelue thouſand
drachmes of ſiluer to ſend to Hieruſalem, to haue prayers made for the
reliefe of the ſoules ſlaine in that
battaile: nether would the multitude
of people haue ether contributed, or
the prieſts of the Temple, receiued
the

the prefent, had they thought (as
thefe men doe) that it had bene fu-
perftition, to pray for the departed,
or no other place had bene, then the
hell of the damned, or the heauen of
the faued. Therfore &c.

See more 2. Tim. 1. 18. 1. Iohn 5. 16.
Ifay. 4. 4. Ifay 9. 18. Acts 2. 24. Mat.
3. 11. Mat. 12. 32. Mat. 5. 26. Micheas
7. 8. pfal. 66. 12. Tobie 4. 18. Phil.
2. 10. Zacharie 9. 11.

See Fathers that affirme the fame.
S. Amb. vpon the 1. Cor. 3. & ferm.
20. in pfal. 118. S. Hier. lib. 2. cap.
13. aduerf. Iouin. S. Greg. lib. 4. Dia-
log. cap. 39. Origen hom. 6. in cap.
15. Exod: with many others.

XLVIII.

That it is not lawfull to make, or
to haue Images.

Ontrary to the expreffe wordes, of their owne Bible, Exod.
25. 18. *And thou shalt make two Cheru-*
bins of gold, of beaten worke shalt thou
make them, in the two endes of the mer-
cie feate. Thefe grauen Angells, were
　　　　　　　　　　　　　　Ima-

Images, of the highest order of Angells (one excepted) which is in
heauen, and were made with faces
of beautifull young men, and commanded to be set vp by God himselfe in the holie of holies: which S.
Hierom witnesseth the Iewes to
haue worshiped, epist. ad Marcellam: Therfore it is lawfull to make
Images.

1. Kinges 6. 35. *And he carued theron, Cherubins, and Palme trees, and
open Flowers, and couered them with
gold, fitted vpon the carued worke.*
Hence is to be gathered, that the precept of not making a grauen Idoll,
doth nothing at all concerne Images, that is to say, the true representation of thinges subsisting, but of
thinges meerely imaginarie and not
subsisting: for as S. Paul saith. 1.
Cor. 8. *An Idoll is nothinge;* So that
the Idoll, representeth that which
is not; the Image, that which is
(a remarkable difference.) Therfore &c.

Againe,

Againe, feeing an Idol is that properly, which being nothing (as S. Paul faith) is reprefented to be fomthinge, or that which reprefents the thinge that is not, if the Reformers beleue the Image of Chrift crucified to be an Idoll, they then beleeue, that Chrift was neuer crucified: for it followeth neceffarily, as thus. The Image of Chrift crucified, is an Idoll: therfore Chrift was neuer crucified.

Heb. 9. 1. 5. *Then verely the firſt couenant, had alfo ordonances of diuine feruice, and a worldly fanƈtuarye &c. and ouer it, the Cherubins of glorie shadowing the mercie feate.* Loe S. Paul calleth the pictures of the Cherubins which Salomon made, *an ordonance of diuine feruice,* which Reformers call , the making of Idolls : whom fhall we now beleeue, whither bleſſed S. Paul, or a Reformed brother before him? Therfore &c.

To conclude, an Image, is fo both of diuine and naturall right, that all vnderſtanding, imagination, and fenfation,

fation, as well interior, as exterior,
is made by way of Images , called
fpecies fenfibiles & infenfibiles : the
body cannot be in light, without its
fhadow: the Moone and the Starres,
imprint their pictures in the water:
a man cannot looke in a glaffe, without making his picture ; Therefore,
ether God and nature it felfe, doth
breake this commandement, as wel
as wee, or elfe it is abfurd to fay, that
we doe breake it in making of Images. Therfore &c.

See more. 1. Kinges 7. 36. 42. 44.
Num. 21. 8. Mat. 22. 20. Exod. 31. 2.
Exod. 35. 30. where painting and
grauing of pictures , is fo far from
being Idolatrie, that it is proued to
be a fcience diuinely infufed into Be-
feleel by God himfelfe : and fo the
inuention of good Images, came firft
from God.

See Fathers that affirme the fame.
Tert. lib. 2. de Pudicitia. S. Greg.
Naz. ep. 49. ad Olymp. S. Bafil orat
in S. Barlaam. S. Aug. lib. 1. de con-
fenf.

ſenſ. euang. cap. 10. witneſſeth, that in his time, Chriſt was to be ſeene painted in many places, betweene S. Peter and S. Paul.

XLIX.

That it is not lawfull to worship Images, nor to giue any honor, to any dead or inſenſible thinge.

COntrary to the expreſſe wordes of their owne Bible. Exod. 3. 5. *And he ſaid. Draw not nigh hither, put off thy shoes from off thy feete, for the place wheron thou ſtandeſt, is holie ground.* Loe how cleare a place is here produced againſt Reformers, wherin an inſenſible creature without reaſon, was commanded by God him ſelfe to be honored: for the refrayning to tread vpon it, was the doing of honor to it. Therfore all dead images, repreſenting vnto vs a holy thinge, may be honored.

Pſal. 99. 5. *Adore yee the foote-ſtoole of his feete.* Which place is ſpoken litterally of the Arke of the Teſtamét, according to that 1. Chronicles 28. 2.

I had

*I had in my hart to build a house of rest,
for the Arke of the couenant of the Lord,
and for the footstoole of our God.* Now
the principall reason, why the Arke
was worshipped, was in regard of
the Images that were set vpon it,
which the Iewes did worship, as S.
Hierom witnesseth, in his epistle ad
Marcellam. Therfore &c.

Philipians 2. 10. *That at the name
of Iesus, euery knee should bow, of thinges in heauen, and thinges in earth, and
thinges vnder the earth .* Now that is
the name of Iesus, which ether is
pronounced by anothers mouth,
printed in a booke, or painted and
grauen in a picture: but at any of
these we are commanded to bow the
knee: Therfore &c.

Againe, if Images ought not to be
worshipped, we may not (whatsoeuer the Apostle saith) bowe our
knee at the name of Iesus : seeing
wordes (as Aristotle saith, and as the
truth is) are signes representatiue of
the thinges they signifie, & are as the

G   pictu-

pictures of the eare, as the others are of the eyes. Therfore &c.

Numb. 21. 8. *And the Lord said vnto Moyses. Make thee a fierie serpent, and set it vp vpon a pole : and it shall come to passe, that euery one that is bit, when he looketh vpon it, shall liue.* Hence are euidently proued diuers thinges, against Reformers. 1. That God commanded the making of this Image. 2. The setting of it vp for a signe. 3. He promised that the lookers theron, should assuredly receiue succour. 4. He warranted the making, the setting vp, the behoulding, and the reuerencing therof, to be exempted from the breach of the first commandement, by working so many, and so manifest miracles, at, and before the presence thereof. Therfore an Image may be made, may be set vp, may be looked on, and be reuerenced, as Doctor Sanders most learnedly concludeth, in his Treatise of Images.

Sec

See Fathers that affirme the same. S. Amb. serm. 1. in psal. 118. S. Aug. lib. 3. de Trinit. S. Greg. lib. 7. epist. 5. ad Ian. Finally, S. Basill saith (in Iulian citatus in 7. sinod.) *I honor the histories of Images, and doe openly worship them, for this being deliuered vs from the holy Apostles, is not to be forbidden.* S. Chrisostom in his Masse, turned into Latin by Erasmus, saith. *The priest boweth his head, to the Image of Christ.* S. Damascen lib. 4. cap. 17. saith. *The worshipping of the Crosse, and of Images, is a Tradition of the Apostles.*

An obiection.

But before I conclude this present controuersie, I desire to solue a few obiections, which vsuallie are brought against the honor of Images. And first, that of the 2. of Kinges. (we 4.) 18. where Kinge Ezechias, broke downe the brasen Serpent (wherof we last of all made mention) when it was the cause of idolatrie.

G 2   The

This indeed is a common place, from whence our aduersaries colle&t sundrie false and sophisticall arguments: to wit, from the abuse of any good thinge, to destroy it vtterly; together with the right vse thereof. But by the same argument, they may as well colle&t, that the Sunne and the Moone should be taken out of the firmament, because they were worshipped by the Gentils as Gods. Likewise that the holie Bible should be burnt, because many an one drawe h damnable heresies forth of the same, to his owne perdition. Yea, this sillie argument borrowed from the abuse of thinges, serues passing well more to proue the quite contrarie, for it followes well. Images were sometimes abused, therfore they were good in them selues: for that thinge which is euill by abuse only, must needes be good being vsed well.

The

The 2. Obiection.

You giue that honor to Images, which is due to God alone, worshipping, adoring, and creeping to them, as to God.

The answere.

We say the contrarie, which thus we proue. The difference of honor, proceedeth principally from the minde, and not from the exterior bowing or demeanor of the bodie. For if I fall downe before an Image and kisse the same, being all the while of the minde it is no God, nor reasonable creature, but only a remembrance of God, towards whom I desire to shew myne affection, God knoweth how far off myne honor is, from that honor which is due to him alone. As contrariwise, if I lay prostrat at Christes feete, kissed them, knocked my breast, held vp my handes vnto him, yea calling him the Sonne of God, yet all this while, thinke him not

to

to be so in my hart, myne honor tru-
lie should be no honor at all , but a
very contumelie vnto Christ. Adde,
that the wordes which betoken
honor, adoration , worship and the
like, are in a maner confounded in
all languages : but the hart from
whence the honor floweth, knowe-
eth the difference of euery thing. Ex
D. Sanders de imag. pag. 10.

The 3. Obiection.

It is expresly forbidden by God
him selfe, to fall downe before any
Image, or to worship it.

The answere.

Reformers themselues confes to
honor the Sacrament of Christs
supper, which they teache to be, an
Image or representation, of Christs
body and blood . And seeing they
beleeue, no other substance to be
in the Sacrament, besides bread and
wine , nor will not giue the honor of *latria* therunto , hence it
doth follow inuincibly, that they
doe serue or honor some Image:
Now,

Now , as they would not for all this, haue vs to iudge, or call them Idolaters : euen fo let it pleafe them (for their owne fakes) to fpare vs . For as they doe not ftay this honor in the bread and wine, but from thence refer it to Chrift him felfe : euen fo doe we tranf- fer all our honor from all Images, vnto the firft forme or patterne, not fuffering our honor to reft or to end, in the Image we honor. Ex eodem pag. 52.

The 4. *Obiection.*

An Image is a creature , and no God , and to fett vpp a crea- ture to be worfhipped , is Ido- latrie .

The *Anfwere.*

Images are fet vp in Churches, not fpecially to the intent that the people fhould worfhip them , but partly to inftruct the fimple , and partly to ftir vp our mindes, to fol- low the example of thofe holy men, whofe Images we doe behould. So
that

that the worship which is giuen to Images, is giuen as it were by a consequent, and rather because it may be lawfully giuen, then because it is principally sought to be giuen. And touching the Idolatrie which is obiected, you are to vnderstand, that the word is compounded of *Latria,* and *Idolum,* and is as much to say, as, the giuing of Latria, or of Gods honor, vnto an Idol. But our Images, are no Idols, nor the honor we giue them, is not Latria; how then can it be said, that Images are set vp to be vsed to Idolatrie?

Thus much haue I thought good to adde in this place, the more to enlarge this present controuersie, for that there are many weake and simple soules, who stumble at the doctrine of the worship of Images, because indeed they vnderstand it not. And hauing proued the worshippe of them, I shall neede to say nothing in proofe of their making, for the one presupposeth the proofe of of the other.

L.

That no man hath feene God in
any forme , and that ther-
fore his picture or I-
mage, cannot be
made.

C Ontrary to the expreſſe wordes
of their owne Bible , Gen. 3. 8.
where God appeared vnto Adam
Walking in the garden of paradiſe , in
a corporall forme . And Gen. 28. 12.
13. to Iacob, *ſtanding aboue the ladder,*
wheron the Angells aſcended, and
deſcended. For we muſt know, that
it is only the outward ſhape and
forme of the thinge, which is expreſſed, ether in this or the like Image, &
not the inward ſubſtance therof,
which is not poſſible for any pain-
ter to expreſſe; which though it expreſſe not all that is therin , yet that
which it expreſſeth is a truth: & thus
may God be expreſſed to vs . Yea,
who may hinder to picture or expres
God in the ſame maner, wherin he
G 5 him-

him selfe manifetted him selfe to
mortall eyes? Therfore his picture
or Image may be made.

Exod. 33. 11. God appeared, and
fpake vnto Moyfes, *face to face*, as
a man fpeaketh vnto his friend.
To the prophet Ifay 6. 1. 5. *Sitting*
vpon a throane. To Daniel 7. 9. *Sit-*
ting, wearing *garments*, and hauing
haire on his head, like pure wolle. How
then can a wife man dout, but that
thinge may be lawfully fet forth, or
expreffed vnto vs in an outward
image, which neceffarilye muft
be conceiued by an inward? Therfore &c.

1. Kinges (we 3.) 22. 19. *I faw*
the Lord fitting on his throane, and
all the hofte of heauen, ſtanding by
him, on his right hand, and on his
left. One would thinke that en-
nough hath now bene faid to proue
this point. But if they fhall yet
anfwere, that God commandeth
vs to heare his word, and the hi-
ftories which fpeake of his apparitions,

tions , but not to paint them . I
anſwere , that ſeeing we learne by
our eies, as well as by our eares,
there is no reaſon, why that may
not be painted before our eyes,
which may be preached to our eares. Againe , ſeeing he that can
reade the holye ſcriptures , muſt
needes finde the aforeſaid viſions
and hiſtories in the Bible, why not
as well ſee them in a picture on the
church wall, as in a booke of white
paper? Therfore &c.

L I.

That bleſſing or ſigning with the ſigne
of the Croſſe , is not founded in
holie ſcripture.

C Ontrary to the expreſſe wordes
of their owne Bible. Reuelations 7.3. Where one Angell, ſaid
to four other Angells. *Hurt not the*
earth , nether the ſea , nor the trees,
till we haue ſealed (we reade, *ſigned*)
the ſeruants of our God in their fore-
heads. Therfore &c.

Marc. 10. 16. *And hee tooke them*
G 6 *vp*

vp in his armes , put his handes vpon them, and bleſſed them. Therfore bleſſing is founded in holy ſcripture.

Luc. 24. 50. And he led them out as far as to Bethanie , and he lift vp his handes, and bleſſed them . Therfore &c.

See Fathers that affirme the ſame.
Dioniſ. Areopagita cap. 4. 5. 6. eccleſ. Hier. Tertul. lib. de corona mi-
lit. Origen in Exod. cap. 5. hom. 6. 5.
S. Cyrill. Cat. 1. S. Baſil lib. de ſpir.
ſanc. cap. 37. S. Chryſoſt. hom. 55. in
Mat. cap. 16.

LII.

That the publique ſeruice of the Church, ought not to be ſaid , but ſo as all the aſſiſtants may vn-
derſtand it.

COntrary to the expreſſe wordes of their owne Bible, Luc. 1.
8. *And it came to paſſe, that while he executed the prieſts office before God, in the order of his courſe , according to the cuſtome of the prieſts office , his lot was to burne incenſe in the temple of*
the

the Lord ; and the whole multitude of people were praying without, at the time of incense . Where note 1. that this was the common custome. 2. All the people were without , and the priest within , how then did they vnderstand him ? Therfore the publiq e seruice of the church may be so said , as all the assistants vnderstand it not.

Leuiticus 16. 17. *And there shal be no man in the Tabernacle of the congregation, when he goeth in to make an attonement in the holy place, vntill he come out, and haue made an attonement for him selfe , and for his houf-hould, and for all the congregation of Israell.* Therfore &c.

What shall I neede to produce authorities of Fathers , when the practise of the whole Christian world, for these many hudred yeares toge her, is directly contrary to Reformers in this point: against which to dispute (as S. Aug. saith) were insolent madnes. See. Rhe. Teit. p. 463.

But

But for that much cauilling and wrangling is made by many, againſt the practiſe of the Church herein, I will therfore enlarge my ſelfe a litle theron, and ſolue what the aduerſaries doe ſay againſt it. Out of ſcripture, their probableſt place, is this which followeth. 1. Cor. 14. 16. *When thou ſhalt bleſſe with the ſpirit, how ſhall he that occupieth the roome of the vnlearned, ſay Amen at thy giuing of thankes, ſeeing he vnderſtandeth not what thou ſayeſt? For thou verely giueſt thankes, but the other is not edifyed.*

We anſwere hereto, that there be two kindes of prayers, or giuing of thankes, in the Church. The one *Priuat*, which euery man ſayes by himſelfe alone. The other *Publique*, which the Prieſte ſayth, in the name & perſon of the whole Church. As cōcerning *Priuat* prayers, no Catholique denies, but it is very expediēt, that euery man pray in his owne tongue, to the end he may vnderſtād
what

what he fayes. But as touching the *Publique* prayers of the Church, it is not neceſſarie that the cōmon people vnderſtand them, becauſe it is not they who pray, but the Prieſt in the name of the whole Church: For as it was enough for the people of the old law, to vnderſtand, that in ſuch a ſacrifice conſiſted the worſhip of God, although they had not ſo cleare an vnderſtanding of euery thinge that was done therin (as hath bene ſaid:) euen ſo in the new law, when the people aſiſt at the ſacrifice of the Maſſe, acknowledging therby that God is worſhipped, and that it is inſtituted for the remembrance of Chriſts death & paſſion, although they vnderſtand not the Latin tongue, yet are they not wholie deſtitute of the vtilitie and fruiᛤ therof: beſides the helpe of the godly ceremonies, which doe inſtruᛤ them in the whole.

Next, this place alleadgeth ſerueth nothing to the purpoſe, but is rather

ther repugnant to the fame, yea pro-
ues, that the common feruice of the
Church, was not then in the vulgar
language, which euery man vnderftood, but in another láguage, which
was not fo comon to euery one. For
S. Paul faying. *How shall the that oc-*
cupieth the roome of the vnlearned, fay
Amē at thy giuing of thāks, feeing he vn-
derftādeth not what thou fayeft? fhewes
that fuch giuing of thankes, was not
acuftomed to be in the vulgar tógue:
and requires, or rather fuppofes, that
in the feruice of the Church, there
fhould be fome other to fupply the
place of the vnlearned, that is, one
that fhould haue further vnderftan-
ding of that tongue, in the which
the feruice of the Church is faid. But
had the feruice bene in the vulgar
tongue, there needed no man, to haue
fupplied, the place of the Idiot that
vnderftandeth not. So that S. Paul
fhewes moft clearly, that fuch feruice
was not exercifed in a vulgar tógue,
but in another which was not common

mon to the whole people (such as
the Latin tongue is in England, as
alſo thorough the whole Eaſt) and
yet was not, in the contrary extre-
mitie, that is to ſay, wholly ſtrange,
or vtterly barbarous.

And ſeeing they haue this place
continually in their mouthes, and
deceiue therby the ſimple people, I
ſhall ſhew vnto you, that this ſaying
of S. Paul, is altogether peruerted by
the Reformers them ſelues, becauſe
where the Greeke and Latin text
hath. *He who ſupplies the place of an I-*
diot, how ſhall he ſay Amen ? The Miniſters of Geneua, in many of their
Bibles, haue turned the ſame moſt
deceitfully and maliciouſly, thus.
He that is an idiot, how ſhall he ſay A-
men ? As if there were no difference
betwixt an Idiot, and he who ſupplies the place of an Idiot?

Moreouer, the thankſgiuing, to
which S. Paul ſayeth, Amen ſhould
be anſwered, is at all not practiſed
in many of your Reformed Churches,

ches, where nether your Idiots, nor
thofe who fupply the place of your
Idiots, doe anfwere Amen, as S. Paul
willeth, but haue altered Amen, into
So be it, which is plainly repugnant
to his meaning, as alfo to the practice
of the whole Church: for they can
not fay for their excufe, that S. Paul
wrote to thofe, who fpake the Hebrue tongue (as Amen is Hebrue) for
he wrote to the Corinthiãs, who had
their publike feruice in Greeke, and
not in Hebrue : a fufficient argumẽt,
that the word Amen, ought to be re-
tayned in all languages, as it hitherto
hath euer bene amõgft all Chriftians,
before the dayes of our Reformers; in
fo much that the moft learned S. Au-
guftin writeth, that it is not lawfull
to turne Amen, into any other vulgar language, without the fclander of
the whole whole Church. Aug. epift.
118. & 2. de Doctrina Chrift. cap. 20.

To conclude, I cannot but much
mufe at the great fimplicitie of the
common people, who notwithftan-
ding

ding the great light of their reformed
golpel, fee not the lofeneffe and va-
nitie of this their leaders cauill. For,
are ether the mafters, or fchollers,
fo exceeding fenfles as to fay, that
their owne feruice, cõfifting in part,
of the pfalmes of Dauid (the hardeft
part of all the Bible) and partly of
leffons extracted out of the ould and
new Teftament, that all the affiitants
(I fay) doe vnderftand them ? Sure I
am the greateft deuines that euer
were in all chriftendome, neuer durft
fay fo much of them felues : how
wrongfully then, doe they wrangle
with vs about this matter ? But perhaps they will fay, that though the
fimple vnderftand not the hard places, contayned in their pfalmes and
feruice, yet that to their confort, they
vnderftand at leaft fome part therof:
euen fo fay we of the Maffe, and of
our fimple who afift therat. And fo
conclude as I begunne, in the title of
this booke. *By thine owne mouth I*
iudge thee, naughtie feruant.

LIII,

LIII.

That it is both superfluous, and superstitions, to repeate one and the same prayer, sundry times.

Contrary to the expresse wordes of their owne Bible . The Angells in the prophet Isay cap. 6. And the Beastes in the Reuel. cap. 4. which rest nether day nor night, doe thrice repeate one word to the honor of God, saying. *Holy, holy, holy, Lord God of Saboth.*

Againe, Christ him selfe, praying in the garden, repeated one and the same speeche, three feuerall times. Luc. 22. & Mat. 26. 36.

Finally, we reade, that the three children in the fornace, in lauing and praising almightie God, did in euery verse (being many in number) repeate a certaine halfe verse.

See Fathers that affirme the same. Lactantius lib. 4. diuin. instit. cap. 28. S. Amb. lib. de spir. sancto cap. 20. S. Aug. lib. 1. de serm. Dom in monte cap. 5. & lib. de doctrina Christiana

ſtiana cap. 7. S. Greg. hom. 19. in
Ezech. & lib. 1. Moral. cap. 28.

A TABLE OF THE
CONTROVERSIES
contayned in this Trea-
tiſes.

1.   F *the Rule of faith pag.* 12.

2. *Of the Iudge of contro-
uerſie in matters of faith.
pag.* 18.

3. *Of ſcriptures difficultie. pag.* 20.

4. *Of Traditions. pag.* 24.

5. *Of the priuat ſpirit. pag.* 27.

6. *If S. Peters faith hath fayled. p.* 29.

7. *If the church can erre. pag.* 31.

8. *Of her pretended inuiſibilitie. pag.* 35.

9. *Of her vniuerſallitie. pag.* 37.

10. *Of her vnitie. pag* 40.

11. *Of S. Peters headſhip. pag.* 42.

12. *Of a ſecular Princes headſhip. pag.*
47.

13. *Of*

The Table.

13. Of *Antechrist.* pag. 52.

14 *Whither none but God, can forgiue sinnes* pag. 54.

15. *Whether we ought to confes to none but to God.* pag. 57.

16. Of *Pardons.* pag. 59.

17. *Whither the actions and passions of the Saints, are profitable to vs.* pag. 61.

18. Of *workes of supererogation.* pag. 63.

19. Of *Free will.* pag 65.

20. Of *keeping the Command.* pag. 68.

21. Of *faith and good workes.* pag. 71.

22. *Whither good workes or meritorious.* pag. 74.

23. *Whither faith once had, cannot be lost* pag. 76.

24. Of *Gods ineuitable decre, who shall be damned, and who saued.* pag. 77.

25. *Whither we ought to assure our selues of our saluation* pag. 79.

26. *Whither euery one hath his Angell keeper.* pag. 81.

27. *Whither Angells pray not for vs.* pag.

The Table.

pag. 83.

28. Whither we may not pray to them. pag. 84.

29. Whither they can helpe vs or not. pag. 87.

30. Of Saints apparitions. pag. 88.

31. Whither they know what passeth in earth. pag. 90.

32. Whither they pray not for vs. pag. 92.

33. Whither we may alleage their merits in fauor of our selues. pag. 96

34. Whither we may not pray vnto them. pag. 99.

35. Of the Reliques of Saints. pag. 103.

36. Of hollowing of creatures. pag. 106

37. Of the necessitie of Baptisme. p. 108.

38. Of Confirmation. pag. 110.

39. Of the last supper. pag. 111.

40. Of receiuing vnder one, kinde, pag. 115.

41. Of the sacrifice of the Masse. pag. 117.

42. Of Extreame vnction. pag. 120.

43. Of Orders. pag. 123.

The Table.

44. Of Vowes. pag. 125.
45. Of Fasting. pag. 128.
46. Of Limbus. pag. 130.
47. Of Purgatorie. pag. 135.
48. Of making of Images. pag. 140.
49. Of worshiping Images. pag. 144.
50. Of making of the picture of God. pag. 153.
51. Of blessing with the signe of the Croße. pag. 155.
52. Of seruice in an vnknowen tongue. pag. 156.
53. Of often repeating the same prayer. pag. 164.

Faults escaped.

Pag. 8. numb. 5. line 11. & 12. after, *Christ our Lord.* ad, *his Apostles, or their successors.* pag. 32. in some copies, for Isay 9. 7. read, Isay. 35. 9. pag. 37. line 17. and Church, read, and the Church. Ibid. line 20. for *you heauen,* read, *for yon in heauen.*